Frederic William Farrar

The Epistle of Paul the Apostle to the Hebrews

With Notes and Introduction

Frederic William Farrar

The Epistle of Paul the Apostle to the Hebrews
With Notes and Introduction

ISBN/EAN: 9783337414832

Printed in Europe, USA, Canada, Australia, Japan

Cover: Foto ©Lupo / pixelio.de

More available books at **www.hansebooks.com**

The Cambridge Bible for Schools and Colleges.

General Editor:—J. J. S. PEROWNE, D.D.,
Dean of Peterborough.

THE EPISTLE OF PAUL THE APOSTLE

TO THE

HEBREWS,

WITH NOTES AND INTRODUCTION

BY

THE VEN. F. W. FARRAR, D.D.
ARCHDEACON OF WESTMINSTER.

EDITED FOR THE SYNDICS OF THE UNIVERSITY PRESS.

Cambridge:
AT THE UNIVERSITY PRESS.
1888

PREFACE
BY THE GENERAL EDITOR.

THE General Editor of *The Cambridge Bible for Schools* thinks it right to say that he does not hold himself responsible either for the interpretation of particular passages which the Editors of the several Books have adopted, or for any opinion on points of doctrine that they may have expressed. In the New Testament more especially questions arise of the deepest theological import, on which the ablest and most conscientious interpreters have differed and always will differ. His aim has been in all such cases to leave each Contributor to the unfettered exercise of his own judgment, only taking care that mere controversy should as far as possible be avoided. He has contented himself chiefly with a careful revision of the notes, with pointing out omissions, with suggesting occasionally a reconsideration of some question, or a fuller treatment of difficult passages, and the like.

Beyond this he has not attempted to interfere, feeling it better that each Commentary should have its own individual character, and being convinced that freshness and variety of treatment are more than a compensation for any lack of uniformity in the Series.

DEANERY, PETERBOROUGH.

CONTENTS.

	PAGES
I. INTRODUCTION.	
Chapter I. Character, Analysis, and Object of the Epistle to the Hebrews	9—25
Chapter II. Where was the Epistle written? and to whom?	25—28
Chapter III. The Date	29
Chapter IV. Style and Character of the Epistle	29—32
Chapter V. Theology of the Epistle	32—41
Chapter VI. The Author of the Epistle	41—49
Chapter VII. Canonicity	49—50
II. TEXT AND NOTES	51—194
III. INDEX	195—196

₊ The Text adopted in this Edition is that of Dr Scrivener's *Cambridge Paragraph Bible*. A few variations from the ordinary Text, chiefly in the spelling of certain words, and in the use of italics, will be noticed. For the principles adopted by Dr Scrivener as regards the printing of the Text see his Introduction to the *Paragraph Bible*, published by the Cambridge University Press.

INTRODUCTION.

THE old line,

"*Quis, quid, ubi, quibus auxiliis, cur, quomodo, quando?*"

Who? what? where? with what helps? why? how? when? has sometimes been quoted as summing up the topics which are most necessary by way of "introduction" to the sacred books. The summary is not exhaustive nor exact, but we may be guided by it to some extent. We must, however, take the topics in a different order. Let us then begin with '*quid?*' and '*cur?*' What is the Epistle to the Hebrews? with what object was it written? for what readers was it designed? Of the '*ubi?*' and '*quando?*' we shall find that there is little to be said; but the answer to '*quomodo?*' 'how?' will involve a brief notice of the style and theology of the Epistle, and we may then finally consider the question *quis?* who was the writer?

CHAPTER I.

CHARACTER, ANALYSIS, AND OBJECT OF THE EPISTLE TO THE HEBREWS.

IT has been sometimes said that the Epistle to the Hebrews is rather a treatise than an Epistle. The author is silent as to his own name; he begins with no greeting; he sends no special messages or salutations to individuals. His aim is to furnish an elaborate argument in favour of one definite thesis; and he describes what he has written as "a word of exhortation" (xiii. 22). Nevertheless it is clear that we must regard his work as an Epistle. It was evidently intended for a definite circle of readers to whom the author was personally known. The messages and the appeals, though not addressed to single persons, are addressed to the members of a single community, and the tone of many hortatory passages, as well as the definiteness of the remarks in the last chapter, shew that we are not dealing with a cyclical document, but with one of the missives despatched by some honoured teacher to some special Church. It is probable that many such letters have perished. It was the custom of the scattered Jewish synagogues to keep up a friendly intercourse with each other by an occasional interchange of letters sent as opportunity might serve. This custom was naturally continued among the Christian Churches, of which so many had gathered round a nucleus of Gentile proselytes or Jewish converts. If the letter was of a weighty character, it was preserved among the archives of the Church to which it had been addressed. The fact that this and the other Christian Epistles which are included in the Canon have defied the ravages of time and the accidents of change, is due to their own surpassing importance, and to the overruling Providence of God.

The Epistle to the Hebrews is one of many letters which must have been addressed to the various Christian communities in the first century. Passing over for the present the question of the *particular* Church to whose members it was addressed, we see at once that the superscription "to the Hebrews"—whether it came from the hand of the writer or not—correctly describes the class of Christians by whom the whole argument was specially needed. The word 'Hebrews,' like the word 'Greeks,' was used in different senses. In its wider sense it included all who were of the seed of Abraham (2 Cor. xi. 22), the whole Jewish race alike in Palestine and throughout the vast area of the Dispersion (Phil. iii. 5). But in its narrower sense it meant those Jews only who still used the vernacular Aramaic, which went by the name of 'Hebrew,' though the genuine Hebrew in which the Old Testament was written had for some time been a dead language. In a still narrower sense the designation 'Hebrews' was confined to the inhabitants of Judæa. The letter itself sufficiently shews that the Hebrews, to whom it is addressed, were Jewish converts to Christianity. Although the writer was of the school of St Paul, and adopts some of his phrases, and accords with him in his general tone of thought, yet throughout this Epistle he ignores the very existence of the Gentiles to an extent which would have been hardly possible in any work of "the Apostle of the Gentiles" (Acts xviii. 6; Gal. ii. 7, 9; 2 Tim. i. 11), and least of all when he was handling one of his own great topics—the contrast between Judaism and Christianity. The word Gentiles ($\xi\theta\nu\eta$) does not once occur nor are the Gentiles in any way alluded to. The writer constantly uses the expression "the people" (ii. 17; iv. 9; v. 3; vii. 5, 11, 27; viii. 10; ix. 7, 19; x. 30; xi. 25; xiii. 12), but in every instance he means "the chosen people," nor does he give the slightest indication that he is thinking of any nation but the Jews. We do not for a moment imagine that he doubted the call of the Gentiles. The whole tendency of his arguments, the Pauline character of many of his thoughts and expressions, even the fundamental theme of his Epistle, that Judaism *as such*—Judaism in all its distinctive worship and legislation—was abrogated, are sufficient to shew that he would have held with St Paul that 'all are not Israel who are of Israel,' and that 'they who are of the faith are blessed with the faithful Abraham.' But while he undoubtedly held these truths,—for otherwise he could not have been a Christian at all, and still less a Pauline Christian,—his mind is not so full of them as was the mind of St Paul. It is inconceivable that St Paul, who regarded it as his own special Gospel to proclaim to the *Gentiles* the unsearchable riches of Christ (Eph. iii. 4—8), should have written a long Epistle in which the Gentiles do not once seem to cross the horizon of his thoughts; and this would least of all have been possible in a letter addressed "to the Hebrews." The Jews regarded St Paul with a fury of hatred and suspicion which we find faintly reflected in his Epistles and in the Acts (Acts xxi. 21; 1 Thess. ii. 15; 2 Cor. xi. 24; Phil. iii. 2). Even the

Jewish Christians looked on the most characteristic part of his teaching with a jealousy and alarm which found frequent expression both in words and deeds. It would have been something like unfaithfulness in St Paul, it would have been an unworthy suppression of his intensest convictions, to write to any exclusively 'Hebrew' community without so much as distantly alluding to that phase of the Gospel which it had been his special mission to set forth. The case with the writer of this Epistle is very different. He was not only a Jewish Christian, but a Jewish Christian of the Alexandrian school. We shall again and again have occasion to see that he had been deeply influenced by the thoughts of Philo. Now Philo, liberal as were his philosophical views, was a thoroughly faithful Jew. He never for a moment forgot his nationality. He was so completely entangled in Jewish particularism that he shews no capacity for understanding the universal prophecies of the Old Testament. His LOGOS, or WORD, so far as he assumes any personal distinctness, is essentially and preeminently a Jewish deliverer. Judaism formed for Philo the nearer horizon beyond which he hardly cared to look. Similarly in this Epistle the writer is so exclusively occupied by the relations of Judaism to Christianity, that he does not even glance aside to examine any other point of difference between the New Covenant and the Old. What he sees in Christianity is simply a perfected Judaism. Mankind is to him the ideal Hebrew. Even when he speaks of the Incarnation he speaks of it as 'a taking hold' not 'of humanity' but 'of the seed of Abraham' (ii. 16).

In this Epistle then he is writing to Jewish Christians, and he deals exclusively with the topics which were most needful for the particular body of Jewish Christians which he had in view. All that we know of their circumstances is derived from the letter itself. They like the writer himself, had been converted by the preaching of Apostles, ratified 'by signs, and portents, and various powers, and distributions of the Holy Spirit' (ii. 3, 4). But some time had elapsed since their conversion (v. 12). Some of their original teachers and leaders were already dead (xiii. 7). They had meanwhile been subjected to persecutions, severe indeed (x. 32—34), but not so severe as to have involved martyrdom (xii. 4). But the afflictions to which they had been subjected, together with the delay of the Lord's Coming (x. 36, 37), had caused a relaxation of their efforts (xii. 12), a sluggishness in their spiritual intelligence (vi. 12), a dimming of the brightness of their early faith (x. 32), a tendency to listen to new doctrines (xiii. 9, 17), a neglect of common worship (x. 25), and a tone of spurious independence towards their teachers (xiii. 7, 17, 24), which were evidently creating the peril of apostasy. Like their ancestors of old, the Hebrew Christians were beginning to find that the pure spiritual manna palled upon their taste. In their painful journey through the wilderness of life they were beginning to yearn for the pomp and boast and ease of Jewish externalism, just as their fathers had hankered after the melons and fleshpots of their Egyptian servitude. They were casting backward glances of regret towards the doomed city which they had left (xiii. 12). That the danger was imminent is clear from the awful solemnity of the appeals which again and again the writer addresses to them (ii. 1—4; iii. 7—19; vi. 4—12; x. 26—31; xii. 15—17), and which, although they are usually placed in juxtaposition to words of hope and encouragement (iii. 6, 14; vi. 11; x. 39; xii. 18—24; &c.), must yet be reckoned among the sternest passages to be found in the whole New Testament.

A closer examination of the Epistle may lead us to infer that this danger of apostasy—of gradually dragging their anchor and drifting away from the rock of Christ (ii. 1)—arose from two sources; namely—(1) the influence of some one prominent member of the community whose tendency to abandon the Christian covenant (iii. 12) was due to unbelief, and whose unbelief had led to flagrant immorality (xii. 15, 16); and (2) from a tendency to listen to the boastful commemoration of the glories and privileges of Judaism, and to recoil before the taunt that Christians were traitors and renegades, who without any compensatory advantage had forfeited all right to participate in the benefits of the Levitic ritual and its atoning sacrifices (xiii. 10, &c.).

In the communities of Jewish Christians there must have

been many whose faith and zeal—not kindled by hope, not supported by patience, not leavened with absolute sincerity, not maintained by a progressive sanctification—tended to wax dim and cold. And if such men chanced to meet some unconverted Jew, burning with all the patriotism of a zealot, and inflated with all the arrogance of a Pharisee, they would be liable to be shaken by the appeals and arguments of such a fellow-countryman. He would have asked them how they dared to emancipate themselves from a law spoken by Angels? He would have reminded them of the heroic grandeur of Moses; of the priestly dignity of Aaron; of the splendour and significance of the Temple Service; of the disgrace incurred by ceremonial pollution; of the antiquity and revealed efficacy of the Sacrifices; of the right to partake of the sacred offerings; above all, of the grandeur and solemnity of the Great Day of Atonement. He would dwell much on the glorious ritual when the High Priest passed into the immediate presence of God in the Holiest Place, or when "he put on the robe of honour and was clothed with the perfection of glory, when he went up to the holy altar, and made the garment of holiness honourable," and "the sons of Aaron shouted, and sounded the silver trumpets, and made a great noise to be heard for a remembrance before the Most High" (Ecclus. l. 5—16). He would have asked them how they could bear to turn their backs on the splendid history and the splendid hopes of their nation. He would have taunted them with leaving the inspired wisdom of Moses and the venerable legislation of Sinai for the teaching of a poor crucified Nazarene, whom all the Priests and Rulers and Rabbis had rejected. He would have contrasted the glorious Deliverer who should break in pieces the nations like a potter's vessel with the despised, and rejected, and accursed Sufferer—for had not Moses said "Cursed of God is every one who hangeth on a tree"?—whom they had been so infatuated as to accept for the Promised Messiah!

We know that St Paul was charged—charged even by Christians who had been converted from Judaism—with "*apostasy from Moses*" (Acts xxi. 21). So deep indeed was this feeling that, according to Eusebius, the Ebionites rejected all his Epistles on the ground that he was "an apostate from the Law." Such taunts could not move St Paul, but they would be deeply and keenly felt by wavering converts exposed to the fierce flame of Jewish hatred and persecution at an epoch when there arose among their countrymen throughout the world a recrudescence of Messianic excitement and rebellious zeal. The object of this Epistle was to shew that what the Jews called "Apostasy from Moses" was demanded by faithfulness to Christ, and that apostasy from Christ to Moses was not only an inexcusable blindness but an all-but-unpardonable crime.

If such were the dangerous influences to which the Hebrew community here addressed was exposed, it would be impossible to imagine any better method of removing their perplexities, and dissipating the mirage of false argument by which they were being deceived, than that adopted by the writer of this Epistle. It was his object to demonstrate once for all the inferiority of Judaism to Christianity; but although that theme had already been handled with consummate power by the Apostle of the Gentiles, alike the arguments and the method of this Epistle differ from those adopted in St Paul's Epistles to the Galatians and the Romans.

The *arguments* of the Epistle are different. In the Epistles to the Galatians and the Romans St Paul, with the sledge-hammer force of his direct and impassioned dialectics, had shattered all possibility of trusting in legal prescriptions, and demonstrated that the Law was no longer obligatory upon Gentiles. He had shewn that the distinction between clean and unclean meats was to the enlightened conscience a matter of indifference; that circumcision was now nothing better than a physical mutilation; that the Levitic system was composed of "weak and beggarly elements;" that ceremonialism was a yoke with which the free converted Gentile had nothing to do; that we are saved by faith and not by works; that the Law was a dispensation of wrath and menace, introduced "for the sake of transgressions" (Gal. iii. 19; Rom. v. 20); that so far from being (as all the Rabbis asserted) the one thing on account of which the Universe had been created, the Mosaic Code only possessed a transitory, subordinate, and intermediate character, coming in (as it were in a secondary way) between the Promise to Abraham and the fulfilment of that promise in the Gospel of Christ. To him therefore the whole treatment of the question was necessarily and essentially polemical, and in the course of these polemics he had again and again used expressions which, however unavoidable and salutary, could not fail to be otherwise than deeply wounding to the inflamed susceptibilities of the Jews at that epoch. There was scarcely an expression which he had applied to the observance of the Mosaic law which would not sound, to a Jewish ear, deprecatory or even contemptuous. No Jew who had rejected the Lord of Glory, and wilfully closed his reason against the force of conviction, would have been able to read those Epistles of St Paul without something like a transport of fury and indignation. They would declare that pushed to their logical consequences, such views could only lead (as in fact, when extravagantly perverted, they did lead) to Antinomian Gnosticism; and the reaction against them might tend to harden Jewish Christians in those Ebionite tendencies which found expression a century later in the Pseudo-Clementine writings. Those writings still breathe a spirit of bitter hatred against St Paul, and are "the literary memorial of a manœuvre which had for its aim the absorption of the Roman Church into Judæo-Christianity."

Now the arguments of the Epistle to the Hebrews turn on another set of considerations. They were urged from a different point of view. They do not lead the writer, except in the most incidental and the least wounding manner, to use expressions which would have shocked the prejudices of his unconverted countrymen He does not touch on the once-burning question of Circumcision. It is only towards the close of his Epistle (xiii. 9) that he has occasion to allude, even incidentally, to the distinction of meats. His subject does not require him to enter upon the controversy as to the degree to which Gentile proselytes were obliged to observe the Mosaic Law. He is nowhere compelled to break down the bristling hedge of Jewish exclusiveness. If he proves the boundless superiority of the New Covenant he does not do this at the expense of the majesty of the old. To him the richer privileges of Christianity are the developed germ of the Mosaic Dispensation, and he only contemplates them in their relation to the Jews. He was able to soothe the rankling pride of an offended Levitism by recognising Levitism as an essential link in an unbroken continuity. The difference between the Law and the Gospel in the controversial theology of St Paul was the difference of an absolute *antithesis*. In this Epistle the difference is not of kind but of degree. The difference of degree was indeed transcendent, but still it represented a progress and an evolution. His letter is therefore, as Baur says, "a thoroughly original attempt to establish the main results of St Paul's teaching upon new presuppositions and in an entirely independent way."

All this advantage arose from the point of view at which he was able to place himself. His Alexandrian training, his Jewish sympathies, the nature of his immediate argument, led him to see in Judaism not so much A LAW as a SYSTEM OF WORSHIP. The fact that the Jews who were trying to pervert his Christian converts had evidently contrasted the humility and the sufferings of Christ with the sacerdotal magnificence of the Jewish hierarchs, enabled him to seize on PRIESTHOOD and SACRIFICE rather than on Levitic ordinances as the central point of his treatment. Hence his whole reasoning turns on a different pivot from that of St Paul. The main thing which he has to shew is that Christianity is the perfect fulfilment of a Type. It is therefore not only needless for him to disparage the Type, but he can even extol its grandeur and beauty *as* a type. The antitheses of St Paul's controversy are of necessity far more sharp and hard. To him the contrast between the Law and the Gospel was a contrast between an awful menace and a free deliverance; between the threat of inevitable death and the gift of Eternal life. To St Paul the Law was an ended servitude, a superfluous discipline, a broken fetter, a torn and cancelled bond (Rom. viii. 2; Gal. iii. 24, 25; iv. 9, 25; Col. ii. 14, &c.): to this writer the Mosaic system, of which the Law was only a part, was a needless scaffolding, a superannuated symbol. To St Paul the essence of the Old Dispensation was summed up in the words

"*He that doeth them shall live by them*," which, taken alone, involved the exceptionless and pitiless conclusion 'since none have ever perfectly obeyed them, all shall perish by them': to this writer the essence of Mosaism was the direction which bade Moses to "*make all things after the pattern shewed him in the Mount*" (Heb. viii. 5). Hence the contrast between Judaism and Christianity was not, in the view of this writer, a contrast between Sin and Mercy, between Curse and Blessing, between Slavery and Freedom, but a contrast almost exclusively (so far as the direct argument was concerned) between Type and Antitype, between outline and image, between shadow and substance, between indication and reality. Thus St Paul's argument may be described as mainly ethical, and this writer's as mainly metaphysical. The Alexandrian philosophy with which he was familiar had led him to hold that the reality and value of every material thing and of every outward system depended on the nearness with which it approximated to a Præ-existent ideal. The seen world, the world of phenomena, is but a faint adumbration of the unseen world, the world of *Noumena*, the world of Ideas and of Archetypes (see infra § v. 3).

From this different line of his argument rises the complete difference of his method. The attitude which St Paul was forced to adopt was not, and could not be conciliatory. At the beginning of the warfare between Judaism and Christianity the battle had to be internecine till the victory had declared itself on one side or the other. It was as impossible for St Paul to dwell on the grandeur and significance of the Judaic system as it would have been for Luther to write glowing descriptions of the services rendered to humanity by the Mediæval Papacy. It was not until Luther had published his *De captivitate Babylonica* that Protestant writers, secure in their own position, might without danger dwell on the good as well as on the evil deeds which the Popes have done. Similarly, until St Paul had written his two great controversial Epistles, a Jewish Christian could hardly speak freely of the positive value and greatness of the Levitic Law. A Jew, reading for the first time the Epistle to the Hebrews, would be favourably impressed with the evident love and sympathy which the writer displays towards the Tabernacle, its ministers, and its ritual. He would without difficulty concede the position that these were typical. He would thus be led, insensibly and without offence, into a consideration of the argument that these symbols found in Christ their predestined and final fulfilment (x. 1). When he had been taught, by a method of Scriptural application with which he was familiar, that a transference of the Priesthood had always been contemplated, he would be prepared to consider the Melchisedek Priesthood of Christ. When he saw that a transference of the Priesthood involved of necessity a transference of the Law (vii. 11, 12), he would be less indignant when he was at last confronted with such an expression as the *annulment* of the Law (vii. 18). The expressions ultimately applied to the Law are as strongly depreciatory as any in St Paul. The writer speaks of its "weakness and unprofitableness" (vii. 18); describes it as consisting in "carnal ordinances"; and declares that its most solemn sacrifices were utterly and necessarily inefficacious (ix. 13; x. 4). But the condemnation is *relative* rather than *absolute*, and the reader is not led to this point until he has seen that the legal institutions only shrink into insignificance in comparison with the finality and transcendent supremacy of the dispensation of which they were (after all) the appointed type.

The method adopted added therefore greatly to the inherent effectiveness of the line of controversy. It involved an Irony of the most finished kind, and in the original sense of the word. There was nothing biting and malicious in the irony, but it resembled the method often adopted by Socrates. Socrates was accustomed to put forward the argument of an opponent, to treat it with the profoundest deference, to discuss it with the most respectful seriousness, and all the while to rob it step by step of all its apparent validity, until it was left to collapse under the weight of inferences which it undeniably involved. In this Epistle, though with none of the dialectical devices of the great Athenian, we are led by a somewhat similar method to a very similar result. We see all the antiquity and glory of Mosaism. The Tabernacle rises before us in its splendour and beauty. We see the Ark and the Cherubim, and Aaron's rod that budded, and the golden pot of manna, and the wreaths of fragrant incense. We see the Levites in their white ephods busy with the sacrificial victims. We watch the High Priest as he passes with the blood of bulls and goats through the sanctuary into the Holiest Place. We see him come forth in his "golden apparel" and stand before the people with the jewelled Urim on his breast. And while the whole process of the solemn and gorgeous ritual is indicated with loving sympathy, suddenly, as with one wave of the wand, the Tabernacle, its Sacrifices, its Ritual, and its Priesthood seem to have been reduced to a shadow and a nullity, and we recognise the Lord Jesus Christ far above all Mediators and all Priests, and the sole means of perfect, confident, and universal access to the Inmost Sanctuary of God's Presence! We have, all the while, been led to recognise that, by faith in Christ, the Christian, not the Jew, stands forth as the true representative of the old traditions, the child of the glorious forefathers, the predestined heir of the Eternal Realities.

And thus the Epistle was equally effective both for Jews and Christians. The Jew, without one violent wrench of his prejudices, without one rude shock to his lifelong convictions, was drawn along gently, considerately, skilfully, as by a golden chain of fine rhetoric and irresistible reasoning, to see that the New Dispensation was but the glorious fulfilment, not the ruinous overthrow, of the Old; the Jewish Christian, so far from being robbed of a single privilege of Judaism, is taught that he may enjoy those privileges in their very richest significance. So far from being compelled to abandon the viaticum of good examples which had been the glory of his nation's history, he may feed upon those examples with a deeper sympathy: and so far from losing his beneficial participation in Temples and Sacrifices, he is admitted by the blood of the only perfect Sacrifice into the inmost and the eternal Sanctuary of which the Temple of his nation was but a dim and perishable sign.

The Epistle falls into two divisions:—I., chiefly Didactic (i.—x. 18); II., chiefly Hortative (x. 18—xiii. 25).

The general analysis of the Epistle is as follows:

It was the constant boast of the Jews that their Law was given by Angel-ministers, and on this ground, as well as on the historic grandeur of Moses, Aaron, and Joshua, they claimed for it a superiority over every other dispensation. The writer, therefore, after laying down his magnificent thesis that the Gospel is God's full and final Revelation to man (i. 1—4), proceeds to compare the Old and the New Covenants under the double aspect of (I) their ministering agents (i.—viii.), and (II) their advantageous results (ix.—x. 18).

I. Christ superior to the mediators of the Old Covenant.

α. The infinite superiority of Jesus to the Angels is first demonstrated by a method of Scriptural illustration of which the validity was fully recognised by all Jewish interpreters (i. 5—14). After a word of warning exhortation (ii. 1—4) he shews that this superiority is not diminished but rather enhanced by the temporary humiliation which was the voluntary and predestined means whereby alone He could accomplish His redemptive work (ii. 5—18).

β. And since the Jews placed their confidence in the mighty names of Moses and of Joshua, he proceeds to shew that Christ is above Moses by His very nature and office (iii. 1—6). Then after another earnest appeal (iii. 7—19) he proves more incidentally that Christ was above Joshua, in that He led His people into that true, final, and Sabbatic rest of which, as he proves from Scripture, the rest of Canaan was but a poor and imperfect type (iv. 1—10).

γ. But since he regards the Priesthood rather than the Law as the central point of the Mosaic dispensation, he now enters on the subject which is the most prominent in his thoughts, and to which he has already twice alluded (ii. 17; iii. 1), that CHRIST IS OUR HIGH PRIEST, and that His High Priesthood, as an Eternal Priesthood after the order of Melchisedek, is superior to that of the Aaronic High Priests. The development of this topic occupies nearly six chapters (v. 1—x. 18).

He first lays down the two qualifications for every High Priest, (1) that he must be able to sympathise with those for whom he ministers (v. 1—3), and (2) that he must not be self-called, but appointed by God (v. 4): both of which qualifications Christ possessed (v. 5—10).

But it is a characteristic of his style, and it furthered his main purpose, to mingle solemn passages of warning, exhortation, and encouragement with his line of demonstration. Here, therefore, he pauses on the threshold of his chief argument, to complain of their spiritual dulness and backwardness (v. 11—14); to urge them to more earnest endeavours after Christian progress (vi. 1—3); to warn them of the awful danger and hopelessness of wilful apostasy (4—8); to encourage them by an expression of hope founded on their Christian beneficence (9—10); and to stir them to increased zeal (11, 12) by the thought of the immutable certainty of God's oathbound promises (13—18), which are still further assured to us by the Melchisedek Priesthood of Christ our Forerunner within the Veil (19, 20).

Reverting thus to the comparison of Christ's Priesthood with the Levitic Priesthood (to which he had already alluded in v. 6, 10), he shews that the High Priesthood of Christ, being "after the order of Melchisedek," was superior to that of Aaron,

1. Because it is eternal not transient (vii. 1—3).
2. Because even Abraham paid tithes to Melchisedek (4—6).
3. Because Melchisedek blessed Abraham (7).
4. Because the Levitic Priests die, while Melchisedek stands as the type of an undying Priesthood (8).
5. Because even Levi may be said to have paid tithes to Melchisedek in the person of his ancestor Abraham (9, 10).
6. Because David's reference to Melchisedek shews the contemplated transference of the Priesthood, and therefore of the Law (11, 12). This is confirmed by the fact that Christ was of the tribe of Judah, not of Levi (13, 14). The Melchisedek Priesthood, being eternal, could not be connected with a law which, being weak and profitless, perfected nothing (15—19).
7. Because the Melchisedek Priesthood was founded by an oath (20—22).
8. Because the Levitic priests die, but Christ abideth for ever (23—25).

11. Having thus compared the two orders of Priesthood, he pauses for a moment to dwell on the eternal fitness of Christ's Priesthood to fulfil the conditions which the needs of humanity require (26—28). Into this passage, in his usual skilful manner, he introduces the comparison of the two forms of sacerdotal ministry which he develops in the next three chapters (viii. 1— x. 18).

a. For the Tabernacle which the Levitic Priests serve is— even on their great Day of Atonement—only the shadow of an eternal reality (viii. 1—6). The eternal reality is the new Covenant, which had been promised by Jeremiah, in which the Law should be written on men's hearts, and in which all should know the Lord; and the very fact that a *new* covenant had been promised implies the annulment of the old (viii. 7—13).

β. The Old Tabernacle was glorious and symbolic (ix. 1—5), yet even the High Priest, on the greatest day of its ritual, could only enter once a year into its inmost shrine, and that only with the imperfect and symbolic offerings of a burdensome externalism (6—10). But Christ, the Eternal High Priest of the Ideal Archetype, entered into the Heavenly tabernacle (11) with His own blood, once for all; and for ever (12, 13), offered Himself as a voluntary and sinless offering, eternally efficacious to purge the conscience from dead works (14); and so by His death became the mediator of a new and transcendent covenant, and secured for us the eternal inheritance (14, 15). For a 'Covenant' may also be regarded as a 'Testament,' and that involves the fact of a Death (16, 17). So that just as the Old Covenant was inaugurated by the sprinkling of purifying blood over its Tabernacle, its ministers, its book, its people, and the furniture of its service, in order to secure the remission of transgressions (18—22), the heavenly archetype of these things, into which Christ entered, needed also to be sprinkled with the blood of that better sacrifice (23) which has provided for us, once for all, an all-sufficient expiation (24—28). Then, in one grand finale, in which he gathers the scattered elements of his demonstration into a powerful summary, he speaks of the impotence of the Levitic sacrifices to perfect those who offered them—an impotence attested by their constant repetition (x. 1—4)—and contrasts them with that perfect obedience whereby (as illustrated in Ps. xl. 6, 7) Christ had annulled those sacrifices (5—9). Christ sanctified us for ever by His offered body (10). He did not offer incessant and invalid offerings like the Levitic Priests (11), but one perfect and perfecting sacrifice, as a preliminary to His eternal exaltation (12—14), in accordance with the prophecy of Jeremiah (xxxi. 33, 34), to which the writer had already referred (15—18).

III. The remainder of the Epistle (x. 19—xiii. 17) is mainly hortatory.

He has made good his opening thesis that God 'in the end of these days has spoken unto us by His Son.' This he has done by shewing Christ's superiority to Angels (i. 5—ii. 16) and to Moses and Joshua (iii. 1—iv. 16); His qualifications for High Priesthood (v. 1—10); the superiority of His Melchisedek Priesthood over that of Aaron (vii. 1—28); and the superiority of the ordinances of His New Covenant over those of the Old (viii. 1—x. 15). He has thus set forth to the wavering Hebrew Christians, with many an interwoven appeal, incontrovertible reasons why they should not abandon the better for the worse, the complete for the imperfect, the valid for the inefficacious, the Archetype for the copy, the Eternal for the transient. It only remains for him to apply his arguments by final exhortations. This he does by one more solemn strain of warning and encouragement (x. 19—39), which leads him into a magnificent historic illustration of the nature of faith as manifested by works (xi.). This served to shew the Jewish Christians, that, so far from being compelled to abandon the mighty memories of their past history, they were themselves the true heirs and the nearest representatives of that history, so that their unconverted brethren rather than themselves were aliens from the Commonwealth of Israel and strangers from the Covenants of promise. The Epistle closes with fervent exhortations to moral steadfastness and a holy Christian walk in spite of trial and persecution (xii. 1—14). This is followed by a warning founded on the great contrast which he has developed between the Old and New Covenants

(15—29). He gives them special directions to be loving, hospitable, sympathetic, pure, contented, and gratefully recognizant of their departed teachers (xiii. 1—9). Then with one more glance at the difference between the New and the Old Dispensations (10—15), he adds a few more affectionate exhortations (16—19), and ends with brief messages and blessings (23—25).

We see then that the whole Epistle forms an argument *a minori ad majus*. If Judaism had its own privileges, how great, *a fortiori*, must be the privileges of the Gospel! Hence the constant recurrence of such expressions as "a better hope" (vii. 19); "a better covenant" (vii. 22); "a more excellent ministry" (viii. 6); "a better and more perfect Tabernacle" (ix. 11), "better sacrifices" (ix. 23); "better promises" (viii. 6). It may almost be said that the words "by how much more" (ix. 14; τοσούτῳ κρείττων...ὅσῳ, i. 4, καθ' ὅσον, vii. 20, ὅσῳ, viii. 6, πόσῳ, x. 29) are the keynote of the entire treatment. It was a style of argument of which the Jews had often studied the validity; for the first of the seven famous *Middoth* or 'rules of interpretation' elaborated by the great Rabbi Hillel was called "Light and Heavy" (קל וחומר) which is nothing but the deduction of the greater from the less; a mode of argument which our Lord Himself had used, on more than one occasion, in His controversies with the Pharisees (Matt. x. 29).

We know nothing of the effects produced by the Epistle upon the particular community of Christians to which it was addressed, but we feel that if they could retrograde into Judaism after meditating on these arguments their apostasy must indeed have been of that moral and willing character for which, humanly speaking, there was little hope.

CHAPTER II.

WHERE WAS THE EPISTLE WRITTEN? AND TO WHOM?

1. *Ubi?* Where was the letter written?

The question cannot be answered. The only possible clue to any answer lies in the words "they of Italy salute you" (xiii. 24).

But this furnishes us with no real clue. "They of Italy" means simply "the Italians." The salutation might be sent from any city in the world in which there were Jewish Christians, or even Gentile converts, whose home was or once had been in Italy. It is however a little strange that many, both in ancient and modern times, should have assumed from this passage that the letter was written in Italy. There would indeed be nothing against this in the use of the preposition ἀπὸ, but if the letter were written from Rome or Italy it would be strange to say "those of Italy salute you." If I wrote from Paris or Vienna to an English friend in Russia or elsewhere I might naturally say "our *English* friends salute you," but hardly if I wrote from London or any town in England. Nothing in the way of reasonable conjecture can be deduced from a reference so absolutely vague. Nor again can we found any conclusion on the fact that Timothy was known to these Hebrew Christians. There was a constant intercourse by letters and messengers between the small and suffering communities of early Christians, and Timothy was probably known by name to every Church in Proconsular Asia, in Palestine, in Greece, in Italy, and in the islands and along the shores of the entire Mediterranean.

2. To whom was this Epistle written?

We have seen that the writer evidently had some *one* community in view. This is proved by the specific character of his messages and admonitions. Even if the last four verses were a special postscript to some particular Church we should draw the same conclusion. We must therefore reject the supposition of Euthalius and others that it was addressed 'to *all* the converted Hebrews of the Circumcision'—"les Judéo-chrétiens en général considérés au point de vue théorique" (Reuss). Where then did these Hebrew Christians reside? To what city was the letter originally sent? The genuine superscription gives us no help, for it is simply "To the Hebrews."

a. The general tradition, originated by some of the Greek fathers (e.g. Chrysostom and Theodoret), assumes that the letter was addressed to the Palestinian Jews, and specially to the Church of JERUSALEM. This was partly deduced from the erroneous notion that the members of the Mother Church were exclusively designated by the title of "the saints." Ebrard supposes that it was written to encourage Christian neophytes at Jerusalem, who were rendered anxious by being excluded from the Temple worship and from participation in the sacrifices. No doubt this supposition would suit such expressions as those in xiii. 10, 13, and much of the Epistle would have had a deep interest for those who were daily witnesses of, and possibly even worshippers in, the services of the Temple. Yet the opinion is untenable. The Judaists of Palestine would be little likely to welcome the letter of a Hellenist, who apparently knew no Hebrew, and who only quotes the Septuagint even when it differs from the sacred text (e.g. i. 6, x. 5); nor would they feel any special interest in a half-Gentile convert like Timothy. Further, it would hardly be true of them that "they had not yet resisted unto blood" (xii. 4). Again, they were little likely to have forgotten their dead leaders (xiii. 7); they had received the Gospel first-hand, not second-hand; and many of them may even have heard the Gospel from the Lord Himself (ii. 3). Nor were they in a position to minister to the saints (vi. 10), since they were themselves plunged in the deepest poverty. Least of all is it probable that an Alexandrian Hellenist, of the school of one so little acceptable to the Palestinian Judaists as that of St Paul, would have ventured not only to address them in a tone of authority, but even to reproach these Churches of the earliest Saints in words of severe rebuke for their ignorance and childishness (v. 11—14).

β. The Church of CORINTH is perhaps excluded by ii. 3, which seems to refer to some community founded by one of the original Twelve Apostles.

γ. That the letter was addressed to the Church of ALEXANDRIA is by no means improbable. It has been supposed that there is an allusion to this Epistle in the Muratorian Canon under the name of 'an Epistle to the Alexandrians;' and in the Manuscript D is a reading ($\dot{\epsilon}\nu$ $\tau\hat{\eta}$ $\pi\alpha\tau\rho\dot{\iota}\delta\iota$) in Acts xviii. 25, which implies that Apollos, the probable writer of the Epistle, had been converted to Christianity in Alexandria. This opinion, with the modification that it was addressed to Jewish Christian *ascetics* in Alexandria (Dr Plumptre), or to a *section* only of the Alexandrian Church (Hilgenfeld), has been widely accepted by modern critics. There are however several objections to this view. (1) The Church of Alexandria is believed to have been founded by St Mark, and not by one of the Twelve. (2) Alexandria is a Church with which neither St Paul nor Timothy had any direct connexion. (3) The Epistle is not heard of in the Alexandrian Church till nearly a century later. (4) The authorship of the Epistle was not certainly known in the school of Alexandria, which indeed did more than any other school to originate the mistaken impression that it was written by St Paul.

δ. Some critics have supposed that it was addressed to the Jewish-Christian community at ROME. The suggestion suits the references in ii. 3; xiii. 7, 9; x. 32. It also suits the fact that the writer seems to have been acquainted with the Epistle to the Romans (see x. 30; xiii. 1—6, 9—20), and that the Roman Church was from the first aware that the Epistle was *not* written by St Paul. But this view is excluded by the very probable conjecture that Timothy had been imprisoned at Rome during his last visit to St Paul (xiii. 23); by the silence of St Clement as to the author; by the absence of any trace that Apollos had ever visited Rome; by the fact that the persecutions to which allusion is made had, for some time, expended their severity (x. 32); as well as by the certainty that the Church of Rome, more than any other, had been deluged with the blood of martyrdom (xii. 4); and by the absence of all allusion to the Church of the Gentiles.

ε. Other isolated conjectures—as that it was addressed to Ravenna (Ewald), or Jamnia (Willib. Grimm), or Antioch (Hofmann)—may be passed over; but it may be worth considering whether it was not addressed to the Jewish Christians at EPHESUS. They must have been a numerous and important body, and both Apollos and Timothy had laboured among them.

CHAPTER III.

THE DATE.

Quando? The date at which the Epistle was written cannot be fixed with precision. All that we can say is that it was certainly written before the Fall of Jerusalem, A.D. 70. This conclusion is not mainly founded on the use of the present tense in speaking of the Temple services (ix. 6, 7; x. 1, &c.), because this might conceivably be due to the same figure of speech which accounts for the use of the present tense in speaking of the Jewish ministrations in Josephus, Clemens Romanus, Justin Martyr, and even in the Talmud. It is founded on the whole scope of the argument. No one who was capable of writing the Epistle to the Hebrews at all (there being no question of *pseudonymity* in this instance) could possibly have foregone all mention of the tremendous corroboration—nay, the absolutely demonstrative force—which had been added to his arguments by the work of God in History. The destruction of Jerusalem came as a divine comment on all the truths which are here set forth. While it in no way derogates from the permanent value of the Epistle as a possession for all time, it would have rendered superfluous its *immediate* aim and object. The seductions of Judaism, the temptation to apostatise to the Mosaic system, were done away with by that awful Advent which for ever closed the era of the Old Dispensation. We therefore infer that the Epistle was written when Timothy was (apparently) liberated from prison, soon after the martyrdom of St Paul, about the close of A.D. 67 or the beginning of A.D. 68.

CHAPTER IV.

STYLE AND CHARACTER OF THE EPISTLE.

1. THE notion that the Epistle was a translation from the Hebrew is found in St Clement of Alexandria, and is repeated

by Eusebius, Jerome, Theodoret, and by many others down to recent times. It seems to have originated in the attempt to account for the marked differences of style which separate it from the writings of St Paul. But this conjecture is wholly devoid of probability. St Clement couples it with the suggestion that it was translated by St Luke, because the style has some points of resemblance to that of the Acts of the Apostles. But St Luke (as we shall see) cannot have been the author, and the notion that it was written in Aramaic is now generally abandoned. No writing of antiquity shews fewer traces of being a translation. The Greek is eminently original and eminently polished. It abounds in paronomasiæ (plays on words, i. 1; ii. 8; v. 14; vii. 3, 19, 22, 23, 24; viii. 7, 8; ix. 28; x. 29, 34—38, 39; xi. 27; xiii. 14, &c.). It is full of phrases, and turns of idiom, which could scarcely be rendered in Hebrew at all, or only by the help of cumbrous periphrases. The numerous quotations which it contains are taken not from the Hebrew but from the LXX., and the argument is sometimes built on expressions in which the LXX. differs from the original (i. 6, 7; ii. 7; x. 5). It touches in one passage (ix. 15) on the Greek meaning of the word $\delta\iota\alpha\theta\acute{\eta}\kappa\eta$, 'a testament,' which has no equivalent in the Hebrew *Berith*, 'a covenant[1].' The hypothesis that the Epistle was not originally written in Greek violates every canon of literary probability.

2. The style of the Epistle attracted notice even in the earliest times. It is as different as possible from the style of St Paul. "*Omnibus notis dissidet*" said the great scholar Erasmus. More than a thousand years ago Origen remarked that it is written in better and more periodic Greek. In its rhythm and balance it has been described as "elaborately and faultlessly rhetorical." The style of St Paul, whenever his emotions are deeply stirred, is indeed eloquent, but with a fervid, spontaneous, impassioned eloquence, which never pauses to round a

---

[1] Heb. ix. 16. Calvin says with his usual strong sense, "$\Delta\iota\alpha\theta\acute{\eta}\kappa\eta$ ambiguam apud Graecos significationem habet; *berith* autem Hebraeis non nisi *foedus* significat; haec una ratio sano judicii hominibus sufficiet ad probandum quod dixi, Graeco sermone scriptam fuisse epistolam."

period or to select a sonorous expression. He constantly mingles two constructions; breaks off into personal allusions; does not hesitate to use the roughest terms; goes off at a word; and leaves sentences unfinished. He writes like a man who thought in Aramaic while he expressed himself in Greek. The style of this writer bears the stamp of a wholly different individuality. He writes like a man of genius who is thinking in Greek as well as writing in it. He builds up his paragraphs on a wholly different model. He delights in the most majestic amplifications, in the most effective collocation of words, in the musical euphony of compound terms (see in the original i. 3; viii. 1; xii. 2, &c.). He is never ungrammatical, never irregular, never personal; he never struggles for expression; he never loses himself in a parenthesis; he is never hurried into an unfinished clause. He has less of burning passion, and more of conscious literary self-control. As I have said elsewhere, the movement of this writer resembles that of an Oriental Sheykh with his robes of honour wrapped around him; the movement of St Paul is that of an athlete girded for the race. The eloquence of this writer, even when it is at its most majestic volume, resembles the flow of a river; the rhetoric of St Paul is like the rush of a mountain-torrent amid opposing rocks.

3. The writer quotes differently from St Paul. St Paul often reverts to the original Hebrew, and when he uses the LXX. his quotations agree, for the most part, with the Vatican Manuscript. This writer (as I have already observed) follows the LXX. even when it differs from the Hebrew, and his citations usually agree with the Alexandrian Manuscript. St Paul introduces his references to the Old Testament by some such formula as "as it is written," or "the Scripture saith" (Rom. ix. 17; i. 17), whereas this writer adopts the Rabbinic and Alexandrian expressions, "He saith" (i. 5, 6; v. 6; vii. 13), "He hath said" (iv. 3); "Some one somewhere testifieth" (ii. 6); "as the Holy Spirit saith," or "He testifieth" (ii. 6; iii. 7; x. 15; vii. 17)—forms which are not used by St Paul.

4. Again, he constructs his sentences differently, and combines them by different connecting particles (see in the original

ii. 16 to iii. 16, &c.); and has at least six special peculiarities of style not found, or found but rarely, in St Paul—such as the constant use of "all;" the verb "to sit" used intransitively (i. 3; viii. 1); the phrase "even though" (ἐάνπερ); "whence" (ὅθεν), used in the sense of "wherefore;" "to perpetuity" instead of "always;" and his mode of heightening the comparative by a following preposition.

5. Once more, St Paul usually speaks of the Saviour as "our Lord Jesus Christ," or "Christ Jesus our Lord"—forms which occur sixty-eight times in his Epistles; this writer, on the other hand, usually refers to Him as "Jesus," or "the Lord," or "Christ," or "our Lord" (vii. 14), or "the Lord" (ii. 3), or, once only, as "our Lord Jesus" (xiii. 20), whereas the distinctive Pauline combination, "Christ Jesus," does not occur once (see note on iii. 1). The explanation of this fact is that, as time went on, the title "Christ" became more and more a personal name, and the name "Jesus" (most frequently used in this Epistle, ii. 9; iii. 1; vi. 20; vii. 22; x. 19; xii. 2, 24; xiii. 12) became more and more connotative of such supreme reverence and exaltation as to need no further addition or description.

CHAPTER V.

THEOLOGY OF THE EPISTLE.

THE author of this Epistle, though he is writing exclusively to Jewish Christians, and though he shews himself eminently Judaic in his sympathies, is yet distinctly of the same school as the Apostle of the Gentiles.

Of the four great topics which occupy so large a place in St Paul's Epistles—the relation of Judaism to Christianity, the redemptive work of Christ, justification by faith, and the call of the Gentiles—the first forms the main topic of this Epistle; the second occupies one large section of it (v. 1—x. 18); and the third is involved in one entire chapter (xi.). The fourth is indeed conspicuously absent, but its absence is primarily due to the concentration of the Epistle upon the needs of those readers to whom it was addressed. He says expressly that Christ died on behalf of every man (ii. 9), and no one has ever doubted respecting his full belief in the Universality of the Gospel. As the circumstances which occasioned the composition of the Epistle furnished no opportunity to dwell upon the subject, he leaves it on one side. It is probable that even in the most bigoted of the Jewish Christian communities the rights of the Gentiles to equal participation in the privileges of the Gospel without any obligation to obey the Levitic law had been fully established, partly by the decree of the Synod of Jerusalem (Acts xv. 1—29), and partly by the unanswerable demonstrations of St Paul.

It need hardly be said that the writer of this Epistle is at one with St Paul upon all great fundamental doctrines. Both of the sacred writers speak of the heavenly exaltation of Christ (Eph. iv. 10; Heb. ix. 24); of His prevailing intercession (Rom. viii. 34; Heb. vii. 25); of the elementary character of the ceremonial Law (Gal. iv. 3; Heb. vii. 19); of Christ as "the end of the Law" (Rom. x. 4; Heb. x. 4—7); and of a multitude of other deep religious truths which were the common heritage of all Christians.

But while he deals with the same great topics as the Apostle of the Gentiles, he handles them in a very distinct manner, and with considerable variation of theological terminology.

a. In his mode of dealing with the Old and New Covenants we have already seen that he starts from a different point of view. He does not mention the subject of circumcision, so prominent throughout the Epistle to the Galatians; and while his proof that Christ is superior to Moses only occupies a few verses (iii. 1—6), he devotes a large and most important part of his letter to the proof that Christ's Priesthood is superior to that of Aaron, and that it is a Priesthood after the order of Melchisedek—whom St Paul does not so much as name. Indeed, while in this Epistle the titles Priest and High Priest occur no less than 32 times, in accordance with their extreme prominence in the theological conceptions of the writer, it is remarkable that neither word occurs so much as once in all the 13 Epistles of St Paul.

β. In speaking of the Redemptive work of Christ he is evidently at one with St Paul (ix. 15, 22), but does not enter so fully upon the *mysterious* aspect of Christ's death as an expiatory sacrifice. As though he could assume all which St Paul had written on that subject, he leaves (as it were) "a gap between the means and the end," asserting only again and again, but without explanation and comment, the simple fact that Christ offered Himself as a sacrifice, and that man was thereby sanctified and purified (ii. 11; ix. 13, 14; x. 2, 10, 14, 22). In his favourite conception of 'perfectionment' (*teleiōsis*) he seems to include justification, sanctification, and glorification. His conception of Christ is less that of a Crucified and Risen Redeemer, than that of a sympathising and glorified High Priest. And the result of His work is described not as leading to a mystic oneness with Him, but as securing us a free access to Him, and through Him into the Inmost Sanctuary of God.

γ. Again, there is a difference between the writer and St Paul in their use of the terms Justification and Faith. In St Paul the term 'Justification by Faith' succinctly describes the method by which the righteousness of God can become the justification of man—the word for 'righteousness' and 'justification' being the same (*dikaiosunē*). But in this Epistle the word 'righteousness' is used in its simple and original sense of moral rectitude. The *result* of Christ's redemptive work, which St Paul describes by his use of *dikaiosunē* in the sense of 'justification,' this writer indicates by other words, such as 'sanctification,' 'purification,' and 'bringing to perfection.' He does not allude to the notion of "*imputed*" righteousness as a condition freely bestowed by God upon man, but describes 'righteousness' as faith manifested by obedience and so earning the testimony of God (xi. 4, 5). It is regarded not as the Divine gift which man receives, but as the human condition which faith produces. The phrase "to justify," which occurs 28 times in St Paul, is not once found in this Epistle. The writer, like St Paul, quotes the famous verse of Habakkuk, "The just shall live by faith" (perhaps in the slightly different form, "My just man shall live by faith[1]") but the sense in which he quotes it is not the *distinctive* sense which it bears in St Paul—where it implies that 'the man who has been justified by that trust in Christ which ends in perfect union with Him shall enjoy eternal life,'— but rather in its simpler and more original sense that 'the upright man shall be saved by his faithfulness.' For 'faith' when used by St Paul in the sense peculiar to his writings, means the life in Christ, the absolute personal communion with His death and resurrection. But the central conception, "in Christ"— Christ not only for me but *in* me—is scarcely alluded to by the author of this Epistle. He uses the word 'faith' in its more common sense of 'trust in the Unseen.' He regards it less as the instrument of justification than as the condition of access (iii. 14; iv. 2, 16; vi. 1; vii. 25; x. 1, 22; xi. 1, 6).

δ. Again, one of the characteristics of this Epistle is the recurrence of passages which breathe a spirit peculiarly severe (ii. 1—3; iv. 1; vi. 4—8; x. 26—31; xii. 15—17), such as does indeed resemble a few passages of Philo, but finds no exact parallel even in the sternest passages of St Paul. Luther speaks of one of these passages as "a hard knot which seems in its obvious import to run counter to all the Gospels and the Epistles of St Paul." Both Tertullian and Luther missed the real significance of these passages, but the very interpretation which made the Epistle dear to the Montanistic hardness of Tertullian made it displeasing to the larger heart of the great Reformer.

ε. But the most marked feature of the Epistle to the Hebrews is its Alexandrian character, and the resemblances which it contains to the writings of Philo, the chief Jewish philosopher of the Alexandrian school of thought:—

1. Thus, it is Alexandrian in its quotations, which are (1) from the Septuagint version, and (2) agree mainly with the Alexan-

---

[1] The "my" is found in the LXX. sometimes after "just," sometimes after "faith;" and is read after "just" in ℵ, A, N, and after "faith" in D. See note on Heb. x. 38.

3—2

drian manuscript of that version, and (3) are introduced by formulæ prevalent in the Alexandrian school (see supra IV. § 3).

2. It is Alexandrian in its unusual expressions. Many of these (e.g. 'in many parts' i. 1, 'effluence' i. 2, 'hypostasis' i. 3, 'servant' (*therapon*) iii. 5; 'place of repentance' xii. 17; 'confirmation' vi. 16; 'issue' (*ekbasis*) xiii. 7, &c.), are common to this Epistle with the Alexandrian Book of Wisdom. So great indeed is the affinity between these books in their sonorous style, their use of compound terms, their rare phrases, and their accumulation of epithets that they are mentioned in juxtaposition by Irenæus (Euseb. *H. E.* v. 26), and nearly so in the Muratorian Canon. The writers of both had evidently studied Philo, and it has even been supposed by some that Philo, and by others that the writer of this Epistle, also wrote the Book of Wisdom.

3. It is Alexandrian in its method of dealing with Scripture. In the important section about Melchisedek the whole structure of the argument is built on two passing and isolated allusions to Melchisedek, of which the second was written nine hundred years after the death of the Priest-king. They are the only allusions to him in the Jewish literature of more than 1500 years. Yet upon these two brief allusions—partly by the method of allegory, partly by the method of bringing different passages together (iii. 11; iv. 8, 9), partly by the significance attached to names, (vii. 2), partly by the extreme emphasis attributed to single words (viii. 13), partly by pressing the silence of Scripture as though it were pregnant with latent meanings (i. 5; ii. 16; vii. 3)—the writer builds up a theological system of unequalled grandeur. But this whole method of treatment is essentially Rabbinic and Alexandrian. That it was, however, derived by the writer from his training in the methods of Alexandrian and not of Rabbinic exegesis arises from the fact that he is ignorant of Hebrew, and that the typical resemblance of Melchisedek to the Logos or Word of God had already excited the attention of Philo, who speaks of the Logos as "shadowed forth by Melchisedek" and as "the great High Priest." (*Leg. Alleg.* iii. 25, 26; *De Somn.* i. 38.)

4. It is Alexandrian in its fundamental conception of the

antithesis between the world of fleeting phenomena and the world of Eternal Realities, between the copies and the Ideas, between the shadows and the substance, between the visible material world and the world of divine Præ-existent Archetypes. The school of Philo had learnt from the school of Plato that "earth

> Is but the shadow of heaven, and things therein
> Each to the other like more than on earth is thought."

Hence (as I have said) the writer seizes on the passage "See that thou make all things according to the pattern shewed thee in the Mount" (viii. 5; ix. 23). To him the contrast between the Old and New Covenants turns on the fundamental antithesis between the Shadow and the Reality. Levitism was the shadow, Christianity is not a shadow but a substantial image; the *absolute* reality—to which Christianity is so much nearer an approximation, of which Christianity is so much closer a copy—is in the world to come. The Mosaic system, as concentrated in its Tabernacle, Priesthood, and Sacrifices is only "a copy" (viii. 5); "a shadow" (x. 1), "a parable" (ix. 9); 'a præfiguration' (ix. 24); whereas Christianity is by comparison, and by virtue of its closer participation in the Idea, 'the type,' 'the perfect,' 'the genuine' (viii. 2) 'the very image' (x. 1). The visible world (xi. 3) is "this creation" (ix. 11); it is "made with hands" (ix. 11); it is capable of being touched and grasped (xii. 18); it is but a quivering, unstable, transient semblance (xii. 27): but the invisible world is supersensuous, immaterial, immovable, eternal. It is the world of "Heavenly things" (ix. 23), the archetypal world, the true "House of God" (x. 21), "the genuine Tabernacle" (viii. 2), "the City which hath the foundations" (xi. 10), the true "fatherland" (xi. 14), "the heavenly Jerusalem" (xii. 22), "the kingdom unshaken" and that "cannot be shaken" (xii. 27, 28). And this invisible world is the world of the heirs of the Gospel. It is so now, and it will be so yet more fully. In the True Temple of Christianity the Visible and the Invisible melt into each other. The salvation is now subjectively enjoyed, it will hereafter be objectively realised (vi. 4, 5; xii. 28).

5. But the Alexandrianism of the Epistle appears most clearly in the constant parallels which it furnishes to the writings of Philo. We have already called attention to some of these, and they will be frequently referred to in the notes. Even in the general structure and style of the Epistle there are not only a multitude of phrases and expressions which are common to the writer with Philo, but we notice in both the same perpetual interweaving of argument with exhortation; the same methods of referring to and dealing with the Old Testament; the same exclusive prominence of the Hebrew people; the same sternness of tone in isolated passages; and the same general turns of phraseology (see Bleek's notes on i. 6; ii. 2; v. 11; vi. 1, &c.). If we find in Heb. ii. 6, "someone somewhere testified" and in iv. 4, "He hath spoken somewhere thus," we find the very same phrases in Philo (*De Plant.* § 21; *De Ebriet.* § 14, &c.). If we find in Heb. vii. 8, "being testified of that he liveth," we find also in Philo, "Moses being testified of that he was faithful in all his house" (comp. Heb. iii. 2). If in Heb. xiii. 5 we have the modified quotation, "I will never leave thee, nor will I ever in any wise forsake thee," we find it in the very same form in Philo (*De Confus. Lingu.* § 33).

We may here collect a few passages of marked resemblance.

i. Heb. i. 3, "who being the effluence of His glory..."
Philo *De Opif. Mundi* § 51. "Every man...having become an impression or fragment or effluence of the blessed nature."

ii. Heb. i. 3, 'the stamp of His substance.'
Philo (*Quod det. pot.* § 23) speaks of the spirit of man as "a type and stamp of the divine power," and (*De Plant.* § 5) of the soul, as "impressed by the seal of God of which the stamp is the everlasting Word."

iii. Heb. i. 6, "the First-begotten."
Philo (*De Agricult.* § 12) speaks of the Word as "the firstborn Son," and (*De Confus. Lingu.* § 14) as 'an eldest Son.'

iv. Heb. i. 2. "By whom also He made the worlds" (*aionas*).
Philo *De Migr. Abraham.* § 1, "You will find the Word of God the instrument by which the world (*kosmos*) was prepared."

v. Heb. xi. 3, "that the worlds (*aionas*) were made by the utterance of God."

Philo (*De Sacrif. Abel*, § 18), "God in saying was at the same time creating."

vi. Heb. i. 3, "And bearing all things by the utterance of His power."

Philo (*Quis Rer. Div. Haer.* § 7), "He that beareth the things that are."

vii. Heb. iii. 3, "in proportion as he that buildeth the house hath more honour than the house."

Philo (*De Plant.* § 16), "Being so much better as the possessor is better than the thing possessed, and that which made than the thing which is made."

viii. Heb. iv. 12, 13, "For living is the Word of God and efficient and more cutting than any two-edged sword, and piercing to the division both of soul and spirit, both of joints and marrow."

Philo (*Quis Rer. Div. Haer.* § 28), commenting on Abraham's "dividing the sacrifices in the midst," says that "God did thus with His Word, which is the cutter of all things, which, whetted to its keenest edge, never ceases to divide all perceptible things, but when it pierces through to the atomistic and so-called indivisible things, again this cutter begins to divide from these the things that can be contemplated in speech into unspeakable and incomprehensible portions;" and farther on he adds, that the soul is "threefold," and that "each of the parts is cut asunder," and that the Word divides "the reasonable and the unreasonable." Elsewhere (*De Cherub.* § 9) he compares the Word to the fiery sword. Philo is applying the metaphors philosophically, not religiously, but it is impossible to suppose that the resemblance between the passages is merely accidental.

ix. Heb. iv. 12, "and is a discerner of the thoughts and intents of the heart."

Philo (*De Leg. Alleg.* iii. 59), "And the Divine Word is most keen-sighted, so as to be capable of inspecting all things."

x. Heb. vi. 5, "tasting that the utterance of God is excellent."

Philo (*De Profug.* § 25), "The souls, tasting (the utterance of God) as a divine word (*logos*) a heavenly nurture." (Comp. *De Leg. Alleg.* iii. 60.)

xi. Heb. iii. 6, "whose house are we."

Philo (*De Somn.* i. 23), "Strive, oh soul, to become a house of God."

xii. Heb. vi. 13, "since He could not swear by any greater He sware by Himself."

Philo (*De Leg. Alleg.* iii. 72). "Thou seest that God sweareth not by another, for nothing is better than Him, but by Himself who is best of all."

xiii. Heb. vii. 27, "who hath not need, *daily*, like those High Priests..."

Philo (*De Spec. Legg.* §. 23), "The High Priest...offering prayers and sacrifices day by day."

xiv. Heb. ix. 7, "once in the year only the High Priest enters."

Philo (*Leg. ad Caj.* § 39), "into which once in the year the great Priest enters."

xv. We might add many similar references; *e.g.* to Abel's blood (xii. 24); Noah's righteousness (xi. 7); Abraham's obedience, in going he knew not whither (xi. 8); the faithfulness of Moses (iii. 2, 5); milk and solid food (v. 12—14); the fact that sacrifices are meant to *call sin to remembrance* (x. 3); the stress laid on the word "To-day" (iii. 7—15). But it will be sufficient to add a few passages in which Philo speaks of the Logos as High Priest.

xvi. Heb. iv. 14, "Having then a great High Priest..."

Philo (*De Somn.* i. 38), "The great High Priest then," &c.

xvii. Heb. iv. 15, "without sin," vii. 26, "Holy, harmless, undefiled."

Philo (*De Profug.* § 20), "For we say that the High Priest is not a man but the Divine Word, with no participation in any sin whether voluntary or involuntary." *Id.* § 21, "It is his nature to be wholly unconnected with all sin."

xviii. Heb. iv. 15, "able to be touched with a feeling of our infirmities."

Philo (*De Profug.* § 18), "not inexorable is the Divine, but gentle through the mildness of its nature."

xix. Heb. vii. 25, "living to make intercession for them."

Philo (*De Migr. Abraham*, § 21), "But these things He is accustomed to grant, not turning away from His suppliant Word."

xx. Heb. v. 10, "After the order of Melchisedek."

Philo (*De Leg. Alleg.* iii. 26), "For the Logos is a Priest," &c. who, as he proceeds to say, brings righteousness and peace to the soul, and has his type in Melchisedek "the Righteous King" and the King of Salem, *i.e.* of Peace. See also *De congr. quaerend. erudit. grat.* § 18.

xxi. Heb. vii. 3, "without father, without mother."

Philo (*De Profug.* § 20), "For we say that the High Priest is not a man but the Divine word...wherefore I think that He is sprung from incorruptible parents...from God as His Father, and from Wisdom as His mother."

For these and other passages see Siegfried *Philo von Alexandria* 321—330 and Gfrörer's *Philo und die Alex. Theosophie* i. 163—248.

CHAPTER VI.

THE AUTHOR OF THE EPISTLE.

WE now come to the question *Quis?*—who wrote the Epistle to the Hebrews?

In our Authorised Version and even in the Revised Version—which does not however profess to have reconsidered the superscriptions of the Epistles—we find the heading "The Epistle *of Paul the Apostle* to the Hebrews." Now the writer was undoubtedly a Paulinist, i.e. he belongs to the same school of thought as St Paul. Besides the common phrases which form part of the current coin of Christian theology he uses some which are distinctively Pauline. He had been deeply influenced by the companionship of the Apostle and had adopted much of his distinctive teaching. This is universally admitted. The student who will compare ii. 10, vi. 10, x. 30, xii. 14, xiii. 1—6, 18, 20 with Rom. xi. 36; 1 Thess. i. 3; Rom. xii. 19, 18, 1—21; 2 Cor. iv. 2; Rom. xv. 33 respectively, and who will observe the numerous other resemblances to which attention is called in the following notes, will have sufficient proof of this. The writer uses about fifty words which in the N. T. only occur in the Epistles of St Paul or in his speeches as recorded by St Luke, and in the last chapter the resemblances to St Paul are specially numerous. On the other hand, after what we have already seen of the differences of style, of method, of culture, of individuality, of theological standpoint, and of specific terminology between the writer of this Epistle and St Paul, we shall be compelled to admit not only that St Paul could not possibly have been the actual *writer* of the Epistle—a fact which was patent so far back as the days of Origen—but that it could not even indirectly have been due to his authorship. The more we study the similarities between this and the Pauline Epistles—and the more strongly we become convinced that the writers were connected in faith and feeling—the more absolutely incompatible (as Dean Alford has observed) does the notion of their personal identity become. And this is exactly the conclusion to which we are led by a review of the ancient evidence upon the subject. The Early Western Church seems to have *known* that St Paul did not write the Epistle. In the Eastern Church the obvious and superficial points of resemblance gave currency to the common belief in the Pauline authorship, but the deeper-lying differences were sufficient to convince the greatest scholars that (at the best) this could only be admitted in a modified sense.

The Epistle was known at a very early period and is very largely used and imitated by St Clement of Rome, in his letter to the Corinthians (*circ.* A.D. 96), and yet he nowhere mentions the name of the author. He would hardly have used it so extensively without claiming for his quotations the authority of St Paul if he had not been aware that it was *not* the work of the great Apostle.

In the Western Church no single writer of the first, second, or even third century attributed it to St Paul. ST HIPPOLYTUS († A.D. 235 ?) and ST IRENAEUS († A.D. 202) are said to have denied the Pauline authorship[1], though Eusebius tells us that Irenaeus (in a work which he had not seen, and which is not extant) quoted from it and from the Wisdom of Solomon. The Presbyter GAIUS did not number it among St Paul's Epistles. The CANON of MURATORI (*circ.* A.D. 170) either does not notice it, or only with a very damaging allusion under the name of an 'Epistle to the Alexandrians forged in the name of Paul with reference to the heresy of Marcion.' Yet MARCION himself rejected it, and NOVATIAN never refers to it, frequently as he quotes Scripture and useful as it would have been to him. TERTULLIAN († A.D. 240) representing perhaps the tradition of the Church of North Africa, ascribes it to Barnabas. This testimony to the non-Pauline authorship is all the weightier because Tertullian would have been only too eager to quote the authority of St Paul in favour of his Montanism had he been able to do so. St Cyprian († A.D. 258) never alludes to it. Victorinus of Pettau († 303) ignores it. The first writer of the Western Church who attributes it to St Paul (and probably for no other reason than that he found it so ascribed in Greek writers) is Hilary of Poictiers, who died late in the fourth century († A.D. 368). St Ambrose indeed († 397) and Philastrius (*circ.* A.D. 387) follow the Greeks in ascribing it to St Paul, though the latter evidently felt some hesitation about it. But it is certain that for nearly four centuries the Western Church refused in general to recognise the Pauline authorship, and this was probably due to some tradition on the subject which had come down to them from St Clement of Rome. If it had been

---

[1] Stephen Gobar ap. Phot. *Bibl. Cod.* 232.

written by the Apostle of the Gentiles, St Clement of Rome, who was probably a friend and contemporary of St Paul, would have certainly mentioned so precious a truth at least orally to the Church of which he was a Bishop. If he said any thing at all upon the subject it can only have been that whoever was the author *St Paul was not.*

Accordingly, even down to the seventh century we find traces of hesitation as to the Pauline authorship in the Western Church, though by that time a loose habit had sprung up of quoting it as 'the Epistle of Paul to the Hebrews.' This was due to the example of St Jerome († 420) and St Augustine († 430). These great men so far yielded to the stream of irresponsible opinion—which by their time had begun to set in from the East—that they ventured popularly to quote it as St Paul's, although when they touch seriously upon the question of the authorship they fully admit or imply the uncertainty respecting it. Their hesitation as to the Pauline authorship is incidentally shewn by the frequency with which they quote it either without any name, or with the addition of some cautionary phrase. That the Epistle is attributed to St Paul by *later* authors and Councils is a circumstance entirely devoid of any critical importance.

It was from the Eastern Church that the tendency to accept the Epistle as St Paul's derived its chief strength. The Alexandrian School naturally valued an Epistle which expressed their own views, and was founded upon premisses with which they were specially familiar. Apart from close criticism they would be naturally led by phenomena which lay on the surface to conjecture that it might be by St Paul; and (as has frequently happened) the hesitations of theological scholarship were swept away by the strong current of popular tradition. But this tradition cannot be traced farther back than an unsupported guess of the Presbyter PANTAENUS about the middle of the Second Century. St Clemens of Alexandria (in a lost work, quoted by Eusebius) says that the "blessed Presbyter" had endeavoured to account for the absence of St Paul's name (which is found in every one of his genuine Epistles) by two reasons. St Paul, he said, had suppressed it "out of modesty," both because the Lord was the true Apostle to the Hebrews (Heb. iii. 1), and because he was writing to the Hebrews "out of superabundance" being himself the Apostle of the Gentiles. Neither reason will stand a moment's consideration: they are desperate expedients to explain away an insuperable difficulty. For if St Paul had written "to the Hebrews" at all, there is no single writer who would have been less likely to write anonymously. Calvin rightly says "Ego ut Paulum agnoscam auctorem adduci nequeo. Nam qui dicunt nomen fuisse de industria suppressum quod odiosum esset Judaeis nihil afferunt. Cur enim mentionem fecisset Timothei? &c." It never occurred to any Apostle to consider that his title was an arrogant one, and the so-called "Apostolic Compact" no more prevented St Paul from addressing Jews than it prevented St Peter from addressing Gentiles. The fact that Eusebius quotes this allusion to Pantaenus as the earliest reference to the subject which he could find, shews that in spite of the obvious inference from x. 34 (and especially from the wrong reading "my bonds") there was no tradition of importance on the subject even in the Eastern Church during the first two centuries. ST CLEMENS of ALEXANDRIA is himself († A.D. 220) equally unsuccessful in his attempts to maintain even a modified view of the Pauline authorship. He conjectures that the Epistle was written in Hebrew, and had been translated by St Luke; and he tries to account for its anonymity by a most uncritical and untenable surmise. St Paul he says did not wish to divert the attention of the Jews from his arguments, since he knew that they regarded him with prejudice and suspicion. This singular notion—that St Paul wished to entrap the attention of his readers unawares before revealing his identity—has been repeated by writer after writer down to the present day. But no one can read the Epistle with care without seeing that the writer was obviously known to his readers, and intended himself to be known by them. No Apostolic Church would have paid any attention to an anonymous and unauthenticated letter. The letters were necessarily brought to them by accredited messengers; and if this letter had been written by St Paul to any Hebrew Community the fact would have been known to them in the first halfhour after the messenger's arrival.

ORIGEN again in a popular way constantly quotes the Epistle as St Paul's; but when he seriously entered on the question of the authorship, in a passage quoted by Eusebius from the beginning of his lost Homilies on the Epistle, he admits that the style is much more polished than that of St Paul, and while he says that the Pauline character of the thoughts furnishes some ground for the tradition that St Paul wrote it, he adds that the "history" which had come down about it was that it was "written" by Clement of Rome, or by Luke; but, he says, "who actually wrote the Epistle God only knows." Origen's authority has repeatedly been quoted as though it were decisively given in favour of the Pauline authorship of the Epistle. But if any one will examine the passage above referred to he will see that it represents a conflict between historical testimony and scholarlike criticism on one side, and loose local tradition on the other. Origen was glad to regard the Epistle as being *in some sense* St Paul's, and did not like to differ decidedly from Pantaenus, Clemens, and the general popular view prevalent in his own Church; but he decidedly intimates that *in its present form* St Paul did *not* write the Epistle, and that it can only be regarded as belonging to "the School of Paul."

Lastly, EUSEBIUS of CAESAREA shews the same wavering hesitation. He so far defers to indolent and biassed custom as constantly to quote the Epistle as St Paul's, but in one passage he seems to approve of the opinion that it had been translated from Hebrew, and in another he says that it would not be just to ignore that "some have rejected the Epistle to the Hebrews, saying that it is opposed by the Church of Rome as not being by St Paul."

It is hardly worth while to follow the stream of testimony into ages in which independent criticism was dead; but in the sixteenth century with the revival of scholarship the popular tradition once more began to be set aside. Cardinal Cajetan, Erasmus, Luther, Calvin, Melanchthon, and even Estius were all

INTRODUCTION. 47

more or less unfavourable to the direct Pauline authorship. In modern times, in spite of the intensely conservative character of Anglican theology, there are very few critics of any name even in the English Church, and still fewer among German theologians, who any longer maintain, even in a modified sense, that it was written by St Paul.

Who then was the writer?

From the Epistle itself we can gather with a probability which falls but little short of certainty the following facts (some of which it will be observed tell directly against the identity of the writer with St Paul).

1. The writer was a Jew, for he writes solely as a Jew, and as though the Heathen world were non-existent.

2. He was a Hellenist for he quotes from the LXX. without any reference to the original Hebrew, and even when it differs from the Hebrew (i. 6, x. 5).

3. He was familiar with the writings of Philo, and has been deeply influenced by Alexandrian thought.

4. He was 'an eloquent man and mighty in the Scriptures.'

5. He was a friend of Timotheus.

6. He was known to his readers, and addresses them in a tone of authority.

7. He was not an Apostle, but classes himself with those who had been taught by the Apostles (ii. 3).

8. He was acquainted with the thoughts of St Paul, and had read the Epistle to the Romans.

9. Yet his tone while harmonious with that of St Paul is entirely independent of it.

10. He wrote before the destruction of Jerusalem.

11. His references to the Tabernacle rather than to the Temple seem to make it improbable that he had ever been at Jerusalem.

Further than this it is at least a fair assumption that any friend and scholar of St Paul who was a man of sufficient learning and originality to have written such an Epistle as this, would be somewhere alluded to in that large section of the New Testament which is occupied by the writings and the biography of St Paul.

Accordingly there is scarcely one of the companions of St Paul who has not been suggested by some critic as a possible or probable author of this Epistle. Yet of these all but one are directly excluded by one or more of the above indications. AQUILA could not have written it, for he seems to have been of less prominence even than his wife Priscilla (Acts xviii. 18; 2 Tim. iv. 19). TITUS was a Gentile. SILAS was a Hebraist of Jerusalem. BARNABAS was a Levite, and the other Epistle attributed to him (though spurious) is incomparably inferior to the Epistle to the Hebrews. The genuine Epistle of ST CLEMENT of Rome shews that he could not have written the Epistle to the Hebrews, which indeed he largely quotes on a level with Scripture. The Gospel of ST MARK is wholly unlike this Epistle in style. The style of ST LUKE does indeed resemble in many *expressions* the style of this writer; but the Epistle contains passages (such as vi. 4—8, x. 26—29, &c.) which do not seem to resemble his tender and conciliatory tone of mind, and apart from this St Luke seems to have been a Gentile Christian (Col. iv. 10—14), and not improbably a Proselyte of Antioch. The resemblances between the two writers consist only in verbal and idiomatic expressions, and are amply accounted for by their probable familiarity with each other and with St Paul. But the idiosyncrasy is different, and St Luke has nothing of the stately balance or rhetorical amplitude of this Epistle. TIMOTHY is excluded by xiii. 23. No one else is left but that friend and convert to whom by a flash of most happy insight LUTHER attributed the authorship of the Epistle—APOLLOS.

Apollos meets every one of the necessary requirements. (1) He was a Jew. (2) He was a Hellenist. (3) He was an Alexandrian. (4) He was famed for his eloquence and his powerful method of applying Scripture. (5) He was a friend of Timotheus. (6) He had acquired considerable authority in various Churches. (7) He had been taught by an Apostle. (8) He was of the School of St Paul; yet (9) he adopted an independent line of his own (1 Cor. iii. 6). (10) We have no trace that he was ever at

Jerusalem; and yet, we may add to the above considerations, that his style of argument—like that of the writer of this Epistle—was specially effective as addressed to Jewish hearers. The writer's boldness of tone (Acts xviii. 26) and his modest self-suppression (1 Cor. xvi. 12) also point to Apollos. The various allusions to Apollos are found in Acts xviii. 24—28; 1 Cor. iii. 4—6, xvi. 12; Tit. iii. 13; and *in every single particular* they agree with such remarkable cogency in indicating to us a Christian whose powers, whose training, whose character, and whose entire circumstances would have marked him out as a man likely to have written such a treatise as the one before us, that we may safely arrive at the conclusion either that APOLLOS wrote the Epistle or that it is the work of some author who is to us entirely unknown.

CHAPTER VII.

CANONICITY.

THE Canonicity of the Epistle—that is its right to be placed in the Canon of Holy Scripture—rests on the fact that it has been accepted both by the Eastern and Western Churches. It was known from the earliest ages; was probably alluded to by Justin Martyr; was largely used by St Clement of Rome; is quoted on the same footing as the rest of Scripture by many of the Fathers; and both in the earlier Centuries and at the Reformation has been accepted as authoritative and inspired even by those who had been led to the conclusion that the current opinion of the Church after the third century had erred in assigning it to the authorship of St Paul. Its right to be accepted as part of the Canon, and not merely to possess the deutero-Canonical and inferior authority which Luther assigned to it, is all the more clearly established because it triumphed over the objections which some felt towards it. Those objections arose partly from the sterner passages (especially vi. 4—6), which were misinterpreted as favouring the merciless refusal of the Novatians to re-admit the lapsed into Church privileges; and partly from inability to understand the phrase "to Him that made Him" in iii. 2. But in spite of these needless difficulties which are mentioned by Philastrius late in the fourth century, the Epistle has been justly recognised as a part of sacred Scripture— "marching forth," as Delitzsch says, "in lonely royal and sacred dignity, like the great Melchisedek, and like him without lineage—$ἀγενεαλόγητος$." Even those who like Erasmus and Calvin were unable to admit its Pauline authorship, were still agreed in "embracing it, without controversy, among the Apostolical Epistles." They said with St Jerome, "*Nihil interesse cujus sit, dum ecclesiastici viri sit, et quotidie ecclesiarum lectione celebretur.*" It is no small blessing to the Church that in this Epistle we have preserved to us the thoughts of a deep thinker who while he belonged to the School of St Paul expresses the views of that School with an independent force, eloquence, and insight far surpassing that of every Christian treatise which is not included in the Sacred Canon.

THE EPISTLE OF PAUL THE APOSTLE

TO THE

HEBREWS.

G OD, who at sundry times and in divers manners spake in 1
time past unto the fathers by the prophets, hath in these 2

"The Epistle of Paul the Apostle to the Hebrews." This title is wholly without authority. The original title if there was one at all, probably ran simply "to the Hebrews" as in ℵ, A, B, K, and as in the days of Origen. In various MSS. the Epistle is found in different portions. In D, K, L, it stands as here. In ℵ, A, B, C, it is placed after 2 Thess. (See for fuller information Bleek *Hebraerbrief*, p. 45.)

CH. I. FINALITY AND TRANSCENDENCE OF GOD'S FINAL REVELATION IN CHRIST (1—4). ILLUSTRATIONS OF CHRIST'S PRE-EMINENCE **above Angels** (5—14).

1—4. THESIS OF THE EPISTLE.

1. *God, who at sundry times and in divers manners spake*] It is hardly possible in a translation to preserve the majesty and balance of this remarkable opening sentence of the Epistle. It must be regarded as one of the most pregnant and noble passages of Scripture. The author does not begin, as St Paul invariably does, with a greeting which is *almost* invariably followed by a thanksgiving; but at once, and without preface, he strikes the key-note, by stating the thesis which he intends to prove. His object is to secure his Hebrew readers against the peril of an apostasy to which they were tempted by the delay of Christ's personal return, by the persecutions to which they were subjected, and by the splendid memories and exalted claims of the religion in which they had been trained. He wishes therefore, not only to warn and exhort them, but also to prove that Christianity is a Covenant indefinitely superior to the Covenant of Judaism, alike in its **Agents** and its **Results**. The words "*How much more*," "*A better covenant*," "*a more excellent name*," might be regarded as the keynotes of the Epistle (iii. 3, vii. 19, 20, 22, viii. 6, ix. 23, x. 34, xi. 40, xii. 24, &c.). In many respects, it is not so much a letter as an address. Into these opening verses he has compressed a world of meaning, and has also strongly brought out the conceptions of the contrast between the Old and New Dispensations—a contrast which involves the vast superiority of the latter. Literally, the sentence may be rendered, "In many portions and in many ways, God having of old spoken to the fathers in the prophets, at the end of these days spake to us in **a Son**." It was **God** who spoke in both dispensations; of old and in the present epoch: to the fathers and to us; to them in the Prophets, to us in **a Son**; to them "in many portions" and therefore "fragmentarily," but—as the whole Epistle is meant to shew—to us with a full and complete revelation; to them "in many ways," "multifariously," but to us in one way—namely by revealing Himself in human nature, and becoming "a Man with men."

God] In this one word, which admits the divine origin of Mosaism, the writer makes an immense concession to the Jews. Such expressions as St Paul had used in the fervour of controversy—when for instance he spoke of "the Law" as consisting of "weak and beggarly elements"—tended to alienate the Jews by utterly shocking their prejudices; and in very early ages, as we see from the "Epistle of Barnabas" some Christians had developed a tendency to speak of Judaism with an extreme disparagement, which culminated in the Gnostic attribution of the Old Testament to an inferior and even malignant Deity, whom they called "the Demiurge." The author shared no such feelings. In all his sympathies he shews himself a Hebrew of the Hebrews, and at the very outset he speaks of the Old Dispensation as coming from God.

who] There is no relative in the Greek. Instead of "who...spake... hath spoken..." the force of the original would be better conveyed by "having spoken...spake."

at sundry times] In the Greek, one word *polumerōs* "in many parts." The nearest English representative of the word is "fragmentarily," which is not meant as a term of absolute but only of *relative* disparagement. It has never been God's method to reveal all His relations to mankind at once. He revealed Himself "in many portions." He lifted the veil fold by fold. First came the Adamic dispensation; then the Noahic; then the Abrahamic; then the Mosaic; then that widening and deepening system of truth of which the Prophets were ministers; then the yet more advanced and elaborate scheme which dates from Ezra;—the *final* revelation, the "fulness" of revealed truth came with the Gospel. Each of these systems was indeed fragmentary, and therefore (so far) imperfect, and yet it was the best possible system with reference to the end in view, which was the education of the human race in the love and knowledge of God. The first great truth which God prominently revealed was His Unity; then came the earliest germ of the Messianic hope; then came the Moral Law; then the development of Messianism and the belief in Immortality. Isaiah and Ezekiel, Zechariah and Malachi, the son of Sirach and John the Baptist, had each his several "portion" and element of truth to reveal. But all the sevenfold rays were united in the pure and perfect light when God had given us His Son; and when, by the inbreathing of the Spirit, He had made us partakers of Himself, the last era of revelation had arrived. To this final revelation there can be no further addition, though it may be granted to age after age more and more fully to comprehend it. Complete in itself, it yet works as the leaven, and grows as the grain of mustard seed, and brightens and broadens as the Dawn. Yet even the Christian Revelation is itself but "a part;" "we know in part and prophesy," says St Paul, "in part." Man, being finite, is only capable of partial knowledge.

in divers manners] The "sundry" and "divers" of our A. V. are only due to the professed fondness for variety which King James's translators regarded as a merit. The "many manners" of the older revelation were Law and Prophecy, Type and Allegory, Promise and Threatening; the diverse individuality of many of the Prophets, Seers, Warriors, Kings, who were agents of the revelation; the method of various sacrifices; the messages which came by Urim, by dreams, by waking visions, and "face to face" (see Num. xii. 6; Ps. lxxxix. 19; Hosea xii. 10; 2 Pet. i. 21). The mouthpiece of the revelation was now a Gentile sorcerer, now a royal sufferer, now a rough ascetic, now a polished priest, now a gatherer of sycomore fruit. Thus the separate revelations were not complete but partial; and the methods not simple but complex.

spake] This verb (*lalein*) is often used, especially in this Epistle, of Divine revelations (ii. 2, 3, iii. 5, vii. 14, &c.).

in time past] Malachi the last Prophet of the Old Covenant had died more than four centuries before Christ.

unto the fathers] That is to the Jews of old. The writer, a Jew in all his sympathies, leaves unnoticed throughout this Epistle the very existence of the Gentiles. As a friend and follower of St Paul he of course recognised the call of the Gentiles to equal privileges, but the demonstration of their prerogatives had already been furnished by St Paul with a force and fulness to which nothing could be added. This writer, addressing Jews, is not in any way thinking of the Gentiles. To him "the people" means exclusively "the people of God" in the old sense, namely Israel after the flesh. It is hardly conceivable that St Paul, who was the Apostle to the Gentiles, and whose writings were mainly addressed to them, and written to secure their Gospel privileges, should, even in a single letter, have so completely left them out of sight as this author does. On the other hand he always tries to shew his "Hebrew" readers that their conversion does not involve any sudden discontinuity in the religious history of their race.

by the prophets] Rather, "*in* the Prophets." It is true that the "*by*" *may* be only a Hebraism, representing the Hebrew ב in 1 Sam. xxviii. 6; 2 Sam. xxiii. 2. We find ἐν "*in*" used of agents in Matt. ix. 34, "*In* the Prince of the demons casteth He out demons," and in Acts xvii. 31. But, on the other hand, the writer may have meant the preposition to be taken in its proper sense, to imply that the Prophets were only the *organs* of the revelation; so that it is more emphatic than διά, "by means of." The same thought may be in his mind as in that of Philo when he says that "the Prophet is an in-

last days spoken unto us by *his* Son, whom he hath ap-
terpreter, while God from within whispers what he should utter." "The Prophets," says St Thomas Aquinas, "did not speak of themselves, but God spoke in them." Comp. 2 Cor. xiii. 3. The word Prophets is here taken in that larger sense which includes Abraham, Moses, &c.

2. *Hath...spoken*] Rather, "spake." The whole revelation is ideally summed up in the one supreme moment of the Incarnation. This *aoristic* mode of speaking of God's dealings, and of the Christian life, as *single acts*, is common throughout the New Testament, and especially in St Paul, and conveys the thought that

"Are, and were, and will be are but *is*
And all creation is one act at once."

The word "spoke" is here used in its fullest and deepest meaning of Him whose very name is "the Word of God." It is true that this author, unlike St John, does not actually apply the Alexandrian term "Logos" ("Word") to Christ, but it always seems to be in his thoughts, and, so to speak, to be trembling on his lips. The essential and ideal Unity which dominated over the "many parts" and "many modes" of the older revelation is implied in the most striking way by the fact that it was the same God who spake to the Fathers in the Prophets and to us in a Son.

in these last days] The better reading (ℵ, A, B, D, E, &c.) is "at the end of these days." The phrase represents the technical Hebrew expression *be-acharîth ha-yâmîm* (Num. xxiv. 14). The Jews divided the religious history of the world into "*this age*" (*Olam hazzeh*) and "the future age" (*Olam habba*). The "future age" was the one which was to begin at the coming of the Messiah, whose days were spoken of by the Rabbis as "the last days." But, as Christians believed that the Messiah had now come, to them the former period had ended. They were practically living in the age to which their Jewish contemporaries alluded as the "age to come" (ii. 5, vi. 5). They spoke of this epoch as "the fulness of the times" (Gal. iv. 4); "the last days" (Ja. v. 3); "the last hour" (1 John ii. 18); "the crisis of rectification" (Heb. ix. 10); "the close of the ages" (ix. 26). And yet, even to Christians, there was *one* aspect in which the new Messianic dispensation was still to be followed by "a future age," because the kingdom of God had not yet come either completely or in its final development, which depended on the Second Advent. Hence "the last crisis," "the later crises" (1 Pet. i. 5; 1 Tim. iv. 1) are still in the future, though they thought that it would be a near future; after which would follow the "rest," the "Sabbatism" (Heb. iv. 4, 10, 11, xi. 40, xii. 28) which still awaits the people of God. The indistinctness of separation between "this age" and "the future age" arises from different views as to the period in which the actual "days of the Messiah" are to be reckoned. The Rabbis also sometimes include them in the former, sometimes in the latter. But the writer regarded the end as being at hand (x. 13, 25, 37). He felt that

pointed heir of all *things*, by whom also he made the worlds;

the former dispensation was annulled and outworn, and anticipated rightly that it could not have many years to run.

by his Son] Rather, "in a **Son**." The contrast is here the *Relation* rather than the *Person* of Christ, "in Him who was **a Son**." The preposition "*in*" is here most applicable in its strict meaning, because "in Him dwelleth all the fulness of the Godhead bodily." "The Father, *that dwelleth in me*, He doeth the works" (John xiv. 10). The contrast of the New and Old is expressed by St John (i. 17), "The Law was given by Moses, but *grace and truth* came by Jesus Christ." In Christ all the fragments of previous revelation were completed; all the methods of it concentrated; and all its apparent perplexities and contradictions solved and rendered intelligible.

he hath appointed] Rather, "He appointed." The question as to the *special* act of God thus alluded to, is hardly applicable. Our temporal expressions may involve an inherent absurdity when applied to Him whose life is the timeless Now of Eternity and in Whom there is neither before nor after, nor variableness, nor shadow cast by turning, but Who is always in the Meridian of an unconditioned Plenitude (*Pleroma*). See Jas. i. 17.

heir of all things] Sonship naturally suggests heirship (Gal. iv. 7) and in Christ was fulfilled the immense promise to Abraham that his seed should be heir of the world. The allusion, so far as we can enter into these high mysteries of Godhead, is to Christ's mediatorial kingdom. We only darken counsel by the multitude of words without knowledge when we attempt to define and explain the relations of the Persons of the Trinity towards each other. The doctrine of the περιχώρησις, *circuminsessio* or *communicatio idiomatum* as it was technically called—that is the relation of Divinity and Humanity as effected within the Divine Nature itself by the Incarnation—is wholly beyond the limit of our comprehension. We may in part see this from the fact that the Son Himself is (in ver. 3) represented as doing what in this verse the Father does. But that the *Mediatorial* Kingdom is given to the Son by the Father is distinctly stated in John iii. 35; Matt. xxviii. 18 (comp. ii. 6—8 and Ps. ii. 8).

by whom] i.e. "by whose means;" "by whom, as His agent." Comp. "All things were made by Him" (i.e. by the Word) (John i. 3). "By Him were all things created" (Col. i. 16). "By Whom are all things" (1 Cor. viii. 6). What the Alexandrian theosophy attributed to the Logos, had been attributed to "Wisdom" (see Prov. viii. 22—31) in what was called the *Chokhmah* or the Sapiential literature of the Jews. Christians were therefore familiar with the doctrine that Creation was the work of the Præ-existent Christ; which helps to explain verses 10—12. We find in Philo, "You will discover that the cause of it (the world) is God...and the Instrument the Word of God, by whom it was equipped (*kateskeuasthē*)," *De Cherub.* (Opp. I. 162); and again "But the shadow of God is His Word, whom He used as an Instrument in making the World," *De Leg. Alleg.* (Opp. I. 106).

3 who being the brightness of *his* glory, and the express image

also] He who was the heir of all things was also the agent in their creation.

he made the worlds] Literally, "the aeons" or "ages." This word "aeon" was used by the later Gnostics to describe the various "emanations" by which they tried at once to widen and to bridge over the chasm between the Human and the Divine. Over that imaginary chasm St John had thrown the one wide arch of the Incarnation when he wrote "the Word became flesh." In the N.T. the word "aeons" never has this Gnostic meaning. In the singular the word means "an age;" in the plural it sometimes means "ages" like the Hebrew *olamim*. Here it is used in its Rabbinic and post-biblical sense of "the world" as in xi. 3, Wisd. xiii. 9, and as in 1 Tim. i. 17 where God is called "the king of the world" (comp. Tob. xiii. 6). The word *kosmos* (x. 5) means "the material world" in its order and beauty; the word *aiones* means the world as reflected in the mind of man and in the stream of his spiritual history; *oikoumene* (i. 6) means "the inhabited world."

3. *the brightness*] The substitution of "effulgence" for "brightness" in the Revised Version is not, as it has been contemptuously called, "a piece of finery," but is a rendering at once more accurate and more suggestive. It means "efflux of light"—"Light of (i.e. from) Light" ("*effulgentia*" not "*repercussus*") Grotius. It implies not only resemblance—which is all that is involved in the vague and misleading word "brightness," which might apply to a mere *reflexion:* —but also "origin" and "independent existence." The glory of Christ is the glory of the Father just as the sun is only revealed by the rays which stream forth from it. So the "Wisdom of Solomon" (vii. 26)—which offers many resemblances to the Epistle to the Hebrews, and which some have even conjectured to be by the same author— speaks of wisdom as "the effulgence of the everlasting light." The word is also found in Philo where it is applied to man. This passage, like many others in the Epistle, is quoted by St Clement of Rome (*ad Cor.* 36).

of his glory] God was believed in the Old Dispensation to reveal Himself by a cloud of glory called "the Shechinah," and the Alexandrian Jews, in their anxious avoidance of all *anthropomorphism* and *anthropopathy*—i.e. of all expressions which attribute the human form and human passions to God—often substituted "the Glory" for the name of God. Similarly in 2 Pet. i. 17 the Voice from God the Father is a Voice "from the magnificent glory." Comp. Acts vii. 55; Lk. ii. 9. St John says "God is Light," and the indestructible purity and impalpable essence of Light make it the best of all created things to furnish an analogy for the supersensuous light and spiritual splendour of the Being of God. Hence St John also says of the Word "we beheld His glory" (i. 14); and our Lord said to Philip "he who hath seen Me hath seen the Father" (xiv. 9). Comp. Lk. ix. 29.

the express image] Rather, "the stamp" (*character*). The R. V.

of his person, and upholding all *things* by the word of

renders this word by "very image" (after Tyndale), and in the margin by "impress." I prefer the word "stamp" because the Greek "*charactēr*," like the English word "stamp," may, according to its *derivation*, be used either for the *impress* or for the stamping-tool itself. This Epistle has so many resemblances to Philo that the word may have been suggested by a passage (Opp. I. 332) in which Philo compares man to a coin which has been stamped by the Logos with the being and type of God; and in that passage the word seems to bear this unusual sense of a "stamping-tool," for it impresses a man with the mark of God. Similarly St Paul in the Epistle to the Colossians (i. 15)—which most resembles this Epistle in its Christology—called Christ "the image (*eikōn*) of the invisible God;" and Philo says, "But the word is the image (*eikōn*) of God, by Whom the whole world was created," *De Monarch.* (Opp. II. 225).

of his person] Rather, "of His substance" or "essence." The word *hypostasis, substantia* (literally that which "*stands under*") is, in philosophical accuracy, the imaginary substratum which remains when a thing is regarded apart from all its accidents. The word "person" of our A. V. is rather the equivalent to *prosōpon*. *Hypostasis* only came to be used in this sense some centuries later. Perhaps "Being" or "Essence," though it corresponds more strictly to the Greek *ousia*, is the nearest representative which we can find to *hypostasis*, now that "substance," once the most abstract and philosophical of words, has come (in ordinary language) to mean what is solid and concrete. It is only too possible that the word "substance" conveys to many minds the very opposite conception to that which was intended and which alone corresponds to the truth. Athanasius says, "*Hypostasis* is essence" (οὐσία); and the Nicene Council seems to draw no real distinction between the two words. In fact the Western Church admitted that, in the Eastern sense, we might speak of *three hypostaseis* of the Trinity; and in the Western sense, of *one hypostasis*, because in this sense the word meant Essence. For the use of the word in the LXX. see Ps. xxxviii. 6, lxxxviii. 48. It is curiously applied in Wisd. xvi. 21. In the technical language of theology these two clauses represent the Son as co-eternal and co-substantial with the Father.

upholding all things] He is not only the Creative Word, but the Sustaining Providence. He is, as Philo says, "the chain-band of all things," but He is also their guiding force. "In Him all things subsist" (Col. i. 17). Philo calls the Logos "the pilot and steersman of everything."

by the word of his power] Rather, "by the utterance (*rhēmati*) of His power." It is better to keep "word" for *Logos*, and "utterance" for *rhēma*. We find "strength" (κράτος) and "force" (ἰσχύς) attributed to Christ in Eph. vi. 10, as "power" (δύναμις) here.

when he had by himself purged our sins] Rather, "after making purification of sins." The "by Himself" is omitted by some of the best MSS. (ℵ, A, B), and the "our" by many. But the notion of Christ's

his power, when he had by himself purged our sins, sat down on the right hand of the Majesty on high; 4 being made so much better than the angels, as he hath

independent action (Phil. ii. 7) is involved in the middle voice of the verb. On the purification of our sins by Christ (in which there is perhaps a slight reference to the "Day of Atonement," called in the LXX. "the Day of *Purification*," Ex. xxix. 36), see ix. 12, x. 12; 1 Pet. ii. 24; 2 Pet. i. 9 (comp. Job. vii. 21, LXX.).

sat down] His glorification was directly consequent on His voluntary humiliation (see viii. 1, x. 12, xii. 2; Ps. cix. 1), and here the whole description is brought to its destined climax.

on the right hand] As the place of honour comp. viii. 1; Ps. cx. 1; Eph. i. 20. The controversy as to whether "the right hand of God" means "everywhere"—which was called the "Ubiquitarian controversy" —is wholly destitute of meaning, and has long fallen into deserved oblivion.

of the Majesty] In x. 12 he says "at the right hand of God." But he was evidently fond of sonorous amplifications, which belong to the dignity of his style; and also fond of Alexandrian modes of expression. The LXX. sometimes went so far as to substitute for "God" the phrase "the *place*" where God stood (see Ex. xxiv. 10, LXX.).

on high] Literally, "in high places;" like "Glory to God *in the highest*," Lk. ii. 14 (comp. Job xvi. 19); and "in heavenly places," Eph. i. 20 (comp. Ps. xciii. 4, cxii. 5). The description of Christ in these verses differed from the current Messianic conception of the Jews in two respects. 1. He was divine and omnipotent. 2. He was to die for our sins.

4. *being made*] Rather, "becoming," or "*proving himself to be.*" The allusion is to the Redemptive Kingdom of Christ, and the word merely qualifies the "better name." Christ, regarded as the Agent or Minister of the scheme of Redemption, *became* mediatorially superior to the Angel-ministrants of the Old Dispensation, as He always *was* superior to them in dignity and essence.

so much] The familiar classical ὅσῳ...τοσούτῳ (involving the comparison and contrast which runs throughout this Epistle, iii. 3, vii. 20, viii. 6, ix. 27, x. 25) is not found once in St Paul.

better] This word, common as it is, is only thrice used by St Paul (and then somewhat differently), but occurs 13 times in this Epistle alone (vi. 9, vii. 7, 19, 22, viii. 6, ix. 23, x. 34, xi. 16, 35, 40, xii. 24).

so much better than the angels] The writer's object in entering upon the proof of this fact is not to check the tendency of incipient Gnostics to *worship* Angels. Of this there is no trace here, though St Paul in his letter to the Colossians, raised a warning voice against it. Here the object is to shew that the common Jewish boast that "they had received the law by the disposition of Angels" involved no disparagement to the Gospel which had been ministered by One who was "far above all principality, and power, and might, and dominion, and every name that

by inheritance obtained a more excellent name than they.
For unto which of the angels said he at any time, 5

is named, not only in this world, but also in that which is to come"
(Eph. i. 21). Many Jews held, with Philo, that the Decalogue alone
had been uttered by God, and that all the rest of the Law had been
spoken by Angels. The extreme development of Jewish Angelology at
this period may be seen in the Book of Enoch. They are there called
"the stars," "the white ones," "the sleepless ones." St Clement of
Rome found it necessary to reproduce this argument in writing to the
Corinthians, and the 4th Book of Esdras illustrates the tendency of mind
which it was desirable to counteract.

hath by inheritance obtained] Rather, "hath inherited." Comp.
Lk. i. 32, 35. "Wherefore God also hath highly exalted Him and
given Him a name which is above every name" (Phil. ii. 9). He does
not here seem to be speaking of the eternal generation. Christ inherits
His more excellent name, not as the Eternal Son, but as the God-Man.
Possibly too the writer uses the word "inherited" with tacit reference
to the prophetic promises.

a more excellent name than they] Not here the name of "the only-
begotten Son of God" (John iii. 18), which is in its fulness "a name
which no one knoweth save Himself" (Rev. xix. 12). The "name" in
Scripture often indeed implies the inmost essence of a thing. If, then,
with some commentators we suppose the allusion to be to this Eternal
and Essential name of Christ we must understand the word "inheritance" as merely phenomenal, the manifestation to our race of a præ-
existent fact. In that view the glory indicated by the name belonged
essentially to Christ, and His work on earth only *manifested* the name
by which it was known. This is perhaps better than to follow St
Chrysostom in explaining "inherited" to mean "always possessed as
His own." Comp. Lk. i. 32, "He shall be called the Son of the
Highest."

more excellent...than] This construction (παρὰ after a comparative)
is not found once in St Paul's Epistles, but several times in this Epistle
(i. 4, ii. 9, iii. 3, ix. 23, xi. 4, xii. 24). It should be observed, as bearing
on the authorship of the Epistle, that in these four verses alone there
are no less than six expressions and nine constructions which find no—or
no exact—parallel in St Paul's Epistles.

5—14. ILLUSTRATIONS FROM SCRIPTURE OF THE SUPERIORITY OF
CHRIST TO ANGELS.

5. *For*] The following paragraphs prove "the more excellent name."
By His work on earth the God-man Christ Jesus obtained that superiority
of place in the order and hierarchy of salvation which made Him better
than the Angels, not only in intrinsic dignity but in relation to the
redemption of man. In other words the universal heirship of Christ
is here set forth "not as a *metaphysical* but as a *dispensational* pre-
rogative." That it should be *necessary* for the writer to enter upon a
proof of this may well seem strange to us; but that it *was* necessary is

Thou art my Son, this day have I begotten thee?

proved by the earnestness with which he devotes himself to the task. To us the difficulty lies in the mode of proof, not in the result arrived at; but his readers were unconvinced of the result, while they would have freely admitted the validity of this method of reasoning. The line of proof has been thoroughly studied by Dr W. Robertson Smith, in some papers published in the *Expositor* for 1881, to which I am indebted for several suggestions. "There is nothing added," he says, "to the intrinsic superiority of Christ's being, but He occupies towards us a position higher than the angels ever held. The whole argument turns, not on personal dignity, but on dignity of function in the administration of the economy of salvation." It may be due to this Epistle that we find in later Jewish books (like the *Jalkut Shimeoni*) such sentences as "The King Messiah shall be exalted above Abraham, Moses, and the Ministering Angels" (see Schöttgen, p. 905).

For unto which of the angels said he at any time] The "He" is God. This indirect mode of reference to God is common in the Rabbinic writings. The argument here is from the *silence* of Scripture, as in i. 13, ii. 16, vii. 13, 14.

Thou art my Son...] The quotation is from Ps. ii. 7 (comp. Ps. lxxxix. 20, 26, 27). The author does not need to pause in order to prove that this, and the other passages which he quotes, apply to the Christ; still less to prove that Christ is the Son of God. All Christians held the second point; the first point would have been at once conceded by every Jewish reader. Many of the Jews adopted the common view of the Rabbis that everything in the Old Testament prophecies might be applied to the Messiah. St Peter, in Acts xiii. 33, also applies this verse to Christ, and the great Rabbis, Kimchi and Rashi, admit that the Psalm was accepted in a Messianic sense in ancient days. The Divinity of Christ was a truth which the writer might assume in addressing Christians.

It must therefore be observed that these passages are not advanced as *proofs* that Jesus was the Son of God—which, as Christians, the readers in no wise disputed—but as arguments *ad hominem* and *ex concessis*. In other words they were arguments to those whom the writer had immediately in view, and who had no doubt as to the premisses on which he based his reasoning. He had to confirm a vacillating and unprogressive faith (vi. 12, xii. 25), not to convince those who disputed the central truths of Christianity.

Our own conviction on these subjects rests primarily upon historical and spiritual grounds, and only depends in a very subordinate degree on indirect Scriptural applications. Yet even as regards these we cannot but see that, while the more sober-minded interpreters have always admitted that there was a *primary historic* meaning in the passages quoted, and that they were addressed in the first instance to David, Solomon, &c., yet (1) there is a "pre-established harmony" between the language used and its fulfilment in Christ; (2) the language is often so far beyond the scope of its immediate application that it points to an *ideal* and

And again, I will be to him a Father, and he shall

distant fulfilment; (3) it was interpreted for many centuries before Christ in a Messianic sense; (4) that Messianic sense has been amply justified by the slow progress of history. There is surely some medium between regarding these passages as soothsaying vaticinations, definitely and consciously recognised as such by their writers, and setting them aside as though they contained no prophetic element at all. In point of fact the Jews themselves rightly looked on them as mingling the present and the future, the kingly-theocratic and the Messianic. No one will enter into their real meaning who does not see that all the best Jewish literature was in the highest sense prophetic. It centred in that magnificent Messianic hope which arose immediately from the connexion of the Jews with their covenant God, and which elevated them above all other nations. The divine character of this confident hope was justified, and more than justified, by the grandeur of its fulfilment. Genuine, simple, historical exegesis still leaves room in the Old Testament for a glorious and demonstrable Christology. Although the old aphorism—*Novum Testamentum in Vetere latet, Vetus in Novo patet*—has often been extravagantly abused by allegoric interpreters, every instructed Christian will admit its fundamental truth. The germ of a highly-developed Messianic prophecy was involved from the first in the very idea of a theocracy and a separated people.

this day have I begotten thee] St Paul says (Rom. i. 4) that Jesus was "determined" or "constituted" (ὁρισθέντος) Son of God, with power, *by resurrection from the dead*. The aorist in that passage points to a definite time—the Resurrection (comp. Acts xiii. 33). In other senses the expression "to-day" might be applied to the Incarnation (Lk. i. 31), or to the Ascension, or to the Eternal Generation. The latter explanation however,—which explains "to-day" of "God's eternal now" the *nunc stans* of eternity—though adopted by Origen (who finely says that in God's "to-day" there is neither morning nor evening) and by St Augustine—is probably one of the "afterthoughts of theology." Calvin stigmatises it as a "*frivola Augustini argutia*," but the strongest argument in its favour is that Philo has a somewhat similar conception. The words, however, originally applied to the day of David's complete inauguration as king upon Mount Sion. No *one* time can apply to the Eternal Generation, and the adoption of Philo's notion that "to-day" means "for ever," and that "all Eternity" is God's to-day would here be out of place. Possibly the "to-day" is only, so to speak, an accidental part of the quotation: in other words it may belong rather to the literal and primary prophecy than to its Messianic application. The Church shews that she understood the word "to-day" to apply to the Resurrection by appointing the second psalm as one of the special psalms for Easter-day.

I will be to him a Father] 2 Sam. vii. 14 (LXX.). The words were primarily applicable to Solomon, but the quotation would not, without further argument, have helped forward the writer's end if he had not been able to assume with confidence that none of his readers would dis-

6 be to me a Son? And again, when he bringeth in the firstbegotten into the world, he saith, And let all

pute his typological method of exegesis. It is probable that the promise to David here quoted is directly connected with the passage just adduced from Ps. ii.

he shall be to me a Son] The quotation (comp. Philo *De Leg. Allegor.* III. 8) though primarily applied to Solomon, has the wider sense of prophesying the advent of some perfect theocratic king. The "Angels" it might be objected are called "Sons of God" in Gen. vi. 2; Job i. 6, ii. 1, xxxviii. 7; Dan. iii. 25. In these passages, however, the Alexandrian manuscript of the LXX. which this author seems to have used (whereas St Paul seems to quote from another type of manuscript—the Vatican), has "angels" and not "sons." If it be further urged that in Ps. xxix. 1, lxxxix. 7, even the *Alexandrian* MS. also has "sons" we must suppose either that the writer means to distinguish (1) between the higher and lower senses of the word "son;" or (2) between "Sons of *Elohim*" and "Sons of *Jehovah*," since *Elohim* is so much lower and vaguer a name for God than Jehovah, that not only Angels but even human beings are called Elohim; or (3) that he did not regard the name "sons" as in any way *characteristic* of angels. He shews so intimate a knowledge of the Psalms that—on this ground alone, not to dwell on others—the supposition that he forgot or overlooked these passages is hardly admissible.

6. *And again, when he bringeth in the firstbegotten into the world*] The older and literal rendering is as in the R. V., "*and when he, again, shall have brought in...*" The A. V. takes the word "again" (*palin*) as merely introducing a new quotation, as in ver. 5, and in ii. 13, iv. 5, &c. The word "again," says Bp. Wordsworth, serves the purpose of inverted commas (see Rom. xv. 10—12). In that case it is displaced by an accidental *hyperbaton* or *trajection*, as this transmission of a word into another clause is called. If however the "again" belongs to the verb it can only be explained of Christ's second coming to judge the world (Matt. xxv. 31) unless the writer, assuming the point of view of the ancient prophet, alludes to the Resurrection. But since the mere displacement of the *palin* is certainly possible, it is better to accept this simple explanation than either to adopt these latter theories or to suppose that there had been some previous and premundane presentation of the Son to all created beings. *Hypotheses non fingo* is a rule even more necessary for the theologian than for the scientist.

bringeth in] The Greek verb is in the aorist subjunctive (ϵἰσαγάγῃ), and means "shall have brought in," exactly as in Ex. xiii. 5, 11 (where the same word occurs in the LXX.) and as in Lk. xvii 10, "when ye shall have done all that is commanded you" (ποιήσητε).

the firstbegotten] Rather, "first-born." This title (see Ps. lxxxix. 27) was always applied in a Messianic sense to Christ as "the first-born of all creation" (Col. i. 15); and the first-born of many brethren (ii. 10, 11).

the angels of God worship him. And of the angels 7
he saith, Who maketh his angels spirits, and his

into the world] The Greek word here used is not *kosmos* the material world, but *oikoumene* "the habitable world."

he saith] The language of the Scriptures is regarded as a permanent, continuous, and living utterance (iii. 7, v. 6, viii. 8, 9, 10, x. 5, &c.).

And let all the angels of God worship him] It is doubtful whether the quotation is from Ps. xcvii. 7 "worship Him all ye gods (*Elohim*)"—where the word *Elohim* is rendered "angels" in the LXX. as in Ps. viii. 5—or rather from Deut. xxxii. 43, where there is an "and," and where the LXX. either added these words or found them in the Hebrew text. The Messianic application of the word is natural in the latter passage, for there Jehovah is the *speaker*, and if the "*him*" is applied to the ideal Israel, the ideal Israel was the Jasher or "upright man," and was the type of the Messiah. The Apostles and Evangelists always describe Christ as returning "with the Holy Angels" (Matt. xxv. 31; Mark viii. 38), and describe "all Angels and authorities" as "subject unto Him" (1 Pet. iii. 22; Rev. v. 11—13).

7. *And of the angels he saith*] Rather, "And, with reference to the Angels, He saith." He has shewn that the title of "Son" is too special and too super-eminent to be ever addressed to Angels; he proceeds to shew that the Angels are but subordinate ministers, and that often God clothes them with "the changing garment of natural phenomena" transforming them, as it were, into winds and flames.

Who maketh his angels spirits, and his ministers a flame of fire] Rather, "who maketh His Angels *winds*," for the Angels are already "spirits" (ver. 14). This must be the meaning here, though the words might also be rendered "Who maketh winds His messengers, and fiery flame His ministers." This latter rendering, though grammatically difficult, accords best with the context of Ps. civ. 4 where, however, the Targum has "Who maketh His messengers swift as winds, His ministers strong as flaming fire." The Rabbis often refer to the fact that God makes His Angels assume any form He pleases, whether men (Gen. xviii. 2) or women (Zech. v. 9) or wind or flame (Ex. iii. 2; 2 K. vi. 17). Thus Milton says:

> "For spirits as they please
> Can either sex assume, or both; so soft
> And uncompounded is their essence pure;
> Not tied or manacled with joint or limb
> Nor founded on the brittle strength of bones,
> Like cumbrous flesh; *but in what shape they choose*
> Dilated or condensed, bright or obscure,
> Can execute their aery purposes."

But that mutable and fleeting form of existence which is *the glory* of the Angels would be an *inferiority* in the Son. He could not be clothed, as they are at God's will, in the fleeting robes of varying material phenomena. Calvin, therefore, is much too rash and hasty when he says

8 ministers a flame of fire. But unto the Son *he saith*, Thy throne, O God, *is* for ever and ever: a sceptre of righteousness *is* the sceptre of thy kingdom.

that the writer here draws his citation into a sense which does not belong to it, and that nothing is more certain than that the original passage has nothing to do with angels. With a wider knowledge of the views of Philo, and other Rabbis, he would have paused before pronouncing a conclusion so sweepingly dogmatic. The "Hebrew" readers of the Epistle, like the writer, were evidently familiar with Alexandrian conceptions. Now in Philo there is no sharp distinction between the Logos (who is a sort of *non-incarnate* Messiah) and the Logoi who are sometimes regarded as Angels just as the Logos Himself is sometimes regarded as an Archangel (see Siegfried's *Philo*, p. 22). The Rabbis too explained the "us" of Gen. i. 26 ("Let *us* make man") as shewing that the Angels had a share in creation, see Sanhedrin, p. 38, 2. Such a passage as Rev. xix. 10 may help to shew the reader that the proof of Christ's exaltation above the Angels was necessary.

8. *But unto the Son he saith*] Rather "But of (lit., with reference to) the Son." The Psalm (xlv.) from which the quotation is taken, is called in the LXX. "A song for the beloved," and has been Messianically interpreted by Jewish as well as Christian expositors. Hence it is chosen as one of the special Psalms for Christmas Day.

Thy throne, O God, is for ever and ever] The quotation is from Ps. xlv. 6, 7 (LXX.) which in its primary and historic sense is a splendid epithalamium to Solomon, or Joram, or some theocratic king of David's house. But in the idealism and hyperbole of its expression it pointed forward to "the King in His beauty." "Thy throne, O Elohim," is the rendering which seems most natural, and this at once evidences the mystic and ideal character of the language; for though judges and rulers are sometimes collectively and indirectly called *Elohim* (Ex. xxi. 6, xxii. 8; Ps. lxxiii.; John x. 34—36) yet nothing which approaches a title so exalted is ever given to a human person, except in this typical sense (as in Is. ix. 6). The original, however, has been understood by some to mean "Thy divine throne;" and this verse may be rendered "God is Thy throne for ever and ever." Philo had spoken of the Logos as "the eldest Angel," "an Archangel of many names" (*De Conf. Ling.* 28), and it was most necessary for the writer to shew that the Mediator of the New Covenant was not merely an Angel like the ministers of the Old, or even an Archangel, but the Divine Præ-existent Son whose dispensation therefore supersedes that which had been administered by inferior beings. The Targum on this Psalm (xlv. 3) renders it "Thy beauty, O King Messiah, is greater than the sons of men," and Aben Ezra says it refers not so much to David as to his son Messiah.

a sceptre of righteousness] Rather, "the sceptre of rectitude." The Greek word is *euthutētos* not *dikaiosunēs*, which is the word used in the next verse. "*Euthutēs*" occurs here only in the N.T.

of thy kingdom] The two oldest MSS. (ℵ, B) read "of His kingdom."

Thou hast loved righteousness, and hated iniquity; therefore God, *even* thy God, hath anointed thee *with* the oil of gladness above thy fellows. And, Thou, Lord, in the beginning hast laid the foundation of the earth; and the heavens are the works of thine hands: they shall perish; but thou 9 10 11

9. *Thou hast loved*] Rather, "Thou lovedst"—idealising the whole reign to one point. Comp. Is. xxxii. 1, "Behold, a king shall reign in righteousness;" and Jer. xxiii. 5, "I will raise unto David a righteous Branch."

iniquity] Lit., "lawlessness."

therefore] Comp. ii. 9, 16, 17, v. 7, 8, xii. 2.

God, even thy God] The first word might be a vocative "Oh God," and it is so rendered even by the Jewish translator Symmachus. But this is contrary to the usage of the 2nd Book of Psalms. Where the word "God" is taken up and repeated with the suffix, there is no other instance in which the first is a vocative.

even thy God] Comp. John xx. 17, "I ascend to...*my God* and your God."

the oil of gladness] Rather, "of exultation." The word means the joy of perfect triumph, xii. 2. For the "anointing" of Christ by the Spirit see Lk. i. 35; Matt. iii. 16; Acts x. 38; Is. lxi. 1; but the anointing in *this* verse, alludes to His glorification in Heaven.

above thy fellows] In the original Psalm this refers to all contemporary princes; in its present application it means above all the angel-dwellers on Mount Sion (xii. 22) and above all men who have fellowship with God (iii. 14) only in Christ (ii. 11; 1 John i. 3).

10. *Thou, Lord, in the beginning*] The quotation is from Ps. cii. 25—27. The word "Lord" is not in the original, but it is in the LXX.; and the Hebrew Christians who already believed that it was by Christ that "God made the world" (see note on ver. 2) would not dispute the Messianic application of these words to Him. They are a prayer of the afflicted written at some late period of the exile. Calvin (on Eph. iv. 8) goes so far as to say of such passages that the Apostle "by a pious diversion of their meaning (*piâ deflectione*) accommodates them to the Person of Christ." The remark illustrates the courageous honesty and stern good sense of the great Reformer; but no Jewish-Christian exegete would have thought that he was practising a mere pious misapplication of the sacred words, or have admitted the objection of Cardinal Cajetan that "in a matter of such importance it was unbecoming to use such an argument." The writer's object is not *proof* —which was for his readers unnecessary; he wished to *illustrate* acknowledged truths by admitted principles.

in the beginning] Heb. לְפָנִים, "face-wards," i.e. of old.

11. *They shall perish*] Is. xxxiv. 4, &c.; 2 Pet. iii. 12; Rev. xxi. 1.

remainest] The verb means "abidest through all times."

remainest; and they all shall wax old as *doth* a garment; and as a vesture shalt thou fold them up, and they shall be changed: but thou art the same, and thy years shall not fail. But to which of the angels said he at any time, Sit on my right hand, until I make thine enemies thy footstool? Are they not all ministering spirits, sent forth to minister for them who shall be heirs of salvation?

as doth a garment] A common Scripture metaphor. Is. l. 9, &c.
12. *shalt thou fold them up*] Lit., "Thou shalt roll them up." This reading (ἑλίξεις) is found in most MSS. and is perhaps an unconscious reminiscence of Is. xxxiv. 4 (comp. Rev. vi. 14); but ℵ, D read "thou shalt *change* them" (ἀλλάξεις), as in the original, and in the LXX. (*Cod. Alex.*). On this final consummation, and the destruction of the material universe, see Matt. xxiv. 35; 2 Pet. iii. 7; Rev. xxi. 1.
thou art the same] In the Hebrew (literally) "Thou art He."
thy years shall not fail] i.e. they shall never come to an end (xiii. 8; Rev. i. 8).
13. *until I make thine enemies thy footstool*] This same passage from Ps. cx. 1 had been quoted by our Lord, in its Messianic sense, to the Scribes and Pharisees, without any attempt on their part to challenge His application of it (Matt. xxii. 41—44). It is also referred to by St Peter in Acts ii. 34 and by St Paul (1 Cor. xv. 25). The Greek expression for "till" implies entire indefiniteness of time. The reference is to the oriental custom of putting the feet on the necks of conquered kings (Josh. x. 24).
14. *ministering spirits, sent forth to minister*] Here as elsewhere the A.V. obliterates distinctions, which it so often arbitrarily creates out of mere love for variety in other places. The word "ministering" (*leitourgika*) implies sacred ("liturgic") service (viii. 6, ix. 21); the word "ministry" (*diakonian*) implies service to God on behalf of men. It should be rendered "ministrant spirits sent forth for service."

"How oft do they their silver bowers leave
  And come to succour us who succour want,
How oft do they with golden pinions cleave
  The flitting skies like flying pursuivant,
Against foul fiends to aid us militant!
They for us fight, they watch and duly ward
And their bright squadrons round about us plant,
And all for love and nothing for reward.
Oh! why should heavenly God for men have such regard."
SPENSER.

for them who shall be heirs of salvation] Literally, "for the sake of those who are about to inherit salvation." The salvation is both the *state of salvation* here, and its full fruition hereafter. When we are "justified by God's grace" we are "made heirs according to the hope

Therefore we ought to give the more earnest heed to the 2
things which we have heard, lest at any time we should let
them slip. For if the word spoken by angels was stedfast, 2

of eternal life" (Tit. iii. 7). Spenser widens the mission of the Angels when he speaks of
> "Highest God, who loves His creatures so
> That blessed Angels He sends to and fro
> To serve to wicked men—to serve His deadliest foe."

For Scriptural instances of the service of Angels "to them that fear God" see Ps. xxxiv. 7, xci. 11; Gen. xix. 15; Dan. vi. 22; Acts xii. 7.

sent forth] Lit., "being sent forth." The ministry of Angels is regarded as still continuing.

heirs of salvation] The writer recurs to this great word "salvation" in ii. 3, 10.

CH. II. A SOLEMN WARNING AND EXHORTATION (1—4). CHRIST'S TEMPORARY HUMILIATION FOR THE REDEMPTION AND GLORIFICATION OF MANKIND DOES NOT DISPARAGE HIS PRE-EMINENCE OVER ANGELS (5—13), BUT WAS NECESSARY FOR THE PERFECTNESS OF HIS HIGH-PRIESTLY WORK (14—18).

1. *Therefore*] Because we are heirs of a better covenant, administered not by Angels but by a Son, to whom as Mediator an absolute dominion is to be assigned.

we ought] The word implies moral necessity and not mere obligation. The author never loses sight of the fact that his purpose was to warn as well as to teach.

to give the more earnest heed] If the command to "take heed to thyself, and keep thy soul diligently lest thou forget the things that thine eyes have seen" (Deut. iv. 9) came with awful force to those who had only received the Law by the disposition of Angels, how much "more abundantly" should Christians attend to Him of Whom Moses had spoken to their fathers? (Acts iii. 22).

to the things which we have heard] Lit., "to the things heard," i.e. to the Gospel.

lest at any time] Rather, "lest haply."

we should let them slip] Rather, "should drift away from them." Wiclif rendered the word more correctly than the A.V. which here follows the Genevan Bible of 1560—"lest peradventure we fleten away." The verb thus resembles the Latin *praetervehi*. The metaphor is taken from a boat which having no "anchor sure and *stedfast*," *slips* its anchor, and as Luther says in his gloss, "before her landing shoots away into destruction" (Prov. iii. 21 LXX. υἱὲ μὴ παραρρυῇς). It is obvious that these Hebrew converts were in great danger of "drifting away" from the truth under the pressure of trial, and in consequence of the apathy produced by isolation and deferred hopes (iii. 6, vi. 11, x. 25, 36, 37, xii. 1—3).

2. *For*] An argument *a minori ad majus*, of which indeed the whole Epistle is a specimen. It was the commonest form assumed

and every transgression and disobedience received a just
recompence of reward; how shall we escape, if we neglect

by the Rabbinic interpretation of Scripture, and was the first of the seven exegetic rules of Hillel, who called it "light and heavy."

the word spoken by angels] The " by " is not ὑπό but διά, i. e. " by means of," " through the instrumentality of." The presence of Angels at Sinai is but slightly alluded to in the O. T. in Deut. xxxiii. 2; Ps. lxviii. 17; but these allusions had been greatly expanded, and were prominently dwelt upon in Rabbinic teaching—the Talmud, Targums, Midrashim, &c.—until, at last, we find in the tract Maccoth that God was only supposed to have uttered the First Commandment, while all the rest of the Law was delivered by Angels. This notion was at least as old as Josephus, who makes Herod say that the Jews "had learned of God through Angels" the most sacred part of their laws (Jos. *Antt.* xv. 5 § 3). The Alexandrian theology especially, impressed with the truth that "no man hath seen God at any time" (comp. Ex. xxxiii. 20) eagerly seized on the allusions to Angels as proving that every theophany was only indirect, and that God could only be seen through the medium of Angelic appearances. Hence the Jews frequently referred to Ps. civ. 4, and regarded the fire, and smoke, and storm of Sinai as being Angelic vehicles of the divine manifestation. And besides this, their boast of the Angelic ministry of the Law was founded on the allusions to the "Angel of the Presence" (Ex. xxxii. 34, xxxiii. 14; Josh. v. 14; Is. lxiii. 9). In the N. T. the only two other passages which allude to the work of Angels in delivering the Law are Acts vii. 53; Gal. iii. 19 (see my *Life of St Paul,* II. 149). Clearly the Hebrew Christians had to be delivered from the notion that Christ, by being "made under the Law," had *subjected Himself* to the loftier position of the Angels who had ministered the Law.

was stedfast] Rather, "*became*" or "proved" steadfast. The Law was no *brutum fulmen*; no inoperative dead-letter, but effective to vindicate its own majesty, and punish its own violation. Philo uses the very same word (βέβαια) of the institutions of Moses; but the difference of standpoint between him and the writer is illustrated by the fact that Philo also calls them ἀσάλευτα, " not to be shaken" which this writer would not have done (xii. 27).

every transgression and disobedience] i.e. all sins against it, whether of commission or of omission. *Parabasis* is "transgression;" *parakoē* is "mishearing" and neglect (Matt. xviii. 17; Rom. v. 19).

just] This form of the word (*endikos*) occurs only here and in Rom. iii. 8.

received a just recompence of reward] The word *misthos*, "wage" or "pay"—which is used of punishment as well as of reward—would have expressed the same thought; but the writer likes the more sonorous *misthapodosia* (x. 35, xi. 26). This remorseless self-vindication by the Law ("without mercy"), the certainty that it could not be broken with impunity, is alluded to in x. 28. The Israelites found

so great salvation; which at the first began to be spoken by the Lord, and was confirmed unto us by them that heard *him*; God also bearing *them* witness, both with signs and 4 wonders, and with divers miracles, and gifts of the Holy Ghost, according to his own will?

even in the wilderness (Lev. x. 1, 2; Num. xv. 32, 36; Deut. iv. 3, &c.), that such stern warnings as that of Num. xv. 30—threatening excision to offenders—were terribly real, and applied alike to individuals and to the nation.

3. *how shall we escape*] The "*we*" (being expressed in the original) is emphatic—*we* who are sons, not servants. The verb means "how shall we succeed in escaping," or, "make good our escape"—namely, from similar, but yet more awful punishment (comp. xii. 25).

if we neglect] Rather, "after neglecting," or "when we have neglected."

so great salvation] The transcendence (vii. 25) of the safety provided is a measure of the guilt involved in ceasing to pay any attention to it (x. 29; John xii. 48). It came from Christ not from Angels, its sanctions are more eternal, its promises more divine, its whole character more spiritual.

which at the first began to be spoken] Literally, "seeing that it, having at the first been spoken."

by the Lord] The Gospels shew that Jesus was the first preacher of His own Gospel (Mark i. 14). "The Lord," standing alone, is very rarely, if ever, used as a title for Christ in St Paul. (1 Thess. iv. 15; 2 Thess. ii. 2; 2 Tim. iv. 18, are, to say the least, indecisive.)

was confirmed] The "*word*" of this salvation"—the news of this Gospel—was ratified to us (comp. 1 Cor. i. 6), and so it becomes "steadfast." The verb is derived from the adjective so rendered in ver. 2.

by them that heard] We did not indeed receive the Gospel at firsthand, but from those who were its appointed witnesses (Lk. xxiv. 47, 48; Acts i. 8, v. 32). This verse, as Luther and Calvin so clearly saw, furnishes a *decisive* proof that St Paul was not the writer of this Epistle. He always *insisted* on the primary and direct character of the revelation which he had received as his independent Gospel (Gal. i. 1, 12; Acts xxii. 10, xxvi. 16; 1 Cor. xi. 23, xv. 3, &c.). To talk of "accommodation" here is quite beside the mark.

4. *God also bearing them witness*] The original is stronger, "God bearing witness *with them*;" the supernatural witness coincided with the human.

both with signs and wonders, and with divers miracles] "Signs" to shew that there was a power behind their witness; "portents" to awaken the feeling of astonishment, and so arouse interest; and various "powers." These are alluded to, or recorded, in Mark xvi. 20; Acts ii. 43, xix. 11. St Paul himself appealed to his own "mighty signs and wonders" (Rom. xv. 18, 19; 1 Cor. ii. 4).

5   For unto *the* angels hath he not put in subjection the
6   world to come, whereof we speak: but one in a certain place

and gifts of the Holy Ghost, according to his own will] The word "gifts" means rather "*distributions*" (iv. 12, "dividing"), and the words "according to His own will" apply only to this clause—the gifts which the Holy Spirit distributes as He wills (1 Cor. vii. 17, xii. 11; Rom. xii. 3).

5—13. THE VOLUNTARY HUMILIATION OF JESUS WAS A NECESSARY STEP IN THE EXALTATION OF HUMANITY.

5. *For*] The "for" resumes the thread of the argument about the superiority of Jesus over the Angels. He was to be the supreme king, but the necessity of passing through suffering to His Messianic throne lay in His High-Priesthood for the human race. To Him, therefore, and not to Angels, the "future age" is to belong.

unto the angels hath he not put into subjection the world to come] Lit. "for not to Angels did He subject the inhabited earth to come." In *this* "inhabited earth" things in their pre-Christian condition had been subjected to Angels. This is inferred directly from Ps. viii. where the "little" of degree is interpreted as "a little" of time. The authority of Angels over the Mosaic dispensation had been inferred by the Jews from Ps. lxxxii. 1, where "the congregation of Elohim" was interpreted to mean Angels; and from Deut. xxxii. 8, 9, where instead of "He set the bounds of the people *according to the number of the children of Israel*," the LXX. had "according to the number of the Angels of God." From this passage, and Gen. x., Dan. x. 13, &c. they inferred that there were 70 nations of the world, each under its presiding Angel, but that Israel was under the special charge of God, as is expressly stated in Ecclus. xvii. 17 (comp. Is. xxiv. 21, 22, LXX.). The notion is only *modified* when in Dan. x. 13, 20, Michael "the first Prince," and in Tobit xii. 15, "the seven Archangels," are regarded as protectors of Israel. But now the dispensational functions of Angels have ceased, because in "the kingdom of God" they in their turn were subordinated to the man Christ Jesus.

the world to come] The *Olam habba* or "future age" of the Hebrews, although the word here used is not *aion* but *oikoumenē*, properly the inhabited world. In Is. ix. 6 the Theocratic king who is a type of the Messiah is called "the Everlasting Father," which is rendered by the LXX. "father of the future age." In the "new heavens and new earth," as in the Messianic kingdom which is "the kingdom of our Lord and of His Christ," man, whose nature Christ has taken upon Him, is to be specially exalted. Hence, as Calvin acutely observes, Abraham, Joshua, Daniel are not forbidden to bow to Angels, but under the New Covenant St John is twice forbidden (Rev. xix. 10, xxii. 9). But, although the Messianic kingdom, and therefore the "future age," began at the Resurrection, there is yet another "future

testified, saying, What is man, that thou art mindful of him? or the son of man, that thou visitest him? Thou madest him a little lower than the angels; 7 thou crownedst him with glory and honour, and

age" beyond it, which shall only begin when this age is perfected, and Christ's kingdom is *fully* come.

whereof we speak] i.e. which is my present subject.

6. *but one in a certain place testified*] The writer was of course perfectly well aware that the Psalm on which he proceeds to comment is the 8th Psalm. This indefinite mode of quotation ("some one, somewhere") is common in Philo and the Rabbis. Scripture is often quoted by the words "It saith" or "He saith" or "God saith. Possibly the indefinite form (comp. iv. 4)—which is not found in St Paul—is only here adopted because God is Himself addressed in the Psalm. (See Schöttgen, *Nov. Hebr.*, p. 928.)

What is man] The Hebrew word—*enosh*—means man in his weakness and humiliation. The "what" expresses a double feeling—how mean in himself! how great in *Thy* love! The Psalm is only Messianic in so far as it implies man's final exaltation through Christ's incarnation. It applies, in the first instance, and directly, to man; and only in a secondary sense to Jesus as man. But St Paul had already (1 Cor. xv. 27; Eph. i. 22) applied it in a Messianic sense, and "Son of man" was a Messianic title (Dan. vii. 13). Thus the Cabbalists regarded the name Adam as an anagram for Adam, David, Moses, and regarded the Messiah as combining the dignity of all three. David twice makes the exclamation—"What is man?";—once when he is thinking of man's frailty in connection with his exaltation by God (Ps. viii.); and once (Ps. cxliv. 3) when he is thinking only of man's emptiness and worthlessness, as being undeserving of God's care. (comp. Job vii. 17).

7. *a little lower*] The "little" in the original (*meat*) means "little in degree;" but is here applied to time—"for a little while"—as is clear from ver. 9. The writer was only acquainted with the LXX. and in Greek the βραχύ τι would naturally suggest brevity of time (comp. 1 Pet. v. 10). Some of the Old Greek translators who took the other meaning rendered ὀλίγον παρὰ θεόν.

than the angels] The original has "than *Elohim*," i.e. than God; but the name *Elohim* has, as we have seen, a much wider and lower range than "Jehovah," and the rendering "angels" is here found both in the LXX. and the Targum. It must be borne in mind that the writer is only applying the words of the Psalm, and putting them as it were to a fresh use. The Psalm is "a lyric echo of the first chapter of Genesis" and speaks of man's exaltation. The author is applying it to man's lowliness ("ad suum institutum deflectit," says Calvin, "κατ' ἐπεξεργασίαν"). Yet David's notion, like that of Cicero, is that "Man is a mortal God," and the writer is only touching on man's humiliation to illustrate his exaltation of the God-Man. See Perowne on *the Psalms* (I. 144).

8 didst set him over the works of thy hands: thou hast put all *things* in subjection under his feet. For in that *he* put all in subjection under him, he left nothing *that is* not put under him. But now we see not yet all 9 *things* put under him. But we see Jesus, who was made a little lower than the angels, for the suffering of death,

    and didst set him over the works of thy hands] This clause is probably a gloss from the LXX., as it is absent from some of the best MSS. and Versions (e.g. B and the Syriac). The writer omitted it as not bearing on his argument.

    8. *thou hast put*...] Rather, "Thou didst put..." by one eternal decree. This clause should be added to the last verse. The clause applies not to Christ (as in 1 Cor. xv. 25) but to man in his redeemed glory.

    all things] This is defined in the Psalm (viii. 8. 9) to mean specially the animal world, but is here applied to the universe in accordance with its Messianic application (Matt. xxviii. 18).

    For] The "for" continues the reasoning of ver. 5. The writer with deep insight seizes upon the juxtaposition of "humiliation" and "dominion" as a paradox which only found in Christ its full solution.

    he left nothing that is not put under him] The inference intended to be drawn is not "and therefore even angels will be subject to man," but "and therefore the control of angels will come to an end." When however we read such a passage as 1 Cor. vi. 3 ("Know ye not that we shall judge angels?") it is uncertain whether the author would not have admitted even the other inference.

    But now] i.e. but, in this present earthly condition of things man is not as yet supreme. We see as a fact ($\dot{o}\rho\tilde{\omega}\mu\epsilon\nu$) man's humiliation: we perceive by faith the glorification of Jesus, and of all humanity in Him.

    under him] i.e. under man.

    9. *But we see*] Rather, "But we look upon." The verb used is not $\dot{o}\rho\tilde{\omega}\mu\epsilon\nu$ *videmus* as in the previous verse, but $\beta\lambda\acute{\epsilon}\pi o\mu\epsilon\nu$ *cernimus* (as in iii. 19). In accordance with the order of the original the verse should be rendered "*But we look upon Him who has been, for a little while, made low in comparison of angels—even Jesus—on account of the suffering of death crowned*, &c."

    who was made a little lower than the angels] This alludes to the temporal ("for a little while") and voluntary humiliation of the Incarnate Lord. See Phil. ii. 7—11. For a short time Christ was liable to agony and death from which angels are exempt; and even to the "intolerable indignity" of the grave.

    for the suffering of death] Rather, "*because of* the suffering of death." The *Via crucis* was the appointed *via lucis* (comp. v. 7—10, vii. 26, ix. 12). This truth—that the sufferings of Christ were the willing path of His perfectionment as the "Priest upon his throne" (Zech. vi. 13)—is brought out more distinctly in this than in any other Epistle.

crowned with glory and honour; that he by the grace of God should taste death for every *man*. For it became him, 10

crowned with glory and honour] Into the *nature* of this glory it was needless and hardly possible to enter. "On His head were *many* crowns" (Rev. xix. 12).

that] The words refer to the whole of the last clause. The universal efficacy of His death resulted from the double fact of His humiliation and glorification. He was made a little lower than the angels, He suffered death, He was crowned with glory and honour in order that His death might be efficacious for the redemption of the world.

by the grace of God] The work of redemption resulted from the love of the Father no less than from that of the Son (John iii. 16; Rom. v. 8; 2 Cor. v. 21). It is therefore a part of "the grace of God" (Rom. v. 8; Gal. ii. 21; 2 Cor. vi. 1; Tit. ii. 11), and could only have been carried into completion by the aid of that grace of which Christ was full. The Greek is χάριτι Θεοῦ, but there is a very interesting and very ancient various reading χωρὶς Θεοῦ "*apart from God.*" St Jerome says that he only found this reading "in *some* copies" (in quibusdam exemplaribus) whereas Origen had already said that he only found the *other* reading "by the grace of God" in some copies (ἐν τίσιν ἀντιγράφοις). At present however the reading "*apart from God*" is only found in the cursive manuscript 53 (a MS. of the 9th century), and in the margin of 67. It is clear that the reading was once more common than is now the case, and it seems to have been a Western and Syriac reading which has gradually disappeared from the manuscripts. Theodore of Mopsuestia calls the reading "by the grace of God" meaningless, and others have stamped it as Monophysite (i. e. as implying that in Christ there was only one nature). We have seen that this is by no means the case, though the other reading may doubtless have fallen into disfavour from the use made of it by the Nestorians to prove that Christ did not suffer in His divinity but only "apart from God," i. e. in His *humanity* (so too St Ambrose and Fulgentius). But even if the reading be correct (and it is certainly more ancient than the Nestorian controversy) the words may belong to their own proper clause—"that he may taste death for every being *except God;*" the latter words being added as in 1 Cor. xv. 27. But the reading is almost certainly spurious. For (1) in the *Nestorian* sense it is unlike any other passage of Scripture; (2) in the other sense it is unnecessary (since it bears in no way on the immediate argument) and may have been originally added as a superfluous marginal gloss by some pragmatic reader who remembered 1 Cor. xv. 27; or (3) it may have originated from a confusion of letters on the original papyrus. The incorporation of marginal glosses into the text is a familiar phenomenon in textual criticism. Such perhaps are 1 John v. 7; Acts viii. 37; the latter part of Rom. viii. 1; "without cause" in Matt. v. 22; "unworthily" in 1 Cor. xi. 29, &c.

should taste death] The word "taste" is not to be pressed as though it meant that Christ "saw no corruption." "To taste" does not mean merely "*summis labris delibare.*" It is a common Semitic

for whom *are* all *things*, and by whom *are* all *things*, in

and metaphoric paraphrase for death, derived from the notion of Death as an Angel who gives a cup to drink; as in the Arabic poem Antar " Death fed him with a cup of absinth by my hand." Comp. Matt. xvi. 28; John viii. 52.

for] "on behalf of" ($ὑπέρ$), not "as a substitution for" ($ἀντί$).

for every man] Origen and others made this word neuter "for everything" or "for every existence;" but this seems to be expressly excluded by ver. 16, and is not in accordance with the analogy of John i. 29, iii. 16; 2 Cor. v. 21; 1 John ii. 2. It will be seen that the writer deals freely with the Psalm. The Psalmist views man *in his present condition* as being one which involves both glory and humiliation: it is here applied as expressing man's present humiliation and his future glory, which is compared with Christ's *temporal* humiliation leading to his Eternal glory. It is the necessity of this application which required the phrase "a little" to be understood not of degree but of time. No doubt the writer has read into the words a pregnant significance; but (1) he is only applying them by way of illustrating acknowledged truths; and (2) he is doing so in accordance with principles of exegesis which were universally conceded not only by Christians but even by Jews.

10. *For it became him*] Unlike St Paul the writer never enters into what may be called "the philosophy of the plan of salvation." He never attempts to throw any light upon the mysterious subject of the antecedent necessity for the death of Christ. Perhaps he considered that all which could be profitably said on that high mystery had already been said by St Paul (Rom. iii. 25; Gal. iii. 13; 2 Cor. v. 21). He dwells upon Christ's death almost exclusively *in its relation to us*. The expression which he here uses "it was morally fitting for Him" is almost the only one which he devotes to what may be called the *transcendent* side of Christ's sacrifice—the death of Christ as regards its relation to God. He develops no theory of vicarious satisfaction, &c., though he uses the metaphoric words "redemption" and "make reconciliation for" (ix. 15, ii. 17). The "moral fitness" here touched upon is the necessity for absolutely sympathetic unity between the High Priest and those for whom he offered His perfect sacrifice. Compare Lk. xxiv. 46, "thus it behoved Christ to suffer." Philo also uses the phrase "it became Him." It is a very remarkable expression, for though it also occurs in the LXX. (Jer. x. 7), yet in this passage alone does it contemplate the actions of God under the aspect of inherent moral fitness.

for whom] i. e. "for whose sake," "on whose account." The reference here is to God, not to Christ.

by whom] i. e. by whose creative agency. Compare Rom. xi. 36, "of Him, and through Him, and to Him are all things." The same words may also be applied to Christ, but the context here shews that they refer to God the Father.

in bringing] Lit., "having brought." The use of the *aorist* participle is difficult, but the "glory" seems to imply the potential triumph of

bringing many sons unto glory, to make the captain of their salvation perfect through sufferings. For both he that 11 sanctifieth and they who are sanctified *are* all of one: for

man in the one *finished* act of Christ which was due to "the grace of God." The "Him" and the "having brought" refer to God and not to Christ. God led many sons to glory through the Captain of their Salvation, whom—in that process of Redemptive Work which is shared by each "Person" of the Blessed Trinity—He perfected through suffering. On the Cross the future glory of the many sons was won and was potentially consummated.

many] "A great multitude which no man could number" (Rev. vii. 9—14).

sons] This word seems to shew that the "having brought" refers to God, not to Christ, for we are called Christ's "brethren," but never His sons.

the captain] The word also occurs in Acts v. 31. In Acts iii. 15 it means "author," or "originator," as in xii. 2. The word primarily signifies one who goes at the head of a company as their leader (*antesignanus*) and guide (see Is. lv. 4), and then comes to mean "originator." Comp. v. 9.

to make...perfect] Not in the sense of making morally, or otherwise, perfect, but in the sense of leading to a predestined goal or consummation. See the similar uses of this word in v. 9, vii. 28, ix. 9, x. 14, xi. 40, xii. 23. The LXX. uses the word to represent the *consecration* of the High Priest (Lev. xxi. 10). In this Epistle the verb occurs nine times, in all St Paul's Epistles probably not once. (In 2 Cor. xii. 9 the reading of A, B, D, F, G, L is τελεῖται. In Phil. iii. 12 the reading of D, E, F, G is δεδικαίωμαι).

through sufferings] See note on ver. 9, and comp. Rev. v. 9; 1 Pet. v. 10. Jewish Christians were slow to realise the necessity for a crucified Messiah, and when they did so they tried to distinguish between Messiah son of David and a supposed Messiah son of Joseph. There are however some traces of such a belief. See an Appendix to Vol. II. of the last Edition of Dean Perowne on the Psalms.

11. *For*] The next three verses are an illustration of the moral fitness, and therefore of the Divine necessity, that there should be perfect unity and sympathy between the Saviour and the saved.

both he that sanctifieth and they who are sanctified] The idea would perhaps be better, though less literally, expressed by "both the sanctifier and the sanctified," for the idea of sanctification is here not so much that of progressive holiness as that of cleansing (xiii. 12). This writer seems to make but little difference between the words "to sanctify" and "to purify," because in the sphere of the Jewish Ceremonial Law, from which his analogies are largely drawn, "sanctification" meant the setting apart for service by various means of purification. See ix. 13, 14, x. 10, 14, xiii. 12, and comp. John xvii. 17—19; 1 John i. 7. The progressive sanctification is viewed in its ideal result, and in this result

12 which cause he is not ashamed to call them brethren, saying, I will declare thy name unto my brethren, in the midst of the church will I sing praise unto thee. 13 And again, I will put my trust in him. And again, Behold, I, and the children which God hath given me.

the whole Church of Christ shares, so that, like Israel of old, it is ideally "holy."

are all of one] That is, they alike derive their origin from God; in other words the relation in which they stand to each other is due to one and the same divine purpose (John xvii. 17—19). This seems a better view than to refer the "one" to Abraham (Is. li. 2; Ezek. xxxiii. 24, &c.) or to Adam.

he is not ashamed to call them brethren] If the Gospels had been commonly known at the time when this Epistle was written, the author would doubtless have referred not to the Old Testament, but to such direct and tender illustrations as Matt. xii. 49, 50, "Behold my mother and my brethren! For whosoever shall do the will of my Father which is in heaven, the same is my brother, and sister, and mother:" or to John xx. 17, "Go to my brethren, and say unto them, I ascend unto my Father, and your Father; and to my God, and your God:" Matt. xxviii. 10, "go unto my brethren." Or are we to suppose that this application of Messianic Psalms would have come with even greater argumentative force to his Judaising readers?

to call] i.e. to declare them to be His brethren by calling them so.

12. *I will declare thy name unto my brethren*] Ps. xxii. 22. This is a typico-prophetic Psalm, accepted in a Messianic sense, which was supposed to be mystically indicated by its superscription, "*On the hind of the dawn.*" The sense of its prophetic and typical character had doubtless been deepened among Christians by our Lord's quotation from it on the Cross (Matt. xxvii. 46). It is one of our special Psalms for Good Friday. See the references to it in Matt. xxvii. 35; John xix. 24.

in the midst of the church] Rather, "of the congregation."

13. *And again, I will put my trust in him*] The quotation is probably from Is. viii. 17, but nearly the same words are found in Ps. xviii. 2 and 2 Sam. xxii. 3 (LXX.). The necessity of putting His trust in God is a proof of Christ's humanity, and therefore of His brotherhood with us. When He was on the Cross His enemies said by way of taunt, "*He trusted in God*" (Matt. xxvii. 43).

Behold, I, and the children which God hath given me] This verse furnishes a marked instance of the principles of Biblical interpretation, of which we have already seen many specimens. Isaiah by the prophetess has a son to whom he is bidden to give the name Maher-shalal-hash-baz, or "*Speed-plunder-haste-spoil;*" to his elder son he has been bidden to give the name Shear-Jashub, "*a remnant shall remain;*" and as the names of both sons are connected with prophecies concerning Israel he says "Lo! I and the children whom the Lord hath given me *are for signs*

Forasmuch then as the children are partakers of flesh and 14 blood, he also himself likewise took part of the same; that through death he might destroy him that had the power of

and for wonders in Israel from the Lord of hosts." The words are here entirely dissociated from their context and from their primary historical meaning to indicate the relation between Christ and His redeemed children. The LXX. in Is. viii. 17 insert the words "And He will say," and some have supposed that the author (who, like most Alexandrians, was evidently unacquainted with the original Hebrew) understood these words to imply that it was no longer the Prophet but the Messiah who was the speaker. It is however more probable that he took for granted the legitimacy of his application. In this he merely followed the school of interpretation in which he had been trained, in accordance with principles which were at that period universally accepted among Jews and Christians. We must ourselves regard it as a somewhat extreme instance of applying the words of Scripture in a Messianic sense. But we see the bearing of the illustration upon the immediate point in view, when we recall the typical character and position of Isaiah, and therefore the mystic significance which was naturally attached to his words. Our Lord Himself uses, with no reference to Isaiah, a similar expression, "those that thou gavest me," in John xvii. 12.

14—18. A FULLER STATEMENT OF THE MORAL FITNESS OF CHRIST'S PARTICIPATION IN HUMAN SUFFERINGS.

14. *are partakers of flesh and blood*] Rather, "have shared (and do share) in blood and flesh," i.e. are human. They are all inheritors of this common mystery. This is implied by the perfect tense. "Blood and flesh," as in Eph. vi. 12.

likewise] This word furnished the Fathers with a strong argument against the Docetae who regarded the body of Christ not as real but as purely phantasmal.

took part of the same] Because, as he goes on to intimate, it would otherwise have been impossible for Christ to die. Comp. Phil. ii. 8. The aorist implies the one historic fact of the Incarnation.

he might destroy] Rather, "He may bring to nought," or "render impotent." See 2 Tim. i. 10, "Jesus Christ...hath abolished death;" 1 Cor. xv. 51—57; Rev. i. 18. The word occurs 28 times in St Paul, but elsewhere only here and in Lk. xiii. 7, though sometimes found in the LXX.

him that had the power of death] Rather, "him that *hath*," i.e. in the present condition of things. But Christ, by assuming our flesh, became "the Death of death," as in the old epitaph,

"Mors Mortis Morti mortem nisi morte dedisset
    Aeternae vitae janua clausa foret;"

which we may render

"Had not the Death of death to Death by death his death-blow given,
    For ever closèd were the gate, the gate of life and heaven."

15 death, that is, the devil; and deliver them who through fear
16 of death were all their lifetime subject to bondage. For
verily he took not on *him the nature of* angels; but he took

> It is, however, possible that the phrase, "the power of death," does not imply that the devil can, by God's permission, inflict death, but that he has "a sovereignty, of which death is the realm."
>
> *that is, the devil*] This is the only place in this Epistle in which the name "Devil" occurs. It is nowhere very frequent in the N.T. The English reader is liable to be misled by the rendering "devils" for "demons" in the Gospels. Satan has the power of death, if that be the meaning here, not as lord, but as executioner (comp. Rev. ix. 11); his power is only a permissive power (John viii. 44; Rev. xii. 10; Wisdom ii. 24, "Through envy of the devil came death unto the world)." The manner in which Christ shall thus bring Satan to nought is left untouched, but the best general comments on the fact are in 1 Cor. xv. and the Apocalypse. Nor does this expression encourage any Manichean or dualistic views; for, however evil may be the *will* of Satan, he can never exercise his *power* otherwise than in accordance with the just will of God. The Jews spoke of an Angel of Death, whom they called Sammael, and whom they identified with Satan (Eisenmenger, *Entd. Judenth.* II. p. 821.
>
> **15.** *them who*] Lit. "those, as many as," i.e. "all who."
>
> *through fear of death*] This was felt, as we see from the O.T., far more intensely under the old than under the new dispensation. Dr Robertson Smith quotes from the *Midrash Tanchuma*, "In this life death never suffers man to be glad." See Num. xvii. 13, xviii. 5; Ps. vi., xxx., &c., and Is. xxxviii. 10—20, &c. In heathen and savage lands the whole of life is often overshadowed by the terror of death, which thus becomes a veritable "bondage." Philo quotes a line of Euripides to shew that a man who has no fear of death can never be a slave. But, through Christ's death, death has become to the Christian the gate of glory. It is remarkable that in this verse the writer introduces a whole range of conceptions which he not only leaves without further development, but to which he does not ever allude again. They seem to lie aside from the main current of his views.
>
> **16.** *For verily he took not on him the nature of angels*] Rather, "for assuredly it is not angels *whom He takes by the hand*." The word δήπου, "certainly," "I suppose," occurs here only in the N.T. or LXX., though common in Philo. In classic Greek it often has a semi-ironic tinge, "you will doubtless admit that," like *opinor* in Latin. All are now agreed that the verb does not mean "to take the nature of," but "to take by the hand," and so "to help" or "rescue." Beza indeed called it "execrable rashness" (*exsecranda audacia*) to translate it so, when this rendering was first adopted by Castellio in 1551; but the usage of the word proves that this is the only possible rendering, although all the Fathers and Reformers take it in the other way. It is rightly corrected in the R. V. (comp. Is. xlix. 0, 10; Jer. xxxi. 32; Heb. viii. 9; Matt. xiv. 31; Wisd. iv. 11, "Wisdom...*takes*

on *him* the seed of Abraham. Wherefore in all *things* it be- 17
hoved him to be made like unto *his* brethren, that he might
be a merciful and faithful high priest *in things* pertaining to
God, to make reconciliation for the sins of the people. For 18

by the hand those that seek her"). To refer "*he* taketh not hold" to
Death or the Devil is most improbable.

the seed of Abraham] i.e. He was born a Hebrew. He does not at
all mean to imply that our Lord came to the Jews more than to the
Gentiles, though he is only thinking of the former.

17. *Wherefore*] The Greek word ὅθεν, "*whence*," common in this
Epistle, does not occur once in St Paul, but is found in Acts xxvi. 19,
in a report of his speech, and in 1 John ii. 18.

in all things] These words should be taken with "to be made
like."

it behoved him] Stronger than the "it became Him" of ver. 10. It
means that, with reference to the object in view, there lay upon Him a
moral obligation to become a man with men. See v. 1, 2.

that he might be] Rather, "that he might *become*," or, "prove
Himself."

a merciful and faithful high priest] Merciful, or rather, "*compassionate*" to men; "faithful" to God. In Christ "mercy and truth" have
met together. Ps. lxxxv. 10. The expression "a faithful priest" is
found in 1 Sam. ii. 35. Dr Robertson Smith well points out that the
idea of "a **merciful** priest," which is scarcely to be found in the O. T.,
would come home with peculiar force to the Jews of that day, because
mercy was a quality in which the Aaronic Priests had signally failed
(*Yoma*, f. 9. 1), and in the Herodian epoch they were notorious for
cruelty, insolence and greed (see my *Life of Christ*, II. 329, 330). The
Jews said that there had been no less than 28 High Priests in 107 years
of this epoch (Jos. *Antt.* xx. 10) their brief dignity being due to their
wickedness (Prov. x. 27). The conception of the Priesthood hitherto
had been ceremonial rather than ethical; yet it is only "by mercy and
truth" that "iniquity is purged." Prov. xvi. 6. The word "High
Priest," here first introduced, has evidently been entering into the
writer's thoughts (i. 3, ii. 9, 11, 16), and is the most prominent conception throughout the remainder of the Epistle. The consummating
steps in genuine high priesthood are touched upon in v. 10, vi. 20,
ix. 24.

high priest] The Greek word is comparatively new. In the Pentateuch the high priest is merely called "the Priest" (except in Lev. xxi.
10). In later books of Scripture the epithet "head" or "great" is
added. The word occurs 17 times in this Epistle, but not once in any
other.

in things pertaining to God] Comp. v. 1. The phrase is found in
the LXX. of Ex. xviii. 19.

to make reconciliation for the sins of the people] More literally, "to
expiate the sins of the people." Christ is nowhere said in the N. T. to
"expiate" or "propitiate" God or "the wrath of God" (which are

in that he himself hath suffered being tempted, he is able to succour them that are tempted.

heathen, not Christian, conceptions), nor is any such expression found in the LXX. Nor do we find such phrases as "God was propitiated by the death of His Son," or "Christ propitiated the wrath of God by His blood." God Himself fore-ordained the propitiation (Rom. iii. 25). The verb represents the Hebrew *kippeer*, "to cover," whence is derived the name for the day of Atonement (*Kippurim*). In Dan. ix. 24 Theodotion's version has ἐξιλάσασθαι ἀδικίας. We are left to unauthorised theory and conjecture as to the *manner in which* and the *reason for which* "expiation," in the form of "sacrifice," interposes between "sin" and "wrath." All we know is that, *in relation to us*, Christ is "the propitiation for our sins" (1 John ii. 2, iv. 10; Rom. iii. 25). Accepting the blessed result as regards ourselves we shall best shew our wisdom by abstaining from dogmatism and theory respecting the unrevealed and transcendent mystery as it affects God.

the people] Primarily the Jewish people, whom alone the writer has in mind. Angels, so far as we are told, did not need the Redemptive work.

18. *For in that he himself hath suffered being tempted*] These words have been taken, and grammatically may be explained, in eight or nine different ways. One of the best ways is that here given by the A. V. and endorsed by the R. V. This method regards the Greek ἐν ᾧ as equivalent to the Hebrew *ba-asher*, which means "in so far as." "By His *Passion*," says Bp. Wordsworth, "He acquired *compassion*." Of other possible ways, the most tenable is that which takes ἐν ᾧ quite literally. "*In that sphere wherein* He suffered by being tempted"— the sphere being the whole conditions of human life and trial (comp. vi. 17; Rom. viii. 3). But the first way seems to be the better. Temptation of its own nature involves suffering, and it is too generally overlooked that though our Lord's severest temptations came in two great and solemn crises—in the wilderness and at Gethsemane—yet Scripture leads us to the view that He was always *liable* to temptation—though without sin, because the temptation was always repudiated with the whole force of His will throughout the whole course of His life of obedience. After the temptation in the wilderness the devil only left Him "for a season" (Luke iv. 13). We must remember too that the word "temptation" includes all trials.

he is able to succour them that are tempted] Rather, "that are under temptation" (lit. "that are *being* tempted," i.e. men in their mortal life of trial). This thought is the one so prominent throughout the Epistle, viz. the closeness of Christ's High-Priestly sympathy, iv. 15, v. 1, 2.

CH. III. SUPERIORITY OF CHRIST TO MOSES (1—6). EXHORTATION AGAINST HARDENING THE HEART (7—19).

There is a remarkable parallelism between the structure of this and the next chapter, and that of the first and second chapters.

Wherefore, holy brethren, partakers of the heavenly call- 3
ing, consider the Apostle and High Priest of our profession,
Christ Jesus; who was faithful to him that appointed him, 2

Christ higher than angels (i. 5—14).
Exhortation (ii. 1—5).
In Him man is exalted above angels (ii. 6—16).
His Higher Priesthood (ii. 17, 18).

Christ higher than Moses (iii. 1—6).
Exhortation (iii. 7—19).
In Him His people enter into rest (iv. 1—13).
His Higher Priesthood (iv. 14—16).

1. *Wherefore*] The same word (ὅθεν) as in ii. 17, where see the note. It is an inference from the grandeur of Christ's position and the blessedness of His work as set forth in the previous chapters.

holy brethren] This form of address is never used by St Paul. It assumes that they answered to their true ideal, as does the ordinary term "saints."

partakers of the heavenly calling] Rather, "of *a* heavenly calling." It is a heavenly calling because it comes from heaven (xii. 25), and is a call "upwards" (ἄνω) to heavenly things (Phil. iii. 14) and to holiness (1 Thess. iv. 7).

consider] The word means "contemplate," consider attentively, *fix your* thoughts upon (aorist).

the Apostle] Christ is called an "Apostle" as being "sent forth" (*apostellomenon*) from the Father (John xx. 21). The same title is used of Christ by Justin Martyr (*Apol.* i. 12). It corresponds both to the Hebrew *maleach* ("angel" or "messenger") and *sheliach* ("delegate"). The "Apostle" unites the functions of both, for, as Justin says of our Lord, He announces (*apangellei*) and He is sent (*apostelletai*).

and High Priest] Christ was both the Moses and the Aaron of the New Dispensation; an "Apostle" from God to us; an High Priest for us before God. As "Apostle" He, like Moses, pleads God's cause with us; as High Priest he, like Aaron, pleads our cause with God. Just as the High Priest came with *the name Jehovah* on the golden plate of his mitre in the name of God before Israel, and with *the names of the Tribes* graven on his jewelled breastplate in the name of Israel before God, so Christ is "God with us" and the propitiatory representative of men before God. He is above Angels as a Son, and a Lord of the future world; above Aaron as a Priest after the order of Melchisedek; above Moses as a Son over the house is above a servant in it.

of our profession] Rather, "of our *confession*" as Christians (iv. 14; x. 23; 2 Cor. ix. 13; 1 Tim. vi. 12). It is remarkable that in Philo (Opp. I. 654) the Logos is called "the Great High Priest of our Confession;"—but the genuineness of the clause seems doubtful.

Christ Jesus] Rather, according to the best MSS. "Jesus" (A, B, C, D). Such a variation of reading may seem a matter of indifference, but this is very far from being the case. First of all, the traceable differences in the usage of this sacred name mark the advance of Chris-

3 as also Moses *was faithful* in all his house. For this *man* was counted worthy of more glory than Moses, inasmuch as

tianity. In the Gospels Christ is called Jesus and "the Christ;" "the Christ" being still the title of His *office* as the Anointed Messiah, not the name of His *Person*. In the Epistles "Christ" has become a proper name, and He is frequently spoken of as "the Lord," not merely as a title of general respect, but in the use of the word as an equivalent to the Hebrew "Jehovah." Secondly, the difference of nomenclature shews that St Paul was not the author of this Epistle. St Paul uses the title "Christ Jesus" which (if the reading be here untenable) does not occur in this Epistle. This author uses "Jesus Christ" (x. 10, xiii. 8, 21), "the Lord" (ii. 3), "our Lord" (vii. 14), "our Lord Jesus" (xiii. 20), "the Son of God" (vi. 6, vii. 3, x. 29), but most frequently "Jesus" alone, as here (ii. 9, iv. 14, vi. 20, vii. 22, x. 19, xii. 2, 24, xiii. 12) or "Christ" alone (iii. 6, 14, v. 5, vi. 1, ix. 11, &c.). See Prof. Davidson, *On the Hebrews*, p. 73.

2. *who was faithful*] Lit., "Being faithful," i.e. as Cranmer excellently rendered it, "how that he is faithful." The word is suggested by the following contrast between Christ and Moses, of whom it had been said " My servant Moses is not so, who was *faithful* in all mine house," Num. xii. 7.

to him that appointed him] Lit., "to Him that *made* Him." There can be little doubt that the expression means, as in the A.V. "to Him that made Him *such*," i.e. made Him an Apostle and High Priest. For the phrase is doubtless suggested by 1 Sam. xii. 6, where the LXX. has "He that *made* Moses and Aaron" (A.V. "advanced"); comp. Mk. iii. 14, "And He *made* (ἐποίησε) Twelve, that they should be with Him." Acts ii. 36, "God made Him Lord and Christ." The rendering "appointed" is therefore a perfectly faithful one. Still the peculiarity of the phrase was eagerly seized upon by Arians to prove that Christ was *a created Being*, and this was one of the causes which retarded the general acceptance of the Epistle. Yet even if "made" was not here used in the sense of "appointed" the Arians would have had no vantage ground; for the word might have been applied to the Incarnation (so Athanasius, and Primasius), though not (as Bleek and Lünemann take it) to the Eternal Generation of the Son. Theodoret and Chrysostom understood it as our Version does.

as also Moses...in all his house] Rather, "in all *His* (God's) house," Num. xii. 7. The house is *God's* house or household, i.e. the theocratic family of which the Tabernacle was a symbol—"the house of God which is the Church of the living God," 1 Tim. iii. 15. The "faithfulness" of Moses consisted in teaching the Israelites all that God had commanded him (Deut. iv. 5) and himself "doing according to all that the Lord commanded him" (Ex. xl. 16).

3. *For this man*] Rather, "For *He*," i.e. Christ. The "for" depends on the "Consider."

was counted worthy] Rather, "hath been deemed worthy," namely, by God.

he who hath builded the house hath more honour than the house. For every house is builded by some *man*; but he ⁴ that built all *things is* God. And Moses verily *was* faithful 5 in all his house, as a servant, for a testimony of those *things*

more glory] Rather, "a fuller glory" (*amplioris gloriae*, Vulg.).

of more glory than Moses] Eagerly as the writer is pressing forwards to develop his original and central conception of Christ as our Eternal High Priest, he yet has to pause to prove His superiority over Moses, because the Jews had begun to elevate Moses into a position of almost supernatural grandeur which would have its effect on the imaginations of wavering and almost apostatising converts. Thus the Rabbis said that "the soul of Moses was equivalent to the souls of all Israel;" (because by the cabbalistic process called *Gematria* the numerical value of the letters of "Moses our Rabbi" in Hebrew=613, which is also the value of the letters of "Lord God of Israel"). They said that "the face of Moses was like the Sun;" that he alone "saw through a clear glass" not as other prophets "through a dim glass" (comp. St Paul's "through a mirror in a riddle," 1 Cor. xiii. 12) and that whereas there are but fifty gates of understanding in the world, "all but one were opened to Moses." See the Rabbinic references in my *Early days of Christianity*, I. 362. St Paul in 2 Cor. iii. 7, 8 contrasts the evanescing splendour on the face of Moses with the unchanging glory of Christ.

he who hath builded the house] The verb (κατασκευάσας) implies rather "equipped" or "established" than "builded" (see ix. 2, 6, xi. 7 and note on i. 2; Wisd. xiii. 4).

hath more honour than the house] The point of this expression is not very obvious. If taken strictly it would imply that Moses was himself "the house" which Christ built. But οἶκος, "house" or "*household*" means more than the mere building (οἰκία). It means the whole theocratic family, the House of Israel in its covenant relation; and though Moses was not this House, he was more than a servant in it being also its direct representative and human head. (There is a somewhat similar phrase in Philo, *De plant. Noe*, 16.)

4. *For every house is builded by some man*] The real meaning would perhaps be better expressed by "Every *household* is *established* by some one." The establisher of the Old Dispensation as well as of the New was Christ, but yet, in some sense (as an instrument and minister) Moses might be regarded as the founder of the Old Covenant (Acts vii. 38), as Jesus of the New. The verb (*kataskeuazo*) is rendered "prepare" in ix. 6, xi. 7; Lk. i. 17.

he that built all things is God] In His humanity Jesus was but "the Apostle" of God in building His house, the Church. "He (*the man whose name is the Branch*) shall build the temple *of the Lord*," Zech. vi. 12. God is the supreme, ultimate, and universal Founder.

5. *in all his house*] i.e. in all God's house. Two "houses" are contemplated, Mosaism and Christianity, the Law and the Gospel. Both were established by God. In the household of the Law, Moses was the faithful minister; in the household of the Gospel, Christ took on

6 which were to be spoken after; but Christ as a Son over his own house; whose house are we, if we hold fast the confidence and the rejoicing of the hope firm unto the end.

Him, indeed, "the form of a slave," and as such was faithful even unto death, but yet was Son *over* the House. This seems a more natural explanation than that the writer regards both the covenants as one Household, *in* which Moses was a servant, and *over* which Christ was a Son.

as a servant] The word used is not *doulos* "slave," nor *diakonos* "minister," but *therapōn* "voluntary attendant." It is also applied to Moses in the Ep. of Barnabas and in Ex. xiv. 31 (LXX.).

for a testimony of those things which were to be spoken after] They were to be spoken afterwards by Christ, the Prophet to whom Moses had pointed, Deut. xviii. 15. The Law and the Prophets did but *witness* to the righteousness of God which was to be fully revealed in Christ (Rom. iii. 21). They were but a shadow of the coming reality (x. 1). But although it is natural for us to understand the expression in this way, the author possibly meant no more than that the faithfulness of Moses was an attestation of the Law which was about to be delivered.

6. *as a Son over his own house*] Rather, "over His (i.e. God's) house." In the words "Servant" and "Son" we again (as in i. 5, 8) reach the central point of Christ's superiority to Moses. The proof of this superiority did not require more than a brief treatment because it was implicitly involved in the preceding arguments.

whose house are we] This is a metaphor which the writer may well have learnt in his intercourse with St Paul (2 Cor. vi. 16; Eph. ii. 21, 22. Comp. 1 Pet. ii. 5).

the confidence] Literally, "our cheerful confidence," especially of utterance, as in x. 19, 35. The word rendered "confidence" in verse 14 is different. This boldness of speech and access, which were the special glory of the old democracies, are used by St John also to express the highest Christian privilege of filial outspokenness (1 John iii. 21). Apollos, the probable writer of this Epistle, was known for this bold speech (Acts xviii. 26), and evidently feels the duty and privilege of such a mental altitude (Heb. iv. 16, x. 19, 35).

the rejoicing of the hope] Rather, "the glorying of our hope." The Greek word means "an object of boasting," as in Rom. iv. 2; 1 Cor. v. 6, &c. The way in which the writer dwells on the need for "a full assurance of hope" (vi. 11, 18, 19) seems to shew that owing to the delay in Christ's coming his readers were liable to fall into impatience (x. 36, xii. 1) and apathy (vi. 12, x. 25).

firm unto the end] The same phrase occurs in ver. 14. The word "firm" being feminine does not agree with the neuter word "object of boast," and the repetition of the phrase by a writer so faultlessly rhetorical is singular. It cannot however be regarded as a gloss, for it is found in all the best Manuscripts.

unto the end] That is, not "until death," but until hope is lost in

Wherefore, as the Holy Ghost saith, To day if ye will 7
hear his voice, harden not your hearts, as in the 8
provocation, in the day of temptation in the wilder-

fruition; until this dispensation has attained to its final goal. This necessity for perseverance in well-doing is frequently urged in the N. T. because it was especially needed in times of severe trial. Matt. x. 22; Col. i. 23, and see infra x. 35—39.

7—19. A SOLEMN WARNING AGAINST HARDENING THE HEART.

[This constant interweaving of warning and exhortation with argument is characteristic of this Epistle. These passages (ii. 1—4, iii. 7—19, iv. 1—14, vi. 1—9, x. 19—39) cannot, however, be called digressions, because they belong to the object which the writer had most distinctly in view—namely, to check a tendency to relapse from the Gospel into Judaism].

7. *Wherefore*] The verb which depends on this conjunction is delayed by the quotation, but is practically found in ver. 12, "Take heed." Christ was faithful: therefore take heed that ye be not unfaithful.

as the Holy Ghost saith] For this form of quotation see Mk. xii. 36; Acts i. 16; 2 Pet. i. 21.

To day if ye will hear his voice] Rather, "if ye *hear*," or "shall have heard." The quotation is from Ps. xcv. 7—11, and the word means "Oh that ye would hear His voice!"; but the LXX. often renders the Hebrew *im* by "if." The "to-day" is always the Scripture day of salvation, which is *now*, 2 Cor. vi. 2; Is. lv. 6. "If any man hear my voice...I will come in to him," Rev. iii. 20. The sense of the Imminent Presence of God which reigns throughout the prophecies of the O. T. as well as in the N. T. (x. 37; 1. 2. Thess.; 1 Pet. i. 5, &c.) is beautifully illustrated in the Talmudic story of the Rabbi (*Sanhedrin* 98. 1) who went to the Messiah by direction of Elijah, and asked him when he would come; and He answered "to-day." But before the Rabbi could return to Elijah the sun had set, and he asked "Has Messiah then deceived me?" "No," answered Elijah; "he meant 'To-day if ye hear His voice.'"

8. *harden not your hearts*] Comp. Acts xix. 9. Usually *God* is said to harden man's heart (Ex. vii. 3, &c.; Is. lxiii. 17; Rom. ix. 18) an anthropomorphic way of expressing the inevitable results of neglect and of evil habit. But that this is man's own doing and choice is always recognised (Deut. x. 16; 2 Kings xvii. 14, &c.).

as in the provocation] Lit., "in the embitterment." The LXX. here seem to have read Marah (which means "bitter" and which they render by πικρία in Ex. xv. 23) for Meribah which, in Ex. xvii. 1—7, they render by *Loidoresis* "reproach." This is not however certain, for though the substantive does not occur again, the verb "I embitter" is frequently used of provoking God to anger. For the story of Meribah, see Numb. xx. 7—13.

in the day of temptation] Rather, "of the temptation," i.e. at

9 ness: when your fathers tempted me, proved me,
10 and saw my works forty years. Wherefore I was grieved with that generation, and said, They do alway err in *their* heart; and they have not known
11 my ways. So I sware in my wrath, They shall not enter into my rest.

Massah; Ex. xvii. 7; Deut. vi. 16, though the allusion might also be to Num. xiv.

9. *when*] Rather, "where," i.e. at Massah, or in the wilderness. The rendering "wherewith" or "with which temptation," would have been more naturally expressed in other ways.

proved me] The better reading is "by proving me."

saw my works forty years] The "forty years" is purposely transferred from the next verse of the Psalm. The scene at Massah took place in the 40th and that at Meribah in the 1st year of the wanderings. Deut. ix. 7, xxxiii. 8. They indicate the spirit of the Jews through the whole period. The number 40 is in the Bible constantly connected with judgment or trial, and it would have sounded more impressive in this passage if the date of the Epistle was shortly before the Fall of Jerusalem, i.e. about 40 years after the Ascension. The Rabbis had a saying "The days of the Messiah are 40 years."

10. *I was grieved*] Rather, "I was indignant." The Greek word is derived from the dashing of waves against a bank. It only occurs in the N. T. here and in verse 17, but is common in the LXX.

with that generation] The better reading is "with *this* generation," and it is at least possible that the writer intentionally altered the expression to make it sound more directly emphatic. The words "*this* generation" would fall with grave force on ears which had heard the report of our Lord's great discourse (Matt. xxiii. 36; comp. xxiv. 34). To the writer of this Epistle the language of Scripture is not regarded as a thing of the past, but as being in a marked degree, present, living, and permanent.

They do alway err in their heart] See Ps. lxxviii. 40, 41. The word "alway" is not in the original. The Apostles in their quotations are not careful about verbal accuracy. The Hebrew says "they are a people (*am*) of wanderers in heart," and Bleek thought that the LXX. read *ad* and understood it to mean "always."

11. *So I sware in my wrath*] The reference is to Num. xiv. 28—30. xxxii. 13.

They shall not enter] This is the correct rendering of the idiom (here used by a Hebraism) "*if* they shall enter."

my rest] The writer proceeds to argue that this expression could not refer to the past Sabbath-rest of God: or to the partial and symbolic rest of Canaan; and must therefore refer to the final rest of heaven. But he does not of course mean to sanction any inference about the *future and final salvation* either of those who entered Canaan or of those who died in the wilderness.

Take heed, brethren, lest there be in any of you an evil 12 heart of unbelief, in departing from the living God. But 13 exhort one another daily, while it is called To day; lest any of you be hardened through the deceitfulness of sin. For 14 we are made partakers of Christ, if we hold the beginning of *our* confidence stedfast unto the end; whilst it is said, To 15

12. *Take heed, brethren, lest there be...*] It is evident that deep anxiety mixes with the warning.

in any of you] The warning is expressed indefinitely; but if the Epistle was addressed to a small Hebrew community the writer may have had in view some special person who was in danger (comp. x. 25, xii. 15). In any case the use of the singular might lead to individual searching of hearts. He here begins a homily founded on the quotation from the Psalm.

an evil heart of unbelief] Unbelief has its deep source in the heart more often perhaps than in the mind.

in departing] Lit., *in the apostatising from*. In that one word— Apostasy—the moral peril of his Hebrew readers was evidently summed up. To apostatise *after* believing is more dangerous than not to have believed at all.

from the living God] The epithet is not idle. It conveys *directly* the warning that God would not overlook the sin of apostasy, and *indirectly* the thought that Christ was in heaven at the right hand of God.

13. *exhort one another*] The verb implies the mutually *strengthening* intercourse of consolation and moral appeal. It is the verb from which comes the word *Paraclete*, i.e. the Comforter or Strengthener. The literal rendering is "exhort *yourselves*," but this is only an *idiom* which extends reciprocity into identity, and the meaning is "exhort *one another*."

while it is called To day] Another rendering is "so long as to-day is being proclaimed." The meaning is "while the to-day of the Psalm (τὸ σήμερον) can still be regarded as applicable," i.e. while our "day of visitation" lasts, and while we still "have the light." Lk. xix. 44; John xii. 35, 36.

be hardened] See note on ver. 8. The following clause indicates that God only "hardens" the heart, in the sense that man is inevitably suffered to render his own heart callous by indulgence in sin.

14. *we are made*] Rather, "we are become."

partakers of Christ] Rather, "partakers *with* Christ," for the thought of mystical union with Christ extending into spiritual unity and identity, which makes the words "in Christ" the "monogram" of St Paul, is scarcely alluded to by this writer. His thoughts are rather of "Christ *for* us" than of "Christ *in* us." "To him that overcometh will I grant *to sit with me in my throne*," Rev. iii. 21.

the beginning of our confidence] The word *hypostasis* is here rendered confidence, as in Ps. xxxix. 7 ("sure hope"). This meaning of the

day if ye will hear his voice, harden not your hearts,
16 as in the provocation. For some, when they had heard,
did provoke: howbeit not all that came out of Egypt by
17 Moses. But with whom was he grieved forty years? *was it*
not with them that had sinned, whose carcases fell in the
18 wilderness? And to whom sware he that *they* should not
19 enter into his rest, but to them that believed not? So we see
that they could not enter in because of unbelief.

4   Let us therefore fear, lest, a promise being left *us* of en-

word (elsewhere rendered "substance," to which it etymologically corresponds, i. 3, xi. 1), is found only in later Greek. The expression "*beginning*" does not here imply anything inchoate or imperfect, but is merely in contrast with "end."

stedfast unto the end] See note on ver. 6.

16. *some, when they had heard, did provoke*] Rather, "Who (τίνες) when they heard, embittered (Him)"? This is the reading of the Peshito. It would have been absurd to use the word "some" of 600,000 with only two exceptions, Num. xiv. 38; Josh. xiv. 8, 9.

howbeit not all] Rather, "Nay! was it not all?" (i.e. all except Caleb and Joshua). It is true that the rendering is not free from difficulty, since there seems to be no exact parallel to this use of ἀλλ' οὐ. But it involves less harshness than the other.

17. *grieved*] Rather "indignant." See ver. 10.

whose carcases] To us the words read as though there were a deep and awful irony in this term (κῶλα), as though, "dying as it were gradually during their bodily life, they became *walking* corpses" (Delitzsch). It is doubtful, however, whether any such thought was in the mind of the writer. The word properly means "limbs" but is used by the LXX. for the Hebrew *pegarim*, "corpses" Num. xiv. 29.

fell] Compare the use of the word in 1 Cor. x. 8.

18. *to them that believed not*] Rather, "that *disobeyed*."

19. *So we see*] Lit. "*and* we observe." The translators of the A. V. seem by their version to regard the words as a logical inference from the previous reasoning. It is better, however, to regard them as the statement of a fact—"we see by the argument," or *ex historia cognoscimus*. Grotius. See Ps. cvi. 24—26.

that they could not enter in] They did make the attempt to enter, but failed because they lacked the power which only God could give them (Numb. xiv. 40—45).

CH. IV. CONTINUED EXHORTATION TO EMBRACE THE YET OPEN OFFER OF GOD'S REST (1—14). EXHORTATION FOUNDED ON THE HIGH PRIESTHOOD OF CHRIST (14—16).

1. *Let us therefore fear*] The fear to which we are exhorted is not any uncertainty of hope, but solicitude against careless indifference. It is a wholesome fear taught by wisdom (Phil. ii. 12).

tering into his rest, any of you should seem to come short *of it*. For unto us was the gospel preached, as well as unto 2 them: but the word preached did not profit them, not being mixed with faith in them that heard *it*. For we which have 3 believed do enter into rest, as *he* said, As I have sworn

lest] Lit. *lest haply*.
being left us] It is better to omit the word "*us*." It means "since a promise still remains unrealised." The promise has not been exhausted by any previous fulfilment.
any] Rather, "any one." See note on iii. 12.
of you] He cannot say "of us," because he proceeds to describe the case of hardened and defiant apostates.
should seem to come short of it] Rather, "should seem *to have failed in attaining it*." The Greek might also mean "should think that he has come too late for it;" but the writer's object is to stimulate the negligent, not to encourage the despondent. The word "seem" is an instance of the figure called *litotes*, in which a milder term is designedly used to express one which is much stronger. The author of this Epistle, abounding as he does in passages of uncompromising sternness, would not be likely to use any merely euphuistic phrase. The dignity of his expressions adds to their intensity. For a similar delicate yet forcible use of "seem" see 1 Cor. xi. 16. The verb "to fail" or "come short" occurs in xii. 15, together with a terrible example of the thing itself in xii. 17.

2 *For unto us was the gospel preached, as well as unto them*] We should have expected rather "For unto *them*, as well as unto us," if this had been the right translation. The better version however is " For indeed we too, just as they, have had *a Gospel* preached unto us." The "Gospel" in this instance means the glad tidings of a future rest.
the word preached] Lit. "the word of hearing." The function of the *hearer* is no less necessary than that of the *preacher*, if the spoken word is to be profitable.
not being mixed with faith in them that heard it] There is an extraordinary diversity in the MS. readings here. The best supported seems to be "because they were not united (lit. ' tempered together ') by faith with them that heard (i. e. effectually listened to) it." This would mean that the good news of rest produced no benefit to the rebellious Israelites, because they were not blended with Caleb and Joshua in their faith. They *heard*, but only with the ears, not with the heart. But there is probably some ancient corruption of the text. Perhaps instead of "with them that heard," the true reading may have been "with the *things heard*." The reading of our A. V. gives an excellent sense, if it were but well supported. The verb "to mingle" or "temper" occurs in 1 Cor. xii. 24.

3. *For we which have believed do enter into rest*] Rather, "For we who believed" (i. e. we who have accepted the word of hearing) "are entering into that rest."

in my wrath, if they shall enter into my rest: although the works were finished from the foundation of the world. 4 For *he* spake in a certain place of the seventh *day* on this wise, And God did rest the seventh day from all his 5 works. And in this *place* again, If they shall enter into 6 my rest. Seeing therefore it remaineth that some *must* enter therein, and they to whom it was first preached entered 7 not in because of unbelief, again he limiteth a certain day,

if they shall enter] This ought to have been rendered as in iii. 11, "they shall *not* enter." The argument of the verse is (1) God promised a rest to the Israelites. (2) Many of them failed to enter in. (3) Yet this rest of God began on the first sabbath of God, and *some* men were evidently meant to enter into it. (4) Since then the original recipients of the promise had failed to enjoy it through disbelief, the promise was renewed ages afterwards, in Ps. xcv. by the word "To-day." The immense stress of meaning laid on incidental Scriptural expressions was one of the features of Rabbinic as well as of Alexandrian exegesis.

from the foundation of the world] God's rest had begun since the Creation.

4. *he spake in a certain place*] Rather, "He *hath said somewhere*." By the indefinite "He" is meant "God," a form of citation not used in the same way by St Paul, but common in Philo and the Rabbis. The "somewhere" of the original is here expressed in the A.V. by "in a certain place," see note on ii. 6. The reference is to Gen. ii. 2; Ex. xx. 11, xxxi. 17. The writer always regards the Old Testament not as a dead letter, but as a living voice.

5. *If they shall*] i.e. "they shall not."

6. *it remaineth*] The promise is still left open, is unexhausted.

because of unbelief] Rather, "because of *disobedience*" (*apeitheian*). It was not the Israelites of the wilderness, but their descendants, who came to Shiloh, and so enjoyed a sort of earthly type of the heavenly rest (Josh. xviii. 1).

7. *again he limiteth a certain day*...] There is no reason whatever for the parenthesis in the A.V., of which the reading, rendering, and punctuation are here alike infelicitous to an extent which destroys for ordinary readers the meaning of the passage. It should be rendered (putting only a comma at the end of ver. 6), "*Again, he fixes a day, To-day, saying in David, so long afterwards, even as has been said before, To-day if ye will hear,*" &c. In the stress laid upon the word "to-day" we find a resemblance to Philo, who defines "to-day" as "the infinite and interminable aeon," and says "Till to-day, that is for ever" (*Leg. Alleg.* III. 8; *De Profug.* 11). The argument is that "David" (a general name for the "Psalmist") had, nearly five centuries after the time of Moses, and three millenniums after the Creation, still spoken of God's rest as an offer open to mankind. If we regard this as a mere verbal argument, turning on the attribution of deep mystic senses to the

saying in David, To day, after so long a time; as it is said, To day if ye will hear his voice, harden not your hearts. For if Jesus had given them rest, *then* 8

words "rest" and "to-day," and on the trains of inference which are made to depend on these words, we must remember that such a method of dealing with Scripture phraseology was at this period universally current among the Jews. But if we stop at this point all sorts of difficulties arise; for if the "rest" referred to in Ps. xcv. was primarily the land of Canaan (as in Deut. i. 34—36, xii. 9, &c.), the oath of God, "they shall not enter into my rest" only applied to the generation of the wandering, and He had said "Your little ones...them will I bring in, and they shall know the land which ye have despised," Num. xiv. 31. If, on the other hand, "the rest" meant heaven, it would be against all Scripture analogy to assume that all the Israelites who died in the wilderness were excluded from future happiness. And there are many other difficulties which will at once suggest themselves. The better and simpler way of looking at this, and similar trains of reasoning, is to regard them as particular modes of expressing blessed and eternal truths, and to look on the Scripture language applied to them in the light rather of *illustration* than of Scriptural proof: Quite apart from this Alexandrian method of finding recondite and mystic senses in the history and language of the Bible, we see the deep and glorious truths that God's offer of "Rest" in the highest sense—of participation in His own rest—is left open to His people in the eternal to-day of merciful opportunity. The Scripture illustration must be regarded as quite subordinate to the essential truth, and not the essential truth made to depend on the Scripture phraseology. When God says "They shall not enter my rest," the writer—reading as it were between the lines with the eyes of Christian enlightenment—reads the promise "but others *shall* enter into my rest," which was most true.

saying in David] A common abbreviated form of quotation like "saying in Elijah" for "in the part of Scripture about Elijah" (Rom. xi. 2). The quotation may mean no more than "in the Book of Psalms." The 95th Psalm is indeed attributed to David in the LXX; but the superscriptions of the LXX, like those of our A.V., are wholly without authority, and are in some instances entirely erroneous. The date of the Psalm is more probably the close of the Exile. We may here notice the fondness of the writer for the Psalms, of which he quotes no less than *eleven* in this Epistle (Ps. ii., viii., xxii., xl., xlv., xcv., cii., civ., cx., cxviii., cxxxv.).

8. *Jesus*] i.e. Joshua. The needless adoption of the Greek form of the name by the A.V. is here most unfortunately perplexing to uninstructed readers, as also in Acts vii. 45.

had given them rest] He did, indeed, give them *a* rest and, in some sense (Deut. xii. 9), *the* rest partially and primarily intended (Josh. xxiii. 1); but only a dim shadow of the true and final rest offered by Christ (Matt. xi. 28; 2 Thess. iii. 1—6; Rev. xiv. 13).

9 would he not afterward have spoken of another day. There
10 remaineth therefore a rest to the people of God. For he
that is entered into his rest, he also hath ceased from his
11 own works, as God *did* from his. Let us labour therefore
to enter into that rest, lest any *man* fall after the same ex-
12 ample of unbelief. For the word of God *is* quick, and pow-

then would he not afterward have spoken] The "He" is here Jehovah. More literally, "He would not *have been speaking*." The phrases applied to Scripture by the writer always imply his sense of its living power and ideal continuity. The words are as though they had just been uttered ("He hath said," ver. 4) or were still being uttered (as here, and throughout). There is a similar mode of argument in vii. 11, viii. 4, 7, xi. 15.

9. *There remaineth therefore a rest*] Since the word used for "rest" is here a different word (*sabbatismos*) from that which has been used through the earlier part of the argument (*katapausis*), it is a pity that King James's translators, who indulge in so many needless variations, did not here introduce a necessary change of rendering. The word means "*a Sabbath rest*," and supplies an important link in the argument by pointing to the fact that "the rest" which the Author has in view is God's rest, a far higher conception of rest than any of which Canaan could be an adequate type. The Sabbath, which in 2 Macc. xv. 1 is called "the Day of Rest" (*katapausis*), is a nearer type of Heaven than Canaan. Dr Kay supposes that there is an allusion to Joshua's first Sabbatic year, when "the land had rest from war" (Josh. xiv. 15), and adds that Psalms xcii—civ. have a Sabbatic character, and that Ps. xcii. is headed "a song for the sabbath day."

10. *For he that is entered into his rest*] This is not a special reference to Christ, but to any faithful Christian who rests from his labours. The verse is merely an explanation of the newly-introduced term "Sabbath-rest."

11. *Let us labour*] Lit., "let us be zealous," or "give diligence" (2 Pet. i. 10, 11; Phil. iii. 14).

lest any man] See note on iv. 1.

of unbelief] Rather, "of disobedience."

12. *For the word of God is quick*] "Quick" is an old English expression for "living;" hence St Stephen speaks of Scripture as "the living oracles" (Acts vii. 38). The "word of God" is not here the personal Logos; a phrase not distinctly and demonstrably adopted by any of the sacred writers except St John, who in the prologue to his Gospel calls Christ "the Word," and in the Apocalypse "the Word of God." The reference is to the written and spoken word of God, of the force and almost personality of which the writer shews so strong a sense. To him it is no dead utterance of the past, but a living power for ever. At the same time the expressions of this verse could hardly have been used by any one who was not familiar with the personification of the Logos, and St Clemens of Rome applies the words

erful, and sharper than any twoedged sword, piercing even to the dividing asunder of soul and spirit, and of the joints and marrow, and *is* a discerner of the thoughts and intents of the heart. Neither is there any creature *that is* not manifest in his sight: but all *things are* naked and opened unto the eyes of him with whom we have to do. 13

"a searcher of the thoughts and desires" to God. The passage closely resembles several which are found in Philo, though it applies the expressions in a different manner (see Introduction).

powerful] Lit., effective, energetic: The vital power shews itself in acts.

sharper than any twoedged sword]' The same comparison is used by Isaiah (xlix. 2) and St Paul (Eph. vi. 17) and St John (Rev. ii. 16, xix. 15). See too Wisdom xviii. 15, 16, "Thine Almighty Word leaped down from heaven...and brought thine unfeigned commandment as a sharp sword." Philo compares the Logos to the flaming sword of Eden (Gen. iii. 24) and "the fire and knife" (μάχαιραν) of Gen. xxii. 6.

piercing even to the dividing asunder of soul and spirit, and of the joints and marrow] The meaning is not that the word of God divides the soul (the "natural" soul) by which we live *from the* spirit by which we reason and apprehend; but that it pierces not only the natural soul, but even to the Divine Spirit of man, and even to the joints and marrow (i. e. to the inmost depths) of these. Thus Euripides (*Hippol.* 527) speaks of the "marrow of the soul." It is obvious that the writer does not mean anything very specific by each term of the enumeration, which produces its effect by the rhetorical fulness of the expressions. The ψυχή or animal soul is the sphere of that life which makes a man ψυχικός, i. e. carnal, unspiritual; he possesses this element of life (*anima*) in common with the beasts. It is only by virtue of his spirit (πνεῦμα) that he has affinity with God.

a discerner of the thoughts and intents of the heart] These words are a practical explanation of those which have preceded. The phraseology is an evident reminiscence of Philo. Philo compares the Word to the flaming sword of Paradise; and calls the Word "the cutter of all things," and says that "when whetted to the utmost sharpness it is incessantly dividing all sensuous things" (see *Quis Rer. Div. Haeres,* § 27 ; Opp. ed. Mangey I. 491, 503, 506). By *enthumēseis* is meant (strictly) our moral imaginations and desires; by *ennoiai* our intellectual thoughts: but the distinction of meaning is hardly kept (Matt. ix. 4, &c.).

13. *in his sight*] i.e. in the Sight of God, not of "the Word of God." "He seeth all man's goings," Job. xxxiv. 21. "Thou hast set...our secret sins in the light of Thy countenance," Ps. xc. 8; comp. Ps. cxxxix. 1—12.

opened] The Greek word τετραχηλισμένα must have some such meaning, but it is uncertain what is the exact force of the metaphor from which it is derived. It comes from τράχηλος, "the neck," and has been explained to mean: (1) "seized by the throat and thrown on

14 Seeing then that we have a great high priest, that is passed into the heavens, Jesus the Son of God, let us hold fast *our*
15 profession. For we have not a high priest which cannot

the back"; or (2) "with the neck forced back like that of a malefactor compelled to shew his face" (Sueton. *Vitell.* 17); or (3) "with the neck held back like that of animals in order that the Priest may cut their throats"; or (4) "flayed"; or (5) "anatomised" (comp. Lev. i. 6, 9). This anatomic examination of victims by the Priests was called *momoskopia* since it was necessary that every victim should be "without blemish" (*amomos*), and Maimonides says that there were no less than 73 kinds of blemishes. Hence Polycarp (*ad Phil.* IV.) says that "all things are rigidly examined (πάντα μωμοσκοπεῖται) by God." The usage of Philo, however, decisively shews that the word means "*laid prostrate.*" For the truth suggested see Prov. xv. 11; "I try the reins," Jer. xvii. 10; Ps. li. 6; Prov. xx. 27, "the candle of the Lord searching all the inner parts of the belly."

unto the eyes] "The Son of God, who hath His eyes like unto a flame of fire." Rev. ii. 18.

with whom we have to do] This might be rendered, "to whom our account must be given." Thus in Luke xvi. 2, "render thy account" (τὸν λόγον). Perhaps, however, our A. V. correctly represents it "Him with whom our concern is." Comp. 1 Kings ii. 14; 2 Kings ix. 5 (LXX.), where a similar phrase occurs in this sense.

14—16. EXHORTATION FOUNDED ON CHRIST'S HIGH PRIESTHOOD.

14. *Seeing then that we have a great high priest*] These verses refer back to ii. 17, iii. 1, and form the transition to the long proof and illustration of Christ's superiority to the Levitic Priesthood which occupies the Epistle to x. 18. The writer here reverts to his central thought, to which he has already twice alluded (ii. 17, iii. 1). He had proved that Christ is superior to Angels the ministers, and to Moses the servant of the old Dispensation, and (quite incidentally) to Joshua. He has now to prove that He is like Aaron in all that made Aaron's priesthood precious, but infinitely superior to him and his successors, and a pledge to us of the grace by which the true rest can be obtained. Christ is not only a High Priest, but "a *great* High Priest," an expression also found in Philo (Opp. I. 654).

that is passed into the heavens] Rather, "who hath passed through the heavens"—the heavens being here the lower heavens, regarded as a curtain which separates us from the presence of God. Christ has passed not only *into* but *above* the heavens (vii. 26). Transiit, non modo intravit, caelos.—Bengel.

Jesus the Son of God] The title combines His earthly and human name with his divine dignity, and thus describes the two natures which make His Priesthood eternally necessary.

our profession] Rather, "our confession," as in iii. 1.

15. *For*] He gives the reason for holding fast our confession; [we may do so with confidence], for Christ can sympathise with us in our

be touched with the feeling of our infirmities; but was in all *points* tempted like as *we are, yet* without sin. Let us therefore come boldly unto the throne of grace, that we may obtain mercy, and find grace to help in time of need. For 5 weaknesses, since He has suffered with us (συμπάσχειν). Rom. viii. 17; 1 Cor. xii. 26.

with the feeling of our infirmities] Even the heathen could feel the force and beauty of this appeal, for they intensely admired the famous line of Terence,

"I am a man; I feel an interest in everything which is human;"

at the utterance of which, when the play was first acted, it is said that the whole of the audience rose to their feet; and the exquisite words which Virgil puts into the mouth of Dido,

"*Haud ignara mali, miseris succerrere disco.*"

tempted] "Tempted" (πεπειρασμένον) is the best-supported reading, not πεπειραμένον, "having made trial of," "experienced in." It refers alike to the trials of life, which are in themselves *indirect* temptations—sometimes to sin, always to murmuring and discontent; and to the *direct* temptations to sin which are life's severest trials. From both of these our Lord suffered (John xi. 33—35; "ye are they who have continued with me *in my temptations*" Luke xxii. 28, iv. 2, &c.).

like as we are] Lit. "after the likeness;" a stronger way of expressing the resemblance of Christ's "temptations" to ours than if an adverb had been used.

yet without sin] Lit. "apart from sin." Philo had already spoken of the Logos as sinless (*De Profug.* 20; Opp. I. 562). His words are "the High Priest is not Man but the Divine Word, free from all share, not only in willing but even in involuntary wrongdoing." Christ's sinlessness is one of the irrefragable proofs of His divinity. It was both asserted by Himself (John xiv. 30) and by the Apostles (2 Cor. v. 21; 1 Pet. ii. 22; 1 John iii. 5, &c.). Being tempted, Christ could sympathize with us; being sinless, he could plead for us.

16. *Let us therefore come boldly*] Rather, "let us then approach with confidence." The notion of "approach" to God (προσέρχεσθαι) in the Levitical service (Lev. xxi. 17, xxii. 3) is prominent in this Epistle (vii. 25, x. 1, 22, xi. 6, xii. 18—22). In St Paul it only occurs once (1 Tim. vi. 13), and then in a different sense. His ideal of the Christian life is not "access to God" (though he does also allude to this in one Epistle, Eph. ii. 18, iii. 12) but "oneness with Christ." "Boldly," literally, "with confidence" (iii. 6).

throne of grace] Comp. viii. 1. This throne was typified in the mercy-seat above the Ark (Ex. xxv. 21), over which the Shechinah shone between the wings of the cherubim.

obtain mercy, and find grace] Mercy in our wretchedness, and free favour, though it is undeserved.

to help in time of need] Lit. "for a seasonable succour." Seasonable

every high priest taken from among men is ordained for men *in things* pertaining to God, that he may offer both
2 gifts and sacrifices for sins: who can have compassion on the ignorant, and on them that are out of the way; for that

because "it is still called to-day" (iii. 17), and because the help is so deeply needed (ii. 18).

CH. V. TWO QUALIFICATIONS FOR HIGH-PRIESTHOOD: (1) CAPACITY FOR SYMPATHY (1—3); (2) A SPECIAL CALL (4—10). SPIRITUAL DULNESS OF THE HEBREWS (11—14).

1. *For every high priest taken from among men*] Rather, "being taken," or "chosen as he is." (comp. Ex. xxviii. 1). The writer now enters on his proof that in order to fit Him for the functions of a High Priest for men it was necessary that Christ should become Man. He has already called attention to the subject in a marked manner in ii. 7, iii. 1, iv. 14, 15.

is ordained for men] "Is appointed on men's behalf."

in things pertaining to God] ii. 17. It is his part to act as man's representative in the performance of the duties of worship and sacrifice.

both gifts and sacrifices] We have the same phrase in viii. 3, ix. 9. In O.T. usage no distinction is maintained between "gifts" and "sacrifices," for in Gen. iv. 4, Lev. i. 2, 3, "gifts" is used for animal sacrifices; and in Gen. iv. 3, 5, "sacrifices" is used (as in xi. 4) for bloodless gifts. When, however, the words are used together the distinction between them is that which holds in classical Greek, where "sacrifices" is never used except to mean "slain beasts." The word "offer" is generally applied to expiatory sacrifices, and though "gifts" in the strict sense—e.g. "freewill offerings" and "meat offerings"—were not expiatory, yet the "gift" of incense offered by the High Priest on the Day of Atonement had some expiatory significance.

for sins] To make atonement for sins (ii. 17).

2. *have compassion on*] Rather, "*deal gently with*." The word *metriopathein* means properly "to shew moderate emotions." All men are liable to emotions and passions (*pathē*). The Stoics held that these should be absolutely crushed and that "apathy" ($ἀπάθεια$) was the only fit condition for a Philosopher. The Peripatetics on the other hand—the school of Aristotle—held that the philosopher should not aim at apathy, because no man can be absolutely passionless without doing extreme violence to nature; but that he should acquire *metriopathy*, that is a spirit of "moderated emotion" and self-control. The word is found both in Philo and Josephus. In common usage it meant "moderate *compassion;*" since the Stoics held "pity" to be not only a weakness but a vice. The Stoic *apatheia* would have utterly disqualified any one for true Priesthood. Our Lord yielded to human emotions such as pity, sorrow, and just anger; and that He did so and could do so, "yet without sin," is expressly recorded for our instruction.

he himself also is compassed with infirmity. And by reason 3
hereof he ought, as for the people, so also for himself, to
offer for sins. And no *man* taketh *this* honour unto him- 4
self, but he that is called of God, as *was* Aaron. So also 5

on the ignorant, and on them that are out of the way] Highhanded sinners, *willing* sinners, those who, in the Hebrew phrase, sin "with upraised hand" (Num. xv. 30; Deut. xvii. 12), cannot always be treated with compassionate tenderness (x. 26); but the ignorant and the erring (1 Tim. i. 13)—those who sin "inadvertently," "involuntarily" (Lev. iv. 2, 13, &c.)—and even those who under sudden stress of passion and temptation sin wilfully—need pity (Lev. v. 1, xix. 20—22), and Christ's prayer on the cross was for those "who know not what they do." No untempted Angel, no Being removed from the possibility of such falls, could have had the personal sympathy which is an indispensable requisite for perfect Priesthood.

is compassed with infirmity] Moral weakness is *part of the very nature which he wears*, and which makes him bear reasonably with those who are like himself. The same Greek phrase (*perikeimai* with an accusative) occurs in Acts xxviii. 20 ("I am *bound with* this *chain*"). "Under the gorgeous robes of office there were still the galling chains of flesh." Kay.

3. *And by reason hereof*] i.e. because of this moral weakness.

he ought] He is bound not merely as a legal duty, but as a moral necessity.

so also for himself] The Law assumed that this would be necessary for every High Priest (Lev. iv. 3—12). In the High Priest's prayer of intercession he said, "Oh do thou expiate the misdeeds, the crimes, and the sins, wherewith I have done evil, and have sinned before Thee I and my house!" Until he had thus made atonement for himself, he was regarded as guilty, and so could not offer any atonement for others who were guilty (Lev. iv. 3, ix. 7, xvi. 6, and comp. vii. 27).

to offer for sins] The word "offer" may be used absolutely for "to offer sacrifices" (Lk. v. 14); but the words "for sins" are often an equivalent for "sin-offerings" (see x. 6; Lev. vi. 23; Num. viii. 8, &c.).

4. *this honour*] i.e. this honourable office. We have here the second qualification for Priesthood. A man's own caprice must not be the Bishop which ordains him. He must be conscious of a divine call.

but he that is called of God] Rather, "but on being called by God," or "when he is called by God." Great stress is laid on this point in Scripture (Ex. xxviii. 1). Any "stranger that cometh nigh"—i.e. that intruded unbidden into the Priesthood—was to be put to death (Num. iii. 10). The fate of Korah and his company (Num. xvi. 40), and of Uzziah, king though he was (2 Chron. xxvi. 18—21), served as a terrible warning, and it was recorded as a special aggravation of Jeroboam's impiety that "he made priests of the lowest of the people, which were not of the sons of Levi" (1 K. xii. 31). In one of the Jewish Midrashim, Moses says to Korah "if Aaron, my brother, had *taken upon*

Christ glorified not himself to be made a high priest; but he that said unto him, Thou art my Son, to day have I
6 begotten thee. As he saith also in another *place*, Thou *art* a priest for ever after the order of Melchisedec.

himself the priesthood, ye would be excusable for murmuring against him; but God gave it to him." Some have supposed that the writer here reflects obliquely upon the High Priests of that day—alien Sadducees, not descended from Aaron (Jos. *Antt.* xx. 10) who had been introduced into the Priesthood from Babylonian families by Herod the Great, and who kept the highest office, with frequent changes, as a sort of apanage of their own families—the Boethusim, the Kantheras, the Kamhits, the Beni-Hanan. For the characteristics of these Priests, who completely degraded the dignity in the eyes of the people, see my *Life of Christ*, II. 330, 342. In the energetic maledictions pronounced upon them in more than one passage of the Talmud, they are taunted with not being true sons of Aaron. But it is unlikely that the writer should make this oblique allusion. He was an Alexandrian; he was not writing to the Hebrews of Jerusalem; and these High Priests had been in possession of the office for more than half a century.

as was Aaron] The original is more emphatic "exactly as even Aaron was" (Num. xvi.—xviii). The true Priest must be a divinely-appointed Aaron, not a self-constituted Korah.

5. *So also Christ*] Rather, "*So even the Christ.*" Jesus, the Messiah, the true Anointed Priest, possessed both these qualifications.

glorified not himself] He has already called the High Priesthood "an honour," but of Christ's Priesthood he uses a still stronger word "glory" (ii. 9; John xii. 28, xiii. 31).

but he that said unto him] God glorified Him, and the writer again offers the admitted Messianic Prophecies of Ps. ii. 7 and cx. 4, as a sufficient illustration of this. The fact of His Sonship demonstrates that His call to the Priesthood was a call of God. "Jesus said *If I honour myself, my honour is nothing;* it is my Father that honoureth me, of whom ye say that He is your God," John viii. 54.

6. *in another place*] Ps. cx. 4. This Psalm was so universally accepted as Messianic that the Targum of Jonathan paraphrases the first verse of it "The Lord *said to His Word.*"

after the order] al-dibhrathi, "according to the style of." Comp. vii. 15, "after the likeness of Melchisedek."

after the order of Melchisedec] The writer here with consummate literary skill introduces the name Melchisedek, to prepare incidentally for the long argument which is to follow in chapter vii.; just as he twice introduces the idea of High-Priesthood (ii. 17, iii. 1) before directly dealing with it. The reason why the Psalmist had spoken of his ideal Theocratic king as a Priest after the order of Melchisedek, and not after the order of Aaron, lies in the words "for ever," as subsequently explained. In Zech. iv. 14, the Jews explained "the two Anointed ones (*sons of oil*) who stand by the Lord of the whole

Who in the days of his flesh, when he had offered up pray- 7
ers and supplications with strong crying and tears unto him
that was able to save him from death, and was heard in
that *he* feared; though he were a Son, *yet* learned he obe- 8

earth" to be Aaron and Messiah, and from Ps. cx. 4, they agreed that Messiah was the nearer to God.

7. *Who*] i.e. the Christ.

of his flesh] The word "flesh" is here used for His Humanity regarded on the side of its weakness and humiliation. Comp. ii. 14.

when he had offered up] Lit. "having offered up."

prayers and supplications] The idiosyncrasy of the writer, and perhaps his Alexandrian training, which familiarised him with the style of Philo, made him fond of these sonorous amplifications or full expressions. The word rendered "prayers" (*deēseis*) is rather "supplications," i.e. "special prayers" for the supply of needs; the word rendered "entreaties" (which is joined with it in Job xli. 3, comp. 2 Macc. ix. 18) properly meant olive-boughs (*iketēriai*) held forth to entreat protection. Thus the first word refers to the suppliant, the second implies an approach (*ikneomai*) to God. The "supplications and entreaties" referred to are doubtless those in the Agony at Gethsemane (Lk. xxii. 39—46), though there may be a reference to the Cross, and some have even supposed that there is an allusion to Ps. xxii. and cxvi. See Mark xiv. 36; John xii. 27; Matt. xxvi. 38—42.

with strong crying and tears] Though these are not directly *mentioned* in the scene at Gethsemane they are implied. See John xi. 35, xii. 27; Matt. xxvi. 39, 42, 44, 53; Mark xiv. 36; Lk. xix. 41.

and was heard] Rather, "and being heard" or "hearkened to," Luke xxii. 43; John xii. 28 (comp. Ps. xxii. 21, 24).

in that he feared] Rather, "*from his godly fear*," or "because of his reverential awe." The phrase has been explained in different ways. The old Latin (*Vetus Itala*) renders "*exauditus a metu*," and some Latin Fathers and later interpreters explain it to mean "having been freed *from the fear of death*." The Greek might perhaps be made to bear this sense, though the mild word used for "fear" is not in favour of it; but the rendering given above, meaning that His prayer was heard because of His awful submission (*pro suâ reverentiâ*, Vulg.) is the sense in which the words are taken by all the Greek Fathers. The word rendered "from" (*apo*) may certainly mean "because of" as in Lk. xix. 3, "He could not because of (*apo*) the crowd;" xxiv. 41, "disbelieving because of (*apo*) their joy" (comp. John xxi. 6; Acts xxii. 11, &c.). The word rendered "feared" is *eulabeia*, which means "reverent fear," or "reasonable shrinking" as opposed to terror and cowardice. The Stoics said that the wise man could thus cautiously shrink (*eulabeisthai*) but never actually be afraid (*phobeisthai*). Other attempts to explain away the passage arise from the Apollinarian tendency to deny Christ's perfect *manhood:* but He was "perfectly man" as well as "truly God." He was not indeed "saved *from* death," because He had only prayed that "the cup might pass from Him"

9 dience by *the things* which he suffered; and being made perfect, he became the author of eternal salvation unto all

if such were His Father's will (x. 7); but He was saved *out of* (ἐκ) death" by being raised on the third day, so that "He saw no corruption." For the word *eulabeia*, "piety" or "reverent awe" see xii. 28.

8. *Though he were a Son*] Rather, "**Son** though He was," so that it might have been thought that there would be no need for the great sacrifice; no need for His learning obedience from suffering.

yet learned he obedience] Perhaps rather "His obedience." The stress is not on His "*learning*" (of course *as a man*), but the whole expression is taken together, "He learnt from the things which He suffered," in other words "He bowed to the experience of absolute submission." "The things which He suffered" refer not only to the Agony and the Cross, but to the whole of the Saviour's life. Some of the Fathers stumbled at this expression. Theodoret calls it hyperbolical; St Chrysostom is surprised at it; Theophylact goes so far as to say that here Paul (for he accepts the traditional authorship) "for the benefit of his hearers used such accommodation as obviously to say some unreasonable things." All such remarks would have been obviated if these fathers had borne in mind that, as St Paul says, Christ "counted not equality with God a thing at which to grasp" (Phil. ii. 6). Meanwhile passages like these, of which there are several in this Epistle, are valuable as proving how completely the co-equal and co-eternal Son "emptied Himself of His glory." Against the irreverent reverence of the Apollinarian heresy (which denied Christ's perfect manhood) and the Monothelite heresy (which denied His possession of a human will), this passage, and the earlier chapters of St Luke are the best bulwark. The human soul of Christ's perfect manhood "learned" just as His human body grew (Lk. ii. 52). On this learning of "obedience" see Is. l. 5, "I was not rebellious." Phil. ii. 8, "Being found in fashion as a man he became *obedient* unto death." The paronomasia "he learnt (*emathen*) from what He *suffered* (*epathen*)" is one of the commonest in Greek literature. For the use of *paronomasia* in St Paul see my *Life of St Paul*. I. 628.

9. *and being made perfect*] Having been brought to the goal and consummation in the glory which followed this mediatorial work. See ii. 10 and comp. Lk. xiii. 32, "the third day *I shall be perfected*."

he became the author] Literally, "the cause."

of eternal salvation] It is remarkable that the epithet *aionios* is here alone applied to the substantive "salvation."

salvation unto all them that obey him] In an author so polished and rhetorical there seems to be an intentional force and beauty in the repetition in this verse of the two leading words in the last. Christ prayed to God who was able to "*save*" Him out of death, and He became the cause of "eternal *salvation*" from final death; Christ learnt "*obedience*" by His life of self-sacrifice, and He became a Saviour to them that "*obey*" Him.

them that obey him; called of God a high priest after the 10
order of Melchisedec.

Of whom we have many things to say, and hard to be 11
uttered, seeing ye are dull of hearing. For when for the 12
time ye ought to be teachers, ye have need that *one* teach

10. *called*] Lit., "saluted" or "addressed by God as." This is the only place in the N.T. where the verb occurs.

a high priest after the order of Melchisedec] We should here have expected the writer to enter at once on the explanation of this term. But he once more pauses for a solemn exhortation and warning. These pauses and landing-places (as it were) in his argument, cannot be regarded as mere digressions. There is nothing that they less resemble than St Paul's habit of "going off at a word," nor is the writer in the least degree "hurried aside by the violence of his thoughts." There is in him a complete absence of all the hurry and impetuosity which characterise the style of St Paul. His movements are not in the least like those of an eager athlete, but they rather resemble the stately walk of some Oriental Sheykh with all his robes folded around him. He is about to enter on an entirely original and far from obvious argument, which he felt would have great weight in checking the tendency to look back to the rites, the splendours and the memories of Judaism. He therefore stops with the calmest deliberation, and the most wonderful skill, to pave the way for his argument by a powerful mixture of reproach and warning—which assisted the object he had in view, and tended to stimulate the spiritual dulness of his readers.

11—14. COMPLAINT THAT HIS READERS WERE SO SLOW IN THEIR SPIRITUAL PROGRESS.

11. *Of whom*] i.e. of Melchisedek in his typical character. There is no need to render this "of which matter" or to refer it to Christ. The following argument really centres in the word Melchisedek, and its difficulty was the novel application of the facts of his history to Christ.

hard to be uttered] Rather, "respecting whom what I have to say is long, and hard of interpretation." The word "being interpreted" (*hermēnenomenos*, whence comes the word "hermeneutics") occurs in vii. 2.

ye are] Rather, "ye are become," as in v. 12, vi. 12. They were not so sluggish at first, but are become so from indifference and neglect.

dull of hearing] Comp. Matt. xiii. 14, 15. *Nothros* "dull" or "blunted" is the antithesis to ὀξὺs "sharp."

12. *For when for the time ye ought to be teachers*] That is, "though you ought, by this time, to be teachers, considering how long a time has elapsed since your conversion." The passage is important as bearing on the date of the Epistle.

ye have need that one teach you again which be the first principles] Rather, "ye again have need that some one teach you the rudiments of

you again which *be* the first principles of the oracles of God; and are become such as have need of milk, and not of 13 strong meat. For every one that useth milk *is* unskilful in 14 the word of righteousness: for he is a babe. But strong meat belongeth to *them that are* of full age, *even* those who by reason of use have their senses exercised to discern both

the beginning of the oracles of God." It is uncertain whether we should read τινὰ "that *some one* teach you" or τίνα "that (one) teach you *which are*." The difference in sense is not great, but perhaps the indefinite "some one" enhances the irony of a severe remark. For the word "rudiments" see Gal. iv. 3, 9.

the oracles of God] Here not the O.T. as in Rom. iii. 2.

such as have need of milk] So the young students or neophytes in the Rabbinic schools were called *thinokoth* "sucklings." Philo (*De Agric.* Opp. I. 301) has this comparison of preliminary studies to milk, as well as St Paul, 1 Cor. iii. 1, 2.

strong meat] Rather, "solid food."

13. *that useth milk*] The meaning is "who feeds on milk."

unskilful] "Inexperienced."

for he is a babe] This is a frequent metaphor in St Paul, who also contrasts "babes" (*nēpioi*) with the mature (*teleioi*), Gal. iv. 3; 1 Cor. ii. 6; Eph. iv. 13, 14. We are only to be "babes" in wickedness (1 Cor. xiv. 20).

the word of righteousness] i.e. the Scriptures, and especially the Gospel (see 2 Tim. iii. 16; Rom. i. 17, "*therein* is the righteousness of God revealed").

14. *belongeth to them that are of full age*] The solid food of more advanced instruction pertains to the mature or "perfect."

by reason of use] "Because of their habit," i.e. from being habituated to it. This is the only place in the N.T. where this important word ἕξις *habitus* occurs.

their senses] Their spiritual faculties (αἰσθητήρια). It does not occur elsewhere in the N.T.)

exercised] Trained, or disciplined by spiritual practice.

to discern both good and evil] Lit., "*the discrimination* of good and evil." By "good and evil" is not meant "right and wrong" because there is no question here of moral distinctions; but excellence and inferiority in matters of instruction. To the natural man the things of the spirit are foolishness; it is only the spiritual man who can "distinguish between things that differ" and so "discriminate the transcendent" (1 Cor. ii. 14, 15; Rom. ii. 18; Phil. i. 9, 10). The phrase "to know good and evil" is borrowed from Hebrew (Gen. ii. 17, &c.), and is used to describe the first dawn of intelligence (Is. vii. 15, 16).

CH. VI. AN EXHORTATION TO ADVANCE BEYOND ELEMENTARY CATECHETICAL INSTRUCTIONS (1—3). A SOLEMN WARNING AGAINST THE PERIL OF APOSTASY (4—8). A WORD OF EN-

good and evil. Therefore leaving the principles of the doc- 6
trine of Christ, let us go on unto perfection; not laying
again the foundation of repentance from dead works, and
of faith towards God, of the doctrine of baptisms, and of 2

COURAGEMENT AND HOPE (9—12) FOUNDED ON THE IMMUTA-
BILITY OF GOD'S PROMISES (13—15), TO WHICH THEY ARE
EXHORTED TO HOLD FAST (16—20).

1. *leaving the principles of the doctrine of Christ*] Lit., "leaving the discourse of the beginning of Christ," i. e. *getting beyond* the earliest principles of Christian teaching. He does not of course mean that these first principles are to be neglected, still less forgotten, but merely that his readers ought to be so familiar with them as to be able to advance to less obvious knowledge.

let us go on] Lit., "let us be borne along," as by the current of a stream. The question has been discussed whether the Author in saying "let *us*," is referring to himself or to his readers. It is surely clear that he means (as in iv. 14) to imply both, although in the words "laying a foundation" teachers may have been principally in his mind. He invites his readers to advance with him to doctrines which lie beyond the range of rudimentary Christian teaching. They must come with him out of the limits of this Jewish-Christian Catechism.

unto perfection] The "perfection" intended is the "full growth" of those who are mature in Christian knowledge (see v. 14). They ought not to be lingering among the elementary subjects of catechetical instruction which in great measure belonged no less to Jews than to Christians.

not laying again] There is no need for a *foundation* to be laid a *second time*. He is not in the least degree disparaging the importance of the truths and doctrines which he tells them to "leave," but only urging them to build on those deep foundations the necessary superstructure. Hence we need not understand the Greek participle in its other sense of "overthrowing."

the foundation] Lit., "*a* foundation." The subjects here alluded to probably formed the basis of instruction for Christian catechumens. They were not however exclusively Christian; they belonged equally to Jews, and therefore baptised Christian converts ought to have got beyond them.

repentance from dead works] Repentance is the first lesson of the Gospel (Mk. i. 15). "*Dead works*" are such as cause defilement, and require purification (ix. 14) because they are sinful (Gal. v. 19—21) and because their wages is death (Rom. vi. 23); but "the works of the Law," as having no life in them (see our Article xiii.), may be included under the epithet.

faith towards God] This is also one of the *initial* steps in religious knowledge. How little the writer meant any *disparagement* of it may be seen from xi. 1, 2, 6.

2. *of the doctrine of baptisms*] Perhaps rather, "of ablutions" (ix.

laying on of hands, and of resurrection of the dead, and of
3 eternal judgment. And this will we do, if God permit.

10; Mk. vii. 3, 4), both (1) from the use of the plural (which cannot be explained either physically of "triple immersion," or spiritually of the baptisms of "water, spirit, blood"); and (2) because *baptismos* is never used of Christian baptism, but only *baptisma*. If, as we believe, the writer of this Epistle was Apollos, he, as an original adherent "of John's baptism," might feel all the more strongly that the doctrine of "ablutions" belonged, even in its highest forms, to the *elements* of Christianity. Perhaps he, like Josephus (*Antt.* XVIII. 5, § 2), would have used the word *baptismos*, and not *baptisma*, even of John's baptism. But the word probably implies the teaching which enable Christian catechumens to discriminate beween Jewish washings and Christian baptism.

of laying on of hands] For ordination (Num. viii. 10, 11; Acts vi. 6, xiii. 2, 3, xix. 6, &c.), confirmation (Acts viii. 17), healings (Mk. xvi. 18), &c. Dr Mill observes that the *order* of doctrines here enumerated corresponds with the system of teaching respecting them in the Acts of the Apostles—Repentance, Faith, Baptism, Confirmation, Resurrection, Judgment.

and of resurrection of the dead] These topics had been severally prominent in the early Apostolic teaching (Acts ii. 38, iii. 19—21, xxvi. 20). Even the doctrine of the resurrection belonged to Judaism (Lk. xx. 37, 38; Dan. xii. 2; Acts xxiii. 8).

and of eternal judgment] The doctrine respecting that sentence (*krima*, "doom"), whether of the good or of the evil, which shall follow the judgment (*krisis*) in the future life. This was also known under the Old Covenant, Dan. vii. 9, 10.—The surprise with which we first read this passage only arises from our not realising the Author's meaning, which is this,—your Christian maturity ($\tau\epsilon\lambda\epsilon\iota\acute{o}\tau\eta s$, vi. 1) demands that you should rise far above your present vacillating condition. You would have no hankering after Judaism if you understood the more advanced teaching about the Melchisedek Priesthood—that is the Eternal Priesthood—of Christ which I am going to set before you. It is then needless that we should dwell together on the topics which form the training of neophytes and catechumens, the elements of religious teaching which even belonged to your old position as Jews; but let us enter upon topics which belong to the instruction of Christian manhood. The verse has its value for those who think that "Gospel" teaching consists exclusively in the iteration of threadbare shibboleths. We may observe that of these six elements of catechetical instruction two are spiritual qualities—repentance, faith; two are significant and symbolic acts—washings and laying on of hands; two are eschatological truths—resurrection and judgment.

3. *this will we do*] We will advance towards perfection. The MSS., as in nearly all similar cases, vary between "we will do" (ℵ, B, K, L) and "let us do" (A, C, D, E). It is difficult to decide between the two, and the variations may often be due (1) to the tendency of scribes, especially in Lectionaries, to adopt the hortative form as being more edifying; and

For *it is* impossible for those who were once enlightened, 4
and have tasted of the heavenly gift, and were made parta-

(2) to the fact that at this period of Greek the distinction in sound between ποιήσομεν and ποιήσωμεν was small.

if God permit] These sincere and pious formulae became early current among Christians (1 Cor. xvi. 7; Ja. iv. 15).

4—8. THE AWFULNESS OF APOSTASY.

4. *For*] An inference from the previous clauses. We must advance, for in the Christian course stationariness means retrogression—*non progredi est regredi*.

For it is impossible for those] We shall see further on the meaning of the word "impossible." The sentence begins with what is called the accusative of the subject, "For as to those who were, &c., it is impossible, &c." We will first explain the particular expressions in these verses, and then point out the meaning of the paragraph as a whole.

once] The word, a favourite one with the writer, means "*once for all*." It occurs more often in this Epistle than in all the rest of the N. T. It is the direct opposite of πάλιν in ver. 6.

enlightened] illuminated by the Holy Spirit, John i. 9. Comp. x. 26, 32; 2 Cor. iv. 4. In the LXX. "to illuminate" means "to teach" (2 Kings xii. 2). The word in later times came to mean "to baptise," and "enlightenment," even as early as the time of Justin Martyr (A. D. 150), becomes a technical term for "baptism," regarded from the point of view of its results. The Syriac Version here renders it by "baptised." Hence arose the notion of some of the sterner schismatics—such as the Montanists and Novatians—that absolution was to be refused to all such as fell after baptism into apostasy or flagrant sin (Tertull. *De Pudic.* 20). This doctrine was certainly *not held by St Paul* (1 Cor. v. 5; 1 Tim. i. 20), and is rejected by the Church of England in her xvith Article (and see Pearson, *On the Creed*, Art. x.). The Fathers deduced from this passage the unlawfulness of administering Baptism a second time; a perfectly right rule, but one which rests upon other grounds, and not upon this passage. But neither in Scripture nor in the teaching of the Church is the slightest sanction given to the views of the fanatics who assert that "after they have received the Holy Ghost they can no more sin as long as they live here." It will be remembered that Cromwell on his deathbed asked his chaplain as to the doctrine of Final Perseverance, and on being assured that it was a certain truth, said, "Then I am happy, for I am sure that I was once in a state of grace."

and have tasted of the heavenly gift...] These clauses may be rendered "having both tasted of...and being made...and having tasted." It is not possible to determine which heavenly gift is precisely intended; perhaps it means remission, or regeneration, or salvation, which St Paul calls "God's unspeakable gift" (2 Cor. ix. 15); or, generally, "the gift of the Holy Ghost" (Acts x. 44—46). Calvin vainly attempts to make the clause refer only to "those who had but as it were *tasted with their outward lips* the grace of God, and been irradiated *with some*

5 kers of the Holy Ghost, and have tasted the good word of
6 God, and the powers of the world to come, if they shall fall

sparks of His Light." It is clear from 1 Pet. ii. 3 that such a view is not tenable.

partakers of the Holy Ghost] The Holy Spirit worked in many diversities of operations (1 Cor. xii. 8—10).

5. *and have tasted the good word of God*] Rather, "that the word of God is good." The verb "taste," which in the previous verse is constructed with the genitive (as in classical Greek), is here followed by an accusative, as is more common in Hellenistic Greek. It is difficult to establish any difference in meaning between the constructions, though the latter *may* imply something which is more habitual—"feeding on." But possibly the accusative is only used to avoid any entanglement with the genitive "of God" which follows it. There is however no excuse for the attempt of Calvin and others, in the interests of their dogmatic bias, to make "taste of" mean only "have an *inkling* of" without any deep or real participation; and to make the preciousness of the "word of God" in this place only imply its contrast to the rigour of the Mosaic Law. The metaphor means "to partake of," and "enjoy," as in Philo, who speaks of one "who has quaffed much pure wine of God's benevolent power, and banqueted upon sacred words and doctrines" (*De proem. et poen.* Opp. I. 428). Philo also speaks of the utterance (*rhema*) of God, and God, and of its nourishing the soul like manna (Opp. I. 120, 564). The references to Philo are always to Mangey's edition. The names of the special tracts and chapters may be found in my *Early Days of Christianity*, II. 541—543, and *passim*.

the powers of the world to come] Here again it is not easy to see what is *exactly* intended by "the powers of the Future Age." If the Future Age be the *Olam habba* of the Jews, i.e. the Messianic Age, then its "powers" may be as St Chrysostom said, "the earnest of the Spirit," or the powers mentioned in ii. 4; Gal. iii. 5. If on the other hand it mean "the world to come" its "powers" bring the foretaste of its glorious fruition.

It will then be seen that we cannot attach a definitely certain or exact meaning to the separate expressions; on the other hand nothing can be clearer than the fact that, but for dogmatic prepossessions, no one would have dreamed of explaining them to mean anything less than full conversion.

6. *if they shall fall away*] This is one of the most erroneous translations in the A.V. The words can only mean "*and have fallen away*" (comp. ii. 1, iii. 12, x. 26, 29), and the position of the participle gives it tremendous force. It was once thought that our translators had here been influenced by theological bias to give such a rendering as should least conflict with their Calvinistic belief in the "indefectibility of grace" or in "Final Perseverance"—i.e. that no converted person, no one who has ever become regenerate, and belonged to the number of "the elect"—can *ever* fall away. It was thought that, for this reason, they had put this clause in the form of a *mere hypothesis*. It is now

away, to renew *them* again unto repentance; seeing they crucify to themselves the Son of God afresh, and put *him*

known however that the mistake of our translators was derived from older sources (e.g. Tyndale and the Genevan) and was not due to bias. Calvin was himself far too good a scholar to defend this view of the clause. He attempted to get rid of it by denying that the strong expressions in vers. 4, 5 describe the regenerate. He applies them to false converts or half converts who become reprobate—a view which, as we have seen, is not tenable. The falling *away* means apostasy, the complete and wilful renunciation of Christianity. Thus it is used by the LXX. to represent the Hebrew *mâal* which in 2 Chron. xxix. 19 they render by "*apostasy.*"

to renew them again unto repentance] The verb here used (*anakainizein*) came to mean "to rebaptise." If the earlier clauses seemed to clash with the Calvinistic dogma of the "indefectibility of grace," this expression seemed too severe for the milder theology of the Arminians. Holding—and rightly—that Scripture *never* closes the door of forgiveness to any repentant sinner, they argued, wrongly, that the "impossible" of ver. 4 could only mean "very difficult," a translation which is actually given to the word in some Latin Versions. The solution of the difficulty is not to be arrived at by tampering with plain words. What the author says is that "when those who have tasted the heavenly gift...have fallen away, it is *impossible* to renew them to repentance." He does not say that the Hebrews *have* so fallen away; nor does he directly assert that any true convert *can* thus fall away; but he does say that *when such apostasy occurs* and—a point of extreme importance which is constantly overlooked—*so long as it lasts* (see the next clause) a vital renewal is *impossible*. There can, he implies, be no *second* "Second Birth." The sternness of the passage is in exact accordance with x. 26—29 (comp. 2 Pet. ii. 20, 21); but "the impossibility *lies merely within the limits of the hypothesis itself.*" See our Article xvi.

seeing they crucify] Rather, "while crucifying," "*crucifying as they are doing.*" Thus the words imply not only an absolute, but a *continuous* apostasy, for the participle is changed from the past into the present tense. While men continue in wilful and willing sin they preclude all possibility of the action of grace. So long as they cling deliberately to their sins, they shut against themselves the open door of grace. A drop of water will, as the Rabbis said, suffice to purify a man who has accidentally touched a creeping thing, but an ocean will not suffice for his cleansing so long as he purposely keeps it held in his hand. There is such a thing as "doing despite unto the spirit of grace" (x. 29).

to themselves] This is what is called "the dative of disadvantage"—"to their own destruction."

We see then that this passage has been perverted in a multitude of ways from its plain meaning, which is, that so long as wilful apostasy continues there is no visible hope for it. On the other hand the passage does not

7 to an open shame. For the earth which drinketh *in* the rain that cometh oft upon it, and bringeth forth herbs meet for them by whom it is dressed, receiveth blessing from 8 God: but that which beareth thorns and briers *is* rejected, and *is* nigh unto cursing; whose end *is* to be burned.

lend itself to the violent oppositions of old controversies. In the recognition that, to our human point of view, there does appear to be such a thing as Divine dereliction this passage and x. 26—29, xii. 15—17 must be compared with the passages which touch on the unpardonable sin, and the sin against the Holy Ghost (1 John v. 16; Matt. xii. 31, 32; comp. Is. viii. 21). On the other hand it is as little meant to be "a rock of despair" as "a pillow of security." He is pointing out to Hebrew Christians with awful faithfulness the fatal end of deliberate and insolent apostasy. But we have no right to suppose that he has anything in view beyond the horizon of *revealed* possibilities. He is thinking of the teaching and ministry of the Church, not of the Omnipotence of God. With men it is impossible that a camel should go through the eye of a needle, but "with God all things are possible," (Matt. xix. 26; Mk. x. 20—27; Lk. xviii. 27). In the face of sin—above all of deliberate wretchlessness—we must remember that "God is not mocked" (Gal. vi. 7), and that our human remedies are then exhausted. On the other hand to *close* the gate of repentance against any contrite sinner is to contradict all the Gospels and all the Epistles alike, as well as the Law and the Prophets.

and put him to an open shame] Expose Him to scorn (comp. Matt. i. 19 where the simple verb is used).

7. *For the earth which drinketh in*] Rather, "For land which has drunk." Land of this kind, blessed and fruitful, resembles true and faithful Christians. The expression that the earth "drinks in" the rain is common (Deut. xi. 11). Comp. Virg. *Ecl.* III. 111, "*sat prata biberunt.*" For the moral significance of the comparison—namely that there is a point at which God's husbandry seems to be rendered finally useless,—see Is. v. 1—6, 24.

by whom it is dressed] Rather, "for whose sake (*propter quos.* Tert.) it is also tilled"—namely for the sake of the *owners* of the land.

blessing] Gen. xxvii. 27, "a field which the Lord hath blessed." Ps. lxv. 10, "Thou blessest the increase of it."

8. *that which beareth thorns*] Rather, "if it bear thorns" (Is. v. 6; Prov. xxiv. 31). This neglected land resembles converts who have fallen away.

rejected] The same word, in another metaphor, occurs in Jer. vi. 30.

nigh unto cursing] Lit., "near a curse." Doubtless there is a reference to Gen. iii. 18. St Chrysostom sees in this expression a sign of mercy, because he only says "*near a* curse." "He who has *not yet* fallen into a curse, but has got *near* it, will also be able to get afar from it;" so that we ought, he says, to cut up and burn the thorns, and then we shall be approved. And he might have added that the older "curse"

But, beloved, we are persuaded better *things* of you, and ⁹ *things* that accompany salvation, though we thus speak. For God *is* not unrighteous to forget your work and labour ¹⁰ of love, which ye have shewed toward his name, in that ye have ministered to the saints, and do minister. And we ¹¹

of the land to which he refers, was by God's mercy over-ruled into a blessing.

whose end is to be burned] Lit., "whose end is for burning." Comp. Is. xliv. 15, "that it may be for burning." It is probably a mistake to imagine that there is any reference to the supposed *advantage* of burning the surface of the soil (Virg. *Georg.* I. 84 *sqq.*; Pliny, *H. N.* XVIII. 39, 72), for we find no traces of such a procedure among the Jews. More probably the reference is to land like the Vale of Siddim, or "Burnt Phrygia," or "the Solfatara,"—like that described in Gen. xix. 24; Deut. xxix. 23. Comp. Heb. x. 27. And such a land Judea itself became within a very few years of this time, because the Jews would not "break up their fallow ground," but still continued "to sow among thorns." Obviously the *"whose"* refers to the "land," not to the "curse."

9—12. WORDS OF ENCOURAGEMENT AND HOPE.

9. *beloved*] The warm expression is introduced to shew that his stern teaching is only inspired by love.

we are persuaded] Lit., "We have been (and are) convinced of." Comp. Rom. xv. 14.

better things] Lit., "the better things." I am convinced that the better alternative holds true of you; that your condition is, and your fate will be, better than what I have described.

that accompany salvation] Rather, "akin to salvation," the antithesis to "near a curse." What leads to salvation is obedience (v. 9).

though we thus speak] in spite of the severe words of warning which I have just used. Comp. x. 39.

thus] As in verses 4—8.

10. *to forget*] The aorist implies "to forget in a moment." Comp. xi. 6, 20. God, even amid your errors, will not overlook the signs of grace working in you. Comp. Jer. xxxi. 16; Ps. ix. 12; Am. viii. 7.

and labour of love] The words "labour of" should be omitted. They are probably a gloss from 1 Thess. i. 3. The passage bears a vague general resemblance to 2 Cor. viii. 24; Col. i. 4.

toward his name] which name is borne by all His children.

in that ye have ministered to the saints] In your past and present ministration to the saints, i.e. to your Christian brethren. It used to be supposed that the title "the saints" applied especially to the Christians at Jerusalem (Rom. xv. 25; Gal. ii. 10; 1 Cor. xvi. 1). This is a mistake; and the saints at Jerusalem, merged in a common poverty, perhaps a result in part of their original Communism, were hardly in a

desire that every one of you do shew the same diligence to
12 the full assurance of hope unto the end: that ye be not
slothful, but followers of them who through faith and pa-
13 tience inherit the promises. For when God made promise
to Abraham, because he could swear by no greater, he

condition to minister to one another. They were (as is the case with most of the Jews now living at Jerusalem) dependent in large measure on the *Chaluka* or distribution of alms sent them from without.

and do minister] The continuance of their well doing proved its sincerity; but perhaps the writer hints, though with infinite delicacy, that their beneficent zeal was less active than it once had been.

11. *And*] Rather, "But."

we desire] A strong word: "we long to see in you."

that every one of you] Here again in the emphasis of the expression we seem to trace, as in other parts of the Epistle, some *individual* reference.

the same diligence] He desires to see as much earnestness (2 Cor. vii. 11) in the work of advancing to spiritual maturity of knowledge as they had shewn in ministering to the saints.

to the full assurance] i.e. with a view to your attaining this full assurance. Comp. x. 22, iii. 14. The word also occurs in 1 Thess. i. 5; Col. ii. 2.

unto the end] till hope becomes fruition (iii. 6, 14).

12. *that ye be not slothful*] Rather, "that ye *become* not slothful" in the advance of Christian hope as you already are (v. 11) in acquiring spiritual knowledge.

followers] Rather, "imitators," as in 1 Cor. iv. 16; Eph. v. 1; 1 Thess. 1, 6, &c.

through faith and patience inherit the promises] See ver. 15, xii. 1; Rom. ii. 7. The word rendered "patience" (*makrothumia*) is often applied to the "long suffering" of God, as in Rom. ii. 4; 1 Pet. iii. 20; but is used of men in Col. i. 11; 2 Cor. vi. 6, &c., and here implies the tolerance of hope deferred. It is a different word from the "endurance" of xii. 1, x. 36.

inherit] Partially, and by faith, here; fully and with the beatific vision in the life to come.

13. *For when God*] The "for" implies "and you may feel absolute confidence about the promises; for," &c.

made promise to Abraham] Abraham is here only selected as "the father of the faithful" (Rom. iv. 13); and not as the *sole* example of persevering constancy, but as an example specially illustrious (Calvin).

because he could swear by no greater] In the Jewish treatise Berachoth (f. 32. 1) Moses is introduced as saying to God, "Hadst thou sworn by Heaven and Earth, I should have said *They* will perish, and therefore so may Thy oath; but as Thou hast sworn by Thy great name, that oath shall endure for ever."

sware by himself, saying, Surely blessing I will bless 14
thee, and multiplying I will multiply thee. And so, 15
after he had patiently endured, he obtained the promise.
For men verily swear by the greater: and an oath for con- 16
firmation *is* to them an end of all strife. Wherein God, 17
willing more abundantly to shew unto the heirs of promise
the immutability of his counsel, confirmed *it* by an oath:

he sware by himself] "By myself have I sworn" (Gen. xxii. 16).
"God sweareth not by another," says Philo, in a passage of which this
may be a reminiscence—"for nothing is superior to Himself—but by
Himself, Who is best of all" (*De Leg. Alleg.* III. 72). There are other
passages in Philo which recall the reasoning of this clause (Opp. I. 622,
II. 39).

14. *blessing I will bless thee*] The repetition represents the emphasis
of the Hebrew, which expresses a superlative by repeating the word
twice.

I will multiply thee] In the Heb. and LXX. we have "I will multiply *thy seed*."

15. *after he had patiently endured*] Lit., "having patiently endured," which may mean "by patient endurance." The participles in
this passage are really contemporaneous with the principal verbs.

he obtained the promise] Gen. xv. 1, xxi. 5, xxii. 17, 18, xxv. 7, &c.;
John viii. 56. There is of course no contradiction to xi. 13, 39, which
refers to a farther future and a wider hope.

16. *men verily swear by the greater*] Gen. xxi. 23, xxiv. 3, xxvi.
30—31. The passage is important as shewing the lawfulness of Christian
oaths (see our Article xxxix.).

strife] Rather, "for an oath is to them an end of all gainsaying" (or
"controversy" as *to facts*) "with a view to confirmation." It is meant
that when men swear in confirmation of a disputed point their word is
believed. There is an exactly similar passage in Philo, *De sacr. Abel.
et Cain* (Opp. I. 181).

17. *Wherein*] Rather, "on which principle;" "in accordance with
this human custom."

willing] Rather, "wishing." The verb is not *thelōn*, but *boulome-
nos*.

more abundantly] i.e. than if he had not sworn.

unto the heirs of promise] Rather, "of *the* promise." The heirs of
the promise were primarily Abraham and his seed, and then all Christians
(Gal. iii. 29).

the immutability of his counsel] "I am the Lord, I *change not*"
(Mal. iii. 6). See too Is. xlvi. 10, 11; Ps. xxxiii. 11; Ja. i. 17.) His
changeless "decree" was that in Abraham's seed all the nations of the
world should be blessed. On the other hand the Mosaic law was mutable (vii. 12, xii. 27).

confirmed it by an oath] Rather, "intervened with an oath," i.e. made
His oath intermediate between Himself and Abraham. Philo, with his

13 that by two immutable things, in which *it was* impossible for God to lie, we might have a strong consolation, who have fled for refuge to lay hold upon the hope set before *us:* 19 which *hope* we have as an anchor of the soul, both sure and stedfast, and which entereth into that within the vail;

usual subtle refinements, observes that whereas *our* word is accredited because of an oath, God's oath derives its credit because He is God. On the other hand, Rabbi Eleazer (in the second century) said "the word *Not* has the force of an oath," which he deduced from a comparison of Gen. ix. 11 with Is. liv. 9; and therefore *a fortiori* the word *"yes"* has the force of an oath (Shevuoth. f. 36. 1). The word "intervened," "mediated" (*emesiteusen*) occurs here only in the N. T.

18. *by two immutable things*] Namely, by the *oath* and by the *word* of God. The Targums for "By Myself" have "By My Word have I sworn."

in which it was impossible for God to lie] St Clement of Rome says "*Nothing* is impossible to God, except to lie" (*Ep. ad Cor.* 27). "God that cannot lie" (Tit. i. 2. Comp. Num. xxiii. 19).

consolation] Rather, "encouragement."

who have fled for refuge] As into one of the refuge-cities of old. Num. xxxv. 11.

to lay hold upon the hope set before us] "The hope" is here (by a figure called *metonymy*) used for "*the object of hope* set before us as a prize" (comp. x. 23); "the hope which is laid up for us in heaven," Col. i. 5.

19. *as an anchor of the soul*] An anchor seems to have been an emblem of Hope—being something which enables us to hope for safety in danger—from very early days (Aesch. *Agam.* 488), and is even found as a symbol of Hope on coins. The notion that this metaphor adds anything to the argument in favour of the Pauline authorship of the Epistle, because St Paul too sometimes uses maritime metaphors, shews how little the most ordinary canons of literary criticism are applied to the Scriptures. St Paul never happens to use the metaphor of "an anchor," but it might have been equally well used by a person who had never seen the sea in his life.

"Or if you fear
Put all your trust in God: *that anchor holds.*"
Tennyson, *Enoch Arden.*

and which entereth into that within the vail] This expression is not very clear. The meaning is that the hawser which holds the anchor of our Christian hope passeth into the space which lies behind the veil, i.e. into the very sanctuary of Him who is "the God of Hope" (Rom. xv. 13). "The veil" is the great veil (*Parocheth*) which separated the Holy from the Holy of Holies (Ex. xxvi. 31—35; Heb. x. 20; Matt. xxvii. 51, &c.). The Christian's anchor of hope is not dropped into any earthly sea, but passes as it were through the depths of the aerial ocean, mooring us to the very throne of God.

whither the forerunner is for us entered, *even* Jesus, made a 20
high priest for ever after the order of Melchisedec.

> "Oh! life as futile then as frail!
> What hope of answer or redress?—
> Behind the veil! Behind the veil!"
>
> *In Memoriam.*

The word *katapetasma* usually applies to this veil before the Holy of Holies, while *kalumma* (as in Philo) is strictly used for the *outer* veil.

20. *whither the forerunner is...entered*] Lit. "where a forerunner entered...Jesus;" or "where, as a forerunner" (or harbinger) "Jesus entered."

for us] "on our behalf." This explains the introduction of the remark. Christ's Ascension is a pledge that our Hope will be fulfilled. He is gone to prepare a place for us (John xiv. 2, 3). His entrance into the region behind the veil proves the reality of the hidden kingdom of glory into which our Hope has cast its anchor (Ahlfeld). This is evidently a prominent thought with the writer (iv. 14, ix. 24).

made] Rather, "having become," as the result of His earthly life.

after the order of Melchisedec] By repeating this quotation, as a sort of *refrain*, the writer once more resumes the allusion of v. 10, and brings us face to face with the argument to which he evidently attached extreme importance as the central topic of his epistle. In the dissertation which follows there is nothing which *less* resembles St Paul's manner of "going off at a word" (as in Eph. v. 12—15, &c.). The warning and exhortation which ends at this verse, so far from being "a sudden transition" (or "a digression") "by which he is carried from the main stream of his argument" belongs essentially to his whole design. The disquisition on Melchisedek—for which he has prepared the way by previous allusions and with the utmost deliberation—is prefaced by the same kind of solemn strain as those which we find in ii. 1—3, iii. 2, 12—14, xii. 15—17. So far from being "hurried aside by the violence of his feelings" into these appeals, they are strictly subordinated to his immediate design, and enwoven into the plan of the Epistle with consummate skill. "Hurry" and "vehemence" may often describe the intensity and impetuosity of St Paul's fervent style which was the natural outcome of his impassioned nature; but faultless rhetoric, sustained dignity, perfect smoothness and elaborate eloquence are the very different characteristics of the manner of this writer.

for ever] The words in the Greek come emphatically at the end, and as Dr Kay says strike the keynote of the next chapter (vii. 3, 16, 17, 21, 24, 25, 28).

7 For this Melchisedec, king of Salem, priest of the most

CH. VII. CHRIST, AS AN ETERNAL HIGH PRIEST AFTER THE ORDER OF MELCHISEDEK, IS SUPERIOR TO THE LEVITIC HIGH PRIEST.

Historic reference to Melchisedek (1—4). His Priesthood typically superior to that of Aaron in seven particulars. i. Because even Abraham gave him tithes (4—7). ii. Because he blessed Abraham (7). iii. Because he is the type of an *undying* Priest (8). iv. Because even the yet unborn Levi paid him tithes, in the person of Abraham (9, 10). v. Because the permanence of his Priesthood, continued by Christ, implied the abrogation of the whole Levitic Law (11—19). vi. Because it was founded on the swearing of an oath (20—23). vii. Because it is intransmissible, never being vacated by death (23, 24). Summary and conclusion (25—28).

1. *For this Melchisedec*] All that is historically known of Melchisedek is found in three verses of the book of Genesis (xiv. 18, 19, 20). In all the twenty centuries of sacred history he is only mentioned once, in Ps. cx. 4. This chapter is a mystical explanation of the significance of these two brief allusions. It was not wholly new, since the Jews attached high honour to the name of Melchisedek, whom they identified with Shem, and Philo had already spoken of Melchisedek as a type of the Logos (*De Leg. Alleg.* III. 25, Opp. I. 102).

king of Salem] Salem is probably a town near Shechem. It is the same which is mentioned in Gen. xxxiii. 18 (though there the words rendered "to Shalem" *may* mean "in safety"), and in John iii. 23; and it is the Salumias of Judith iv. 4. This is the view of Jerome, who in his Onomasticon places it eight miles south of Bethshean. The site is marked by a ruined well still called *Sheikh Salim* (Robinson, *Bibl. Res.* III. 333). In Jerome's time the ruins of a large palace were shewn in this place as "the palace of Melchisedek;" and this agrees with the Samaritan tradition that Abraham had been met by Melchisedek not at Jerusalem but at Gerizim. The same tradition is mentioned by Eupolemos (Euseb. *Praep. Evang.* IX. 17. See Stanley, *Sin. and Pal.* p. 237). The more common view has been that Salem is a shortened form of Jerusalem, but this is very improbable; for (1) only a single instance of this abbreviation has been adduced, and that only as a poetic license in a late Psalm which the LXX. describe as "A Psalm with reference to the Assyrian" (Ps. lxxvi. 2). (2) Even this instance is very dubious, for (*a*) the Psalmist *may* be intending to *contrast* the sanctuary of Melchisedek with that of David; or (β) even here the true rendering may be "His place has been made *in peace*" as the Vulgate renders it. (3) Jerusalem in the days of Abraham, and for centuries afterwards was only known by the name Jebus. (4) The typical character of Melchisedek would be rather impaired than enhanced by his being a king *at Jerusalem*, for that was the holy city of the Aaronic priesthood of which he was wholly independent,

high God, who met Abraham returning from the slaughter

being a type of One in whose priesthood men should worship the Father in all places alike if they offered a spiritual worship. We must then regard Salem as being a different place from Jerusalem, if any place at all is intended. For though both the Targums and Josephus (*Antt.* I. 10 § 2) here identify Salem with Jerusalem, the Bereshith Rabba interprets the word Salem as an appellative, and says that it means "Perfect King," and that this title was given to him because he was circumcised (see Wünsche, *Bibl. Rabbinica.* Beresh. Rabba, p. 198). Philo too says "king of peace, for that is the meaning of Salem" (*Leg. Alleg.* III. 25, comp. Is. ix. 5; Col. i. 20). Nothing depends on the solution of the question, for in any case the fact that "Salem" means "peace" or "peaceful" is pressed into the typology. But the Salem near Sichem was itself in a neighbourhood hallowed by reminiscences scarcely less sacred than those of Jerusalem. Besides this connexion with the name of Melchisedek, it was the place where Jacob built the altar *El-Elohe-Israel;* the scene of John's baptism; and the region in which Christ first revealed Himself to the woman of Samaria as the Messiah.

priest of the most high God] The union of Royalty and Priesthood in the same person gave him peculiar sacredness ("He shall be a Priest upon His throne" (Zech. vi. 13). "Rex Anius, rex idem hominum, Phoebique sacerdos" (Virg. *Aen.* III. 80 and Servius *ad loc.*). The expression "God most high" is *El Eliôn*, and this was also a title of God among the Phoenicians. It is however certain that Moses meant that Melchisedek was a Priest of God, for though this is the earliest occurrence of the name *El Eliôn* it is afterwards combined with "Jehovah" in Gen. xiv. 22, and in other parts of the Pentateuch and the Psalms. There is no difficulty in supposing that the worship of the One True God was not absolutely confined to the family of Abraham. The longevity of the early Patriarchs facilitated the preservation of Monotheism at least among some tribes of mankind, and this perhaps explains the existence of the name *Elion* among the Phoenicians (Philo Byblius *ap.* Euseb. *Praep. Evang.* I. 10).

who met Abraham returning from the slaughter of the kings] Amraphel king of Shinar, with three allies, had made war on Bera king of Sodom with four allies, and had carried away plunder and captives from the Cities of the Plain. Among the captives was Lot. Abraham therefore armed his 318 servants, and with the assistance of three Canaanite chiefs, Aner, Mamre, and Eshcol, pursued Amraphel's army to the neighbourhood of Damascus, defeated them, rescued their prisoners, and recovered the spoil. The word here rendered "slaughter" (*kopē* from *kopto* "cut") may perhaps mean no more than "smiting," i.e. defeat. On his return the king of Sodom going forth to greet and thank him met him at "the valley of Shaveh, which is the king's dale," a place of which nothing is known, but which was probably somewhere in the tribe of Ephraim near mount Gerizim. This seems to have been in the little domain of Melchisedek

₂ of the kings, and blessed him; to whom also Abraham gave a tenth *part* of all; first being by interpretation King of righteousness, and after that also King of Salem, which is, ₃ King of peace; without father, without mother, without de-

for we are not told that "he went forth to meet" Abraham, but only that (being apparently at the place where Bera met Abraham) he humanely and hospitably brought out bread and wine for the weary victors, and blessed Abraham, and blessed God for granting him the victory. In acknowledgment of this friendly blessing, Abraham "gave him tithes of all," i.e. of all the spoils.

and blessed him] Evidently as a priestly act. Gen. xiv. 19, 20.

2. *first being*] This seems to imply that of his two names or titles "Melchisedec," and "King of Salem," the *first* means "King of Righteousness" and the second "King of Peace." In a passage of mystic interpretation like this, however, the writer may intend to suggest that there is a direct connexion between the two titles, and that "Righteousness" is *the necessary antecedent* to "Peace," as is intimated in Ps. lxxii. 7, lxxxv. 10. Comp. Rom. v. 1.

by interpretation King of righteousness] The name Melchisedek may mean "King of Righteousness." This is the paraphrase of the Targums, perhaps with tacit reference to Is. xxxii. 1, where it is said of the Messiah "Behold a king shall reign in righteousness." (Comp. Zech. ix. 9; Jer. xxiii. 5.) In the Bereshith Rabba *Tzedek* is explained to mean Jerusalem with reference to Is. i. 21, "Righteousness lodged in it." Josephus (*Antt.* 1. 19, § 12; *B. J.* VI. 10) and Philo, however, render it "Righteous King." Later on in Jewish history (Josh. x. 3) we read of Adonizedek ("Lord of righteousness") who was a king of Jerusalem. Apart from any deeper meaning "Righteousness" or "Justice" was one of the most necessary qualifications of Eastern Kings who are also Judges. In the mystic sense the interpretation of the names Melchizedek and Salem made him a fit type of "the Lord our Righteousness" (Jer. xxiii. 6) and "the Prince of Peace" (Is. ix. 6): and he was also a fit type of Christ because he was a Kingly Priest; a Priest who blessed Abraham; a Priest who, so far as we are told, offered no animal-sacrifices; and a Priest over whom Scripture casts "the shadow of Eternity." See Bishop Wordsworth's note on this passage.

King of peace] "The work of Righteousness shall be Peace, and the effect of Righteousness quietness and assurance for ever" (Is. xxxii. 17; Eph. ii. 14, 15, 17; Rom. v. 1. Comp. Philo *Leg. Alleg.* III. 25, Opp. I. 102).

3. *without father, without mother, without descent*] Rather, "without lineage" or "pedigree" as in ver. 6. The mistake is an ancient one, for in consequence of it Irenæus claims Melchisedek as one who had lived a celibate life (which in any case would not follow). The simple and undoubted meaning of these words is that the father, mother, and lineage of Melchisedek are *not recorded*, so that he becomes more naturally a type of Christ. In the Alexandrian School, to which

scent, having neither beginning of days, nor end of life;

the writer of this Epistle belonged, the custom of allegorising Scripture had received an immense development, and the *silence* of Scripture was regarded as the suggestion of mysterious truths. The Jewish interpreters naturally looked on the passage about Melchisedek as full of deep significance because the Psalmist in the 110th Psalm, which was universally accepted as a Psalm directly Messianic (Matt. xxii. 44) had found in Melchisedek a Priest-King, who, centuries before Aaron, had been honoured by their great ancestor, and who was therefore a most fitting type of Him who was to be "a Priest upon his Throne." The fact that he had no recorded father, mother, or lineage enhanced his dignity because the Aaronic priesthood depended exclusively on the power to prove direct descent from Aaron which necessitated a most scrupulous care in the preservation of the priestly genealogies. (See Ezra ii. 61, 62; Nehem. vii. 63, 64, where families which could not actually produce their pedigree are excluded from the priesthood.) The idiom by which a person is said to have *no* father or ancestry when they are not recorded, or are otherwise quite unimportant, was common to Greek, Latin, and Hebrew. In a Greek tragedy "Ion" calls himself "*motherless*" when he supposes that his mother is a slave (Eurip. *Ion*, 850). Scipio taunted the mob of the Forum as people "who had *neither father nor mother*" (Cic. *De Orat.* II. 64). Horace calls himself "a man *sprung from no ancestors*" (Hor. *Sat.* I. 6, 10). In the Bereshith Rabba we find the rule "a Gentile *has no father*," i.e. the father of a proselyte is not counted in Jewish pedigrees. Further the Jews mystically applied the same sort of rule which holds in legal matters which says "that things not producible are regarded as non-existent." Hence their kabbalistic interpretation of particulars not mentioned in Scripture. From the fact that Cain's death is nowhere recorded in Genesis, Philo draws the lesson that evil never dies among the human race; and he calls Sarah "motherless" because her mother is nowhere mentioned. There is then no difficulty either as to the idiom or its interpretation.

without mother] The mention of this particular may seem to have no bearing on the type, unless a contrast be intended to the Jewish Priests who were descended from Elisheba the wife of Aaron (Ex. vi. 23). But "Christ as God, has no mother, as man no Father." The early Church neither used nor sanctioned the name *Theotokos* "Mother of God" as applied to the Virgin Mary.

without descent] Rather, "without a genealogy." Melchisedek has no recorded predecessor or successor. Bishop Wordsworth quotes "Who shall declare His generation?"

having neither beginning of days, nor end of life]. The meaning of this clause is exactly the same as that of the last—namely that neither the birth nor death of Melchisedek are recorded, which makes him all the more fit to be a *type* of the Son of God. Dean Alford's remark that it is "almost childish" to suppose that nothing more than this is intended, arises from imperfect familiarity with the methods of Rabbinic and Alexandrian exegesis. The notion that Melchisedek was

but made like unto the Son of God; abideth a priest con-

the Holy Spirit (which was held by an absurd sect who called themselves Melchisedekites); or "the Angel of the Presence;" or "God the Word, previous to Incarnation;" or "the Shechinah;" or "the Captain of the Lord's Host;" or "an Angel;" or "a reappearance of Enoch;" or an "*ensarkosis* of the Holy Ghost;" are, on all sound hermeneutical principles, not only "almost" but quite "childish." They belong to methods of interpretation which turn Scripture into an enigma and neglect all the lessons which result so plainly from the laws which govern its expression, and the history of its interpretation. No Hebrew, reading these words, would have been led to these idle and fantastic conclusions about the super-human dignity of the Canaanite prince. If the expressions here used had been meant *literally*, Melchisedek would not have been a man, but a Divine Being—and not the *type* of one—and he could not therefore have been "a Priest" at all. It would then have been not only inexplicable, but meaningless that in all Scripture he should only have been incidentally mentioned in three verses, of a perfectly simple, and straightforward narrative, and only once again alluded to in the isolated reference of a Psalm written centuries later. The fact that some of these notions about him may plead the authority of great names is no more than can be said of thousands of the most absolute and even absurd misinterpretations in the melancholy history of slowly-corrected errors which pass under the name of Scripture exegesis. Less utterly groundless is the belief of the Jews that Melchisedek was the Patriarch Shem, who, as they shewed, might have survived to this time (Avodath Hakkodesh, III. 20, &c. and in two of the Targums). Yet even this view cannot be correct; for if Melchisedek had been Shem (1) there was every reason why he should be called by his own name; and (2) Canaan was in the territory of Ham's descendants, not those of Shem; and (3) Shem was in no sense, whether mystical or literal, "without pedigree." Yet this opinion satisfied Lyra, Cajetan, Luther, Melanchthon, Lightfoot, &c.

Who then was Melchisedek? Josephus and some of the most learned fathers (Hippolytus, Eusebius, &c.), and many of the ablest modern commentators, rightly hold that he was neither more nor less than what Moses tells us that he was—the Priest-King of a little Canaanite town, to whom, because he acted as a Priest of the True God, Abraham gave tithes; and whom his neighbours honoured because he was not sensual and turbulent as they were, but righteous and peaceful, not joining in their wars and raids, yet mingling with them in acts of mercy and kindness. How little the writer of this Epistle meant to exaggerate the typology is shewn by the fact that he does not so much as allude to the "bread and wine" to which an unreal significance has been attached both by Jewish and Christian commentators. He does not make it in any way a type of the shewbread and libations; or an offering characteristic of his Priesthood; nor does he make him (as Philo does) offer any sacrifice at all. How much force would he have added to the typology if he had ventured to treat these gifts as prophecies of the Eucharist,

tinually. Now consider how great this *man was*, unto 4
whom even the patriarch Abraham gave the tenth of the
spoils. And verily they that are of the sons of Levi who 5
receive the office of the priesthood have a commandment
to take tithes of the people according to the law, that is, of

as some of the Fathers do! His silence on a point which would have
been so germane to his purpose is decisive against such a view.
 made like unto the Son of God] Lit. "having been likened to the Son
of God," i.e. having been invested with a typical resemblance to
Christ. The expression explains the writer's meaning. It is a combination of the passage in Genesis with the allusion in Ps. cx., shewing
that the two together constitute Melchisedek a Divinely appointed type
of a Priesthood received from no ancestors and transmitted to no
descendants. The *personal* importance of Melchisedek was very
small; but he is eminently typical, because of the suddenness with
which he is introduced into the sacred narrative, and the subsequent
silence respecting him. He was born, and lived, and died, and had a
father and mother no less than any one else, but by not mentioning
these facts, the Scripture, interpreted on mystic principles, "throws on
him a shadow of Eternity: gives him a *typical* Eternity." The expressions used of him are only *literally* true of Him whose type he was. In
himself only the Priest-prince of a little Canaanite community, his
venerable figure was seized upon, first by the Psalmist, then by the writer
of this Epistle, as the type of an Eternal Priest. As far as Scripture is
concerned it may be said of him, that "he lives without dying fixed for
ever as one who lives by the pen of the sacred historian, and thus
stamped as a type of the Son, the ever-living Priest."
 continually] The Greek expression is like the Latin *in perpetuum*.
 4. *Now consider*] The verb means "to contemplate spiritually."
 how great this man was] Here begin the seven particulars of the
typical superiority of Melchisedek's Priesthood over that of Aaron.
FIRST. Even Abraham gave him tithes.
 the patriarch Abraham] There is great rhetoric force in the order of
the original "to whom even Abraham gave a tithe out of his best spoils
—he the patriarch." Here not only is the ear of the writer gratified by
the sonorous conclusion of the sentence with an *Ionicus a minore*
pătrĭārchēs; but a whole argument about the dignity of Abraham is
condensed into the position of one emphatic word. The word in the
N. T. occurs only here and in Acts ii. 29, vii. 8, 9.
 of the spoils] The word rendered "spoils" properly means that
which is taken from the top of a heap (ἄκρος θἰς); hence some translate
it "the best of the spoils," and Philo describes the tithe given by
Abraham in similar terms.
 5. *who receive the office of the priesthood*] The word used for
"priesthood" is defined by Aristotle to mean "care concerning the
gods."
 to take tithes of the people according to the law] Indirectly, through the

their brethren, though they come out of the loins of Abra-
6 ham: but he whose descent is not counted from them
received tithes of Abraham, and blessed him that had the
7 promises. And without all contradiction the less is blessed
8 of the better. And here men that die receive tithes; but
there he *receiveth them*, of whom it is witnessed that he
9 liveth. And as *I* may so say, Levi also, who receiveth
10 tithes, payed tithes in Abraham. For he was yet in the
11 loins of his father, when Melchisedec met him. If therefore
perfection were by the Levitical priesthood, (for under it

agency of the Levites. Delitzsch argues that after the Exile the Priests collected the tithes themselves. It cannot however be proved that the Priests themselves tithed the people. This was done by the Levites, who gave the tithe of *their* tithes to the priests, Num. xviii. 22—26, Nehem. x. 38. There is however no real difficulty about the expression, for the Priests *might* tithe the people, as Jewish tradition *says* that they did in the days of Ezra; and (2) *Qui facit per alium facit per se*. There is therefore no need to alter "the people" (*laon*) into Levi (*Leuin*). The Priests stood alone in *receiving* tithes and giving none.

come out of the loins] A Hebrew expression, Gen. xxxv. 11.

6. *and blessed*] Lit., *and hath blessed*. SECOND point of superiority. The act is regarded as permanent and still continuous in its effects, in accordance with the writer's manner of regarding Scripture as a living and present entity.

7. *of the better*] i.e. the inferior is blessed by one who is (*pro hac vice* or *quoad hoc*) the Superior. Hence blessing was one of the recognised priestly functions (Num. vi. 23—26).

8. *And here*] As things now are; while the Levitic priesthood still continues.

men that die] "Dying men"—men who are under liability to die (comp. verse 23), as in the lines

"He preached as one who ne'er should preach again
And *as a dying man to dying men*."

it is witnessed that he liveth] i.e. he stands as a living man on the eternal page of Scripture, and no word is said about his death; so far then as the letter of Scripture is concerned he stands in a perpetuity of mystic life. This is the THIRD point of superiority.

9. *as I may so say*] Rather, "so to speak;" shewing the writer's consciousness that the expression is somewhat strained, especially as even Isaac was not born till 14 years later. The phrase is classic, and is common in Philo, but occurs here only in the N.T.

Levi...payed tithes] This is the FOURTH point of superiority.

11. *If therefore perfection were by the Levitical priesthood*] At this point begins the argument which occupies the next nine verses. "Perfection" (compare the verb in ix. 9, x. 1, 14, xi. 40) means power of perfectionment, capacity to achieve the end in view; but this was not

the people received the law,) what further need *was there* that another priest should rise after the order of Melchisedec, and not be called after the order of Aaron? For the 12 priesthood being changed, there is made of necessity a change also of the law. For he of whom these *things* are 13 spoken pertaineth to another tribe, of which no *man* gave attendance at the altar. For *it is* evident that our Lord 14

to be attained through the Levitic priesthood. The FIFTH point of superiority is that the Melchisedek Priesthood implies the abrogation of the Levitic, and of the whole law which was based upon it.

for under it] Rather, "for on the basis of it." The writer regards the Priesthood rather than the Law as constituting the basis of the whole Mosaic system; so that into this slight parenthesis he really infuses the essence of his argument. The Priesthood is obviously changed. For otherwise the Theocratic King of Ps. cx. would not have been called "a Priest after the order *of Melchisedec*" but "after the order *of Aaron*." Clearly then "the order of Aaron" admitted of no attainment of perfection through its means. But if the Priesthood was thus condemned as imperfect and inefficient, the Law was equally disparaged as a transitory institution. Righteousness did not "come by the Law;" if it could so have come Christ would have died in vain (Gal. ii. 21. Comp. Heb. x. 1—14).

what further need was there] There could be no need, since none of God's actions or dispensations are superfluous.

another priest] Rather, "a different priest."

and not be called after the order of Aaron] Lit., "and that he should not be said (viz. in P's. cx. 4) to be after the order of Aaron."

12. *being changed*] He here uses the comparatively mild and delicate term "being *transferred*." When he has prepared the mind of his readers by a little further argument, he substitutes for "transference" the much stronger word "*annulment*" (ver. 18). It is a characteristic of the writer to be thus careful not to shock the prejudices of his readers more than was inevitable. His whole style of argument, though no less effective than that of St Paul in its own sphere, is more conciliatory, more deferential, less vehemently iconoclastic. This relation to St Paul is like that of Melanchthon to Luther.

of necessity] The Law and the Priesthood were so inextricably united that the Priesthood could not be altered without disintegrating the whole complex structure of the Law.

13. *pertaineth*] Lit., "hath had part in."

of which no man gave attendance at the altar] Sacerdotal privileges were exclusively assigned to the tribe of Levi (Deut. x. 8; Num. iii. 5—8). The attempt of King Uzziah, who was of the tribe of Judah, to assume priestly functions, had been terribly punished (2 Chr. xxvi. 3, 19).

14. *evident*] "Known to all." The word (*prodēlon*) occurs in 1 Tim. v. 24, 25.

15 sprang out of Juda; of which tribe Moses spake nothing concerning priesthood. And it is yet far more evident: for
16 that after the similitude of Melchisedec there ariseth another priest, who is made, not after the law of a carnal command-
17 ment, but after the power of an endless life. For *he* testi-

our Lord] This is the first time that we find this expression in the N.T. standing alone as a name for Christ. It is from this passage that the designation now so familiar to Christian lips is derived.
sprang] Lit., "hath sprung." The verb is used generally of the sun *rising* (Mal. iv. 2; Lk. xii. 54; 2 Pet. i. 19), but also of the springing up of plants (Zech. iii. 8, vi. 12, &c.). Hence the LXX. choose the word *Anatolē* which usually means sunrise, to translate the Messianic title of "the Branch."
out of Juda] Gen. xlix. 10; Is. xi. 1; Lk. iii. 33. "The Lion of the tribe of Judah," Rev. v. 5.
concerning priesthood] The better reading is "concerning priests." Uzziah, of the tribe of Judah, king though he was, had been punished by lifelong leprosy for usurping the functions of the tribe of Levi.
15. *yet far more evident*] The word used (*katadēlon*) is stronger than that used in ver. 14 (*prodēlon*) and does not occur elsewhere in the N.T. The change of the Law can be *yet more decisively inferred* from the fact that Melchisedek is not only a Priest of a different tribe from Levi, but a priest constituted in a wholly different manner, and even—as he might have said—out of the limits of the Twelve tribes altogether; and yet a Priest was to be raised after *his* order, not after that of Aaron.
for that] Rather, "if" (as is the case), i.e. "seeing that."
16. *is made*] Lit., "is become."
after the law of a carnal commandment] Rather, "in accordance with *the law of a fleshen* (i.e. earthly) *commandment.*" Neither this writer, nor even St Paul, ever called or would have called the Law "carnal" (*sarkikos*), a term which St Paul implicitly disclaims when he says that the Law is "spiritual" (Rom. vii. 14); but to call it "fleshen" (*sarkinos*) is merely to say that it is hedged round with earthly limitations and relationships, and therefore unfit to be adapted to eternal conditions. Its ordinances indeed might be called "ordinances of the flesh" (ix. 10), because they had to do, almost exclusively, with externals. An attentive reader will see that even in the closest apparent resemblances to the language of St Paul there are differences in this Epistle. For instance his relative disparagement of the Law turns almost exclusively on the conditions of its *hierarchy;* and his use of the word "flesh" and "fleshen," refers not to sensual passions but to mortality and transience.
of an endless life] Lit., "of an indissoluble life," the life of a tabernacle which "could not be dissolved." The word (*akatalutos*) is not found elsewhere in the N.T. The Priest of this new Law and Priesthood is "the Prince of Life" (Acts iii. 15).
17. *he testifieth*] Rather, "he is testified of."

fieth, Thou *art* a priest for ever after the order of Melchisedec. For there is verily a disannulling of the commandment going before for the weakness and unprofitableness thereof. For the law made nothing perfect, but the bringing in of a better hope *did;* by the which we draw nigh unto God. And inasmuch as not without an oath *he was made priest:* (for those priests were made without an oath; but this with an oath by him that said unto him, The Lord sware and will not repent, Thou *art* a priest

18. *there is*] Rather, "there occurs" or "results," in accordance with Ps. cx. 4.

a disannulling] See note on ver. 12. Comp. Gal. iii. 15.

of the commandment] Most ancient and modern commentators understand this of the Mosaic Law in general.

for the weakness and unprofitableness thereof] The writer here shews how completely he is of the school of St Paul, notwithstanding the strength of his Judaic sympathies. For St Paul was the first who clearly demonstrated that Christianity involved the abrogation of the Law, and thereby proved its partial, transitory, and inefficacious character as intended only to be a *preparation for* the Gospel (Rom. viii. 3). The law was only the "tutor" or attendant-slave to lead men to Christ, or train their boyhood till it could attain to full Christian manhood (Gal. iii. 23, 24). It was only *after* the consummation of the Gospel that its disciplinary institutions became reduced to "weak and beggarly rudiments" (Gal. iv. 9).

going before] Comp. 1 Tim. i. 18, v. 24. The "commandment" was only a temporary precursor of the final dispensation.

19. *the law made nothing perfect*] This is illustrated in ix. 6—9.

but the bringing in of a better hope did] The better punctuation is "There takes place a disannulment of the preceding commandment on account of its weakness and unprofitableness—for the Law perfected nothing—but the superinduction of a better hope." The latter clause is a nominative not to "perfected," but to "there is," or rather "there takes place," in ver. 18. The "better hope" is that offered us by the Resurrection of Christ; and the whole of the New Testament bears witness that the Gospel had the power of "perfecting," which the Law had not. Rom. iii. 21; Eph. ii. 13—15, &c.

20. *inasmuch as not without an oath*] This is the SIXTH point of superiority. He has lingered at much greater length over the FIFTH than over the others, from the extreme importance of the argument which it incidentally involved. The oath on which the Melchisedek Priesthood was founded is that of Ps. cx. 4. The word used for "oath" is not the common word *horkos* (as in vi. 17), but the more sonorous *horkomosia*.

21. *those priests were made without an oath*] Lit., "these men have been made priests without an oath."

22 for ever after the order of Melchisedec:) by so much
23 was Jesus made a surety of a better testament. And they
truly were many priests, because *they* were not suffered to
24 continue by reason of death: but this *man*, because he con-
25 tinueth ever, hath an unchangeable priesthood. Wherefore
he is able also to save them to the uttermost that come unto

    22. *of a better testament*] A clearer rendering would be "By so much better was the covenant of which Jesus has been made surety." The words—which might be taken as the keynote of the whole Epistle—should undoubtedly be rendered "of a better *covenant*." The Greek word *diathēkē* is the rendering of the Hebrew *Berîth*, which means a covenant. Of "testaments" the Hebrews knew nothing until they learnt the custom of "making a will" from the Romans. So completely was this the case that there is no word in Hebrew which means "a will," and when a writer in the Talmud wants to speak of a "will," he has to put the Greek word *diathēkē* in Hebrew letters. The Hebrew *berith* is rendered *diathēkē* in the LXX., and "covenant" by our translators at least 200 times. When we speak of the "Old" or the "New *Testament*" we have borrowed the word from the Vulgate or Latin translation of St Jerome in 2 Cor. iii. 6. The only exception to this meaning of *diathēkē* is in ix. 15—17. Of the way in which Jesus is "a pledge" of this "better covenant," see ver. 25 and viii. 1, 6, ix. 15, xii. 24. The word for "pledge" (ἔγγυος) occurs here alone in the N. T., but is found in Ecclus. xxix. 15.

    23. *many priests*] Lit., "And they truly have been constituted priests many in number."

    they were not suffered to continue by reason of death] The vacancies caused in their number by the ravages of death required to be constantly replenished (Num. xx. 28; Ezek. xxii. 29, 30).

    24. *but this man*] Rather, "*but He.*"

    hath an unchangeable priesthood] Rather, "hath his priesthood unchangeable" (*sempiternum*, Vulg.) or perhaps "untransmissible;" "a priesthood that doth not pass to another," as it is rendered in the margin of our Revised Version. The rendering "not to be transgressed against," or "inviolate" (*intransgressibile*, Aug.), is not tenable here. This is the SEVENTH particular of superiority. I think it quite needless to enter into tedious modern controversies as to the particular *time* of Christ's ministry at which He assumed His priestly office, because I do not think that they so much as entered into the mind of the author. The one thought which was prominent in his mind was that of Christ passing as our Great High Priest with the offering of His finished sacrifice into the Heaven of Heavens. The *minor details* of Christ's Priestly work are not defined, and those of Melchisedek are passed over in complete silence.

    25. *to save them to the uttermost*] i.e. "to the consummate end." All the Apostles teach that Christ is "able to keep us from falling and to

God by him, seeing he ever liveth to make intercession for them.

For such a high priest became us, *who is* holy, harmless, 26 undefiled, separate from sinners, and made higher than the

present us faultless before the presence of his glory" (Jude 24; Rom. viii. 34; John vi. 37—39.

to save] He saves them in accordance with His name of Jesus, "the Saviour." Bengel.

by him] "No man cometh unto the Father but by me."

to make intercession] "to appear in the presence of God for us" (Heb. ix. 24). Philo also speaks of the Logos as a Mediator and Intercessor (*Vit. Mos.* III. 16).

Having thus proved in seven particulars the transcendence of the Melchisedek Priesthood of Christ, as compared with the Levitic Priesthood, he ends this part of his subject with a weighty summary, into which, with his usual literary skill, he introduces by anticipation the thoughts which he proceeds to develop in the following chapters.

26. *For such a high priest became us*] The "for" clinches the whole argument with a moral consideration. There was *a spiritual fitness* in this annulment of the imperfect Law and Priesthood, and the introduction of a better hope and covenant. So great and so sympathetic and so innocent an High Priest was suited to our necessities. There is much rhetorical beauty in the order of the Greek. He might have written it in the order of the English, but he keeps the word "Priest" by way of emphasis as the last word of the clause, and then substitutes High Priest for it.

holy] towards God (Lev. xx. 26, xxi. 1; Ps. xvi. 10; Acts ii. 27). He bore "holiness to the Lord" not on a golden mitre-plate, but as the inscription of all His life as "the Holy One of God" (Mk. i. 24).

harmless] as regards men.

undefiled] Not stained, Is. liii. 9 (and as the word implies unstainable) with any of the defilements which belonged to the Levitic priests from their confessed sinfulness. Christ was "without sin" (iv. 15); "without spot" (ix. 14; 1 Pet. i. 19). He "knew no sin" (2 Cor. v. 21).

separate from sinners] Lit., "Having been separated from sinners." The writer is already beginning to introduce the subject of the Day of Atonement on which he proceeds to speak. To enable the High Priest to perform the functions of that day aright the most scrupulous precautions were taken to obviate the smallest chance of ceremonial pollution (Lev. xxi. 10—15); yet even these rigid precautions had at least once in living memory been frustrated—when the High Priest Ishmael ben Phabi had been incapacitated from his duties because in conversing with Hareth (Aretas) Emir of Arabia, a speck of the Emir's saliva had fallen upon the High Priest's beard. But Christ was free not only from ceremonial pollution, but from that far graver moral stain of which the ceremonial was a mere external figure; and had now been exalted above all contact with sin in the Heaven of Heavens (iv. 14).

27 heavens; who needeth not daily, as *those* high priests, to offer up sacrifice, first for his own sins, *and* then for the people's: for this he did once, when he offered up himself.
28 For the law maketh men high priests which have infirmity; but the word of the oath, which was since the law, *maketh* the Son, who is consecrated for evermore.

made higher than the heavens] Having "ascended up far above all heavens" (Eph. iv. 10).

27. *daily*] A difficulty is suggested by this word, because the High Priest did not offer sacrifices daily, but only once a year on the Day of Atonement. In any case the phrase would be a mere verbal inaccuracy, since the High Priest could be regarded as *potentially* ministering in the daily sacrifices which were offered by the inferior Priests; or the one yearly sacrifice may be regarded as *summing up* all the daily sacrifices needed to expiate the High Priest's daily sins (so that "daily" would mean "continually"). It appears however that the High Priest might if he chose take actual part in the daily offerings (Ex. xxix. 38, 44; Lev. vi. 19—22; Jos. *B. J.* v. 5—7). It is true that the daily sacrifices and Mincha or "meat offering" had no recorded connexion with any *expiatory* sacrifices; but an expiatory significance seems to have been attached to the daily offering of incense (Lev. xvi. 12, 13, LXX.; Yoma, f. 44. 1). The notion that there is any reference to the Jewish Temple built by Onias at Leontopolis is entirely baseless. Both Philo (*De Spec. Legg.* § 53) and the Talmud use the very same expression as the writer, who seems to have been perfectly well aware that, normally and strictly, the High Priest only offered sacrifices on one day in the year (ix. 25, x. 1, 3). The stress may be on the *necessity*. Those priests *needed* the expiation by sacrifice for daily sins; Christ did not.

he did once] Rather, "once for all" (ix. 12, 26, 28, x. 10; Rom. vi. 10). Christ offered one sacrifice, once offered, but eternally sufficient.

when he offered up himself] The High Priest was also the Victim, viii. 3, ix. 12, 14, 25, x. 10, 12, 14; Eph. v. 2 (Lünemann).

28. *men*] i. e. ordinary "human beings."

the oath, which was since the law] Namely, in Ps. cx. 4.

consecrated] Rather, "*who has been perfected.*" The word "consecrated" in our A.V. is a reminiscence of Lev. xxi. 10; Ex. xxix. 9. The "perfected" has the same meaning as in ii. 10, v. 9.

Ch. VIII. Having compared the two Priesthoods, and shewn the inferiority of the Aaronic priesthood to that of Christ as "a High Priest for ever after the order of Melchisedek," the writer now proceeds to contrast the two Covenants. After fixing the attention of his readers on Christ as the High Priest of the True Sanctuary (1—6) he shews that God, displeased with the disobedience of those who were under the Old Covenant, had by the prophet Jeremiah promised a New Covenant (7—9) which should

Now of the *things* which we have spoken *this is* the sum: **8** We have such a high priest, who is set on the right hand of the throne of the Majesty in the heavens; a minister of the **2** sanctuary, and of the true tabernacle, which the Lord

be superior to the Old in three respects. i. Because the Law of it should be written *on the heart* (10). ii. Because it should be universal (11), and iii. because it should be a covenant of forgiveness (12). The decrepitude of the Old Covenant, indicated by its being called "old" is a sign of its approaching and final evanescence (13).

1. *of the things which we have spoken this is the sum*] Rather, "the chief point in what we are saying is this." The word rendered "sum" (*kephalaion*) may mean, in its classical sense, "chief point," and that must be the meaning here, because these verses are *not* a summary and they add fresh particulars to what he has been saying. Dr Field renders it "now to crown our present discourse;" Tyndale and Cranmer, "*pyth*."

is set] Rather, "sat"—a mark of preeminence (x. 11, 12, xii. 2).

of the throne] This conception seems to be the origin of the Jewish word *Metatron*, a sort of Prince of all the Angels, near the throne (*meta thronios*).

of the Majesty in the heavens] A very Alexandrian expression. See note on i. 3.

2. *a minister*] From this word *leitourgos* (derived from λεώς, "people," and ἔργον, "work") comes our "liturgy."

of the sanctuary] This (and not "of holy things," or "of the saints") is the only tenable rendering of the word in this Epistle.

and] The "and" does not introduce something new; it merely furnishes a more definite explanation of the previous word.

of the true tabernacle] Rather, "of the genuine tabernacle" (*alethinēs* not *alethous*). The word *alethinos* means "*genuine*," and in this Epistle "*ideal*," "*archetypal*." It is the antithesis not to what is spurious, but to what is material, secondary, and transient. The Alexandrian Jews, as well as the Christian scholars of Alexandria, had adopted from Plato the doctrine of Ideas, which they regarded as divine and eternal archetypes of which material and earthly things were but the imperfect copies. They found their chief support for this introduction of Platonic views into the interpretation of the Bible in Ex. xxv. 40, xxvi. 30 (quoted in ver. 5). Accordingly they regarded the Mosaic tabernacle as a mere sketch, copy, or outline of the Divine Idea or Pattern. The Idea is the perfected Reality of its material shadow. They extended this conception much farther:

"What if earth
Be but the shadow of heaven, and things therein
Each to the other like, more than on earth is thought?"

The "genuine tabernacle" is the Heavenly Ideal (ix. 24) shewn to Moses. To interpret it of "the glorified body of Christ" by a mere

3 pitched, and not man. For every high priest is ordained to offer gifts and sacrifices: wherefore *it is* of necessity that
4 this *man* have somewhat also to offer. For if he were on earth, he should not be a priest, seeing that there are priests
5 that offer gifts according to the law: who serve unto the example and shadow of heavenly *things*, as Moses was ad-

verbal comparison of John ii. 19, is to adopt the all-but-universal method of perverting the meaning of Scripture by the artificial elaborations and inferential afterthoughts of a scholastic theology.

pitched] Lit. "fixed."
and not man] Omit "and." Not a man, as Moses was. Comp. ix. 11, 24.

3. *is ordained*] Rather, "is appointed."
gifts and sacrifices] See note on v. 1.
that this man] It would be better as in the R. V. to avoid introducing the word "man" which is not in the original, and to say "that this High Priest."
have somewhat also to offer] Namely, the Blood of His one sacrifice. The point is one of the extremest importance, and though the writer does not pause to explain *what* was the sacrifice which Christ offered as High Priest, he purposely introduces the subject here to prepare for his subsequent development of it in ix. 12, x. 5—7, 11, 12. Similarly St Paul tells us "Christ...hath given Himself for us, an offering and a sacrifice to God for a sweet-smelling savour" (Eph. v. 2).

4. *For if he were*] Rather, "now if He were still on earth."
if he were on earth] His sanctuary *must* be a heavenly one, for in the earthly one He had no standpoint.
he should not be a priest] He would not even be so much as a Priest at all; still less a High Priest; for He was of the Tribe of Judah (vii. 14), and the Law had distinctly ordained that "no stranger, which is not of the seed of Aaron, come near to offer incense before the Lord" (Num. xvi. 40).
seeing that there are priests that offer gifts according to the law] Rather (omitting "priests" with the best MSS.), since "there are (already) those who offer their gifts according to the Law." The writer could not possibly have used these *present tenses* if the Epistle had been written after the Fall of Jerusalem. Jewish institutions are, indeed, spoken of in the present tense, after the fall of Jerusalem, by Barnabas and Clement of Rome; but they are merely using an everyday figure of speech. In case of the Epistle to the Hebrews the argument would have gained such indefinite force and weight in passages like this by appealing to a fact so startling as the annulment of the Mosaic system by God Himself, working by the unmistakeable demonstrations of history, that no writer similarly circumstanced could possibly have passed over such a point in silence.

5. *who serve unto the example and shadow of heavenly things*] Namely, the priests—who are ministering in that which is nothing but an

v. 6.] HEBREWS, VIII. 129

monished of God when he was about to make the tabernacle: for, See, saith *he, that* thou make all *things* according to the pattern shewed to thee in the mount. But now hath he obtained a more excellent ministry, by how 6

outline and shadow (x. 1; Col. ii. 17) of the heavenly things. The verb "minister" usually takes a dative of the *person to whom* the ministry is paid. Here and in xiii. 10 the dative is used of *the thing* in which the service is done. It is conceivable that there is a shade of irony in this—they serve not a Living God, but a dead tabernacle. And this tabernacle is only a sketch, an outline, a ground pattern (1 Chron. xxviii. 11) as it were—at the best a representative image—of the Heavenly Archetype.

of heavenly things] Perhaps rather "of the heavenly sanctuary" (ix. 23, 24).

as Moses was admonished...] "Even as Moses, when about to complete the tabernacle has been divinely admonished".... On this use of the perfect see note on iv. 9, &c. The verb is used of divine intimations in Matt. ii. 12; Luke ii. 26; Acts x. 22, &c.

all things] This expression is not found either in the Hebrew or the LXX. of the passages referred to (Ex. xxv. 40, xxvi. 30); it seems to be due to Philo (*De Leg. Alleg.* III. 33), who *may*, however, have followed some older reading.

according to the pattern shewed to thee in the mount] Here, as is so often the case in comments on Scripture, we are met by the idlest of all speculations, as to whether Moses saw this "pattern" in a dream or with his waking eyes; whether the pattern was something real or merely an impression produced upon his senses; whether the tabernacle was thus a copy or only "a copy of a copy and a shadow of a shadow," &c. Such questions are otiose, because even if they were worth asking at all they do not admit of any answer, and involve no instruction, and no result of the smallest value. The Palestinian Jews in their slavish literal way said that there was in Heaven an exact literal counterpart of the Mosaic Tabernacle with "a fiery Ark, a fiery Table, a fiery Candlestick," &c., which descended from heaven for Moses to see; and that Gabriel, in a workman's apron, shewed Moses how to make the candlestick,—an inference which they founded on Num. viii. 4, "And *this* work of the candlestick" (Menachoth, f. 29. 1). Without any such fetish-worship of the letter it is quite enough to accept the simple statement that Moses worked after a pattern which God had brought before his mind. The chief historical interest in the verse is the fact that it was made the basis for the Scriptural Idealism by which Philo and the Alexandrian Jews tried to combine Judaism with the Platonic philosophy, and to treat the whole material world as a shadow of the spiritual world.

6. *But now*] i. e. but, as it is.

a more excellent ministry, by how much also] Rather, "a ministry more excellent in proportion as He is also." This proportional method

much also he is the mediator of a better covenant, which was established upon better promises. 7 For if that first *covenant* had been faultless, *then* should 8 no place have been sought for the second. For finding

of stating results runs throughout the Epistle (see i. 4, iii. 3, vii. 22). It might be said with truth that the gist of his argument turns on the word "how much more." He constantly adopts the *argumentum a minori ad majus* (vii. 19, 22, ix. 11, 14, 23, x. 29). For his object was to shew the Hebrews that the privileges of Judaism to which they were looking back with such longing eyes were but transitory outlines and quivering shadows of the more blessed, and more eternal privileges which they enjoyed as Christians. Judaism was but a shadow of which Christianity was the substance; Judaism was but a copy of which Christianity was the permanent Idea, and heavenly Archetype; it was but a scaffolding within which the genuine Temple had been built; it was but a chrysalis from which the inward winged life had departed.

the mediator] ix. 15, xii. 24; 1 Tim. ii. 5.

upon better promises] Better, because not physical but spiritual, and not temporal but heavenly and eternal. Bengel notices that the main words in the verse are all Pauline. Rom. ix. 4; 1 Tim. ii. 5.

7—13. THREEFOLD SUPERIORITY OF THE NEW TO THE OLD COVENANT, AS PROPHESIED BY JEREMIAH; BEING A PROOF THAT THE "PROMISES" OF THE NEW COVENANT ARE "BETTER."

7. *if that first covenant had been faultless*] Whereas it was as he has said "weak" and "unprofitable" and "earthly" (vii. 18). The difference between the writer's treatment of the relation between Christianity and Judaism and St Paul's mode of dealing with the same subject consists in this:—to St Paul the contrast between the Law and the Gospel was that between the Letter and the Spirit, between bondage and freedom, between Works and Faith, between Command and Promise, between threatening and mercy. All these polemical elements disappear almost entirely from the Epistle to the Hebrews, which regards the two dispensations as furnishing a contrast between Type and Reality. This was the more possible to Apollos because he regards Judaism not so much in the light of a Law as in the light of a Priesthood and a system of worship. Like those who had been initiated into the ancient mysteries the Christian convert from Judaism could say ἔφυγον κακόν, εὗρον ἄμεινον—"I fled the bad, I found the better;" not that Judaism was in any sense intrinsically and inherently "*bad*" (Rom. vii. 12), but that it became so when it was preferred to something so much more divine.

8. *For finding fault with them*] The "for" introduces his proof that "place for a better covenant was being sought for." The persons blamed are not expressed, for the word "them" belongs to "He says." Perhaps the meaning is "blaming the first covenant, He says to them" (who were under it). The "He" is God speaking to the Prophet.

fault with them, *he* saith, Behold, the days come, saith
the Lord, when I will make a new covenant with
the house of Israel and with the house of Juda:
not according to the covenant that I made with 9
their fathers in the day when I took them by the
hand to lead them out of the land of Egypt; because they continued not in my covenant, and I regarded them not, saith the Lord. For this *is* the 10
covenant that I will make with the house of Israel
after those days, saith the Lord; I will put my laws
into their mind, and write them in their hearts:
and I will be to them a God, and they shall be to
me a people: and they shall not teach every man 11
his neighbour, and every man his brother, saying,
Know the Lord: for all shall know me, from the

Behold, the days come...] The quotation is from Jer. xxxi. 31—34.
I will make] The Hebrew word means literally "I will cut,"
alluding perhaps to the slaying of victims at the inauguration of a
covenant. But the LXX. and the writer of the Epistle substitute a less
literal word.

9. *I took them by the hand*] See note on ii. 16.

because they continued not in my covenant] The disobedience of the
Israelites was a cause for nullifying the covenant which they had trans-
gressed (Judg. ii. 20, 21; 2 Kings xvii. 15—18). Comp. Hos. i. 9, "Ye
are not my people, and I will not be your God."

and I regarded them not] These words correspond to the "though I
was a husband unto them" of the original. The quotation is from the
LXX., who perhaps followed a slightly different reading. Rabbi
Kimchi holds that the rendering of the LXX. is justifiable even with
the present reading.

10. *and write them in their hearts*] The gift of an *inner* law, not
written on granite slabs, but on the fleshen tablets of the heart, is the
first promise of the New Covenant. It involves the difference between
the Voice of the Spirit of the God in the Conscience and a rigid external law; the difference, that is, between spirituality and legalism.
This is brought out in Ezek. xxxvi. 26—29.

I will be to them a God] For similar prophecies see Zech. viii. 8;
Hos. ii. 23; and for their fulfilment 1 Pet. ii. 9, 10; 2 Cor. vi. 16—18.

11. *his neighbour*] Lit. "his fellow-citizen."

for all shall know me] The *second* promise of the New Covenant is
that there shall be no *appropriation* of knowledge; no sacerdotal exclusiveness; no learned caste that shall monopolise the keys of knowledge, and lock out those that desire to enter in. "*All* thy children
shall be taught of the Lord" (Is. liv. 13), and all shall be "a chosen
generation, a royal priesthood, a holy nation, a peculiar people."

9—2

12 least to the greatest. For I will be merciful to their unrighteousness, and their sins and their ini-
13 quities will I remember no more. In that *he* saith, A new *covenant*, he hath made the first old. Now that which decayeth and waxeth old *is* ready to vanish away.

all shall know me] By virtue of the anointing of the Holy Spirit, which "teacheth us of all things" (1 John ii. 27).

from the least to the greatest] That is, from the eldest to the youngest (Gen. xix. 11; Acts viii. 10, &c.).

12. *I will be merciful to their unrighteousness*] Comp. Rom. xi. 27. The *third* promise of the New Covenant is the forgiveness of sins, with a fulness and reality which could not be achieved by the sacrifices of the Old Covenant (see ii. 15, ix. 9, 12, x. 1, 2, 4, 22). Under the Old Covenant there had been a deep feeling of the nullity of sacrifices *in themselves*, which led to an almost startling disparagement of the sacrificial system (1 Sam. xv. 22; Ps. xl. 6, l. 8—10, li. 16; Mic. vi. 6, 7; Is. i. 11; Hos. vi. 6; Am. v. 21, 22, &c.).

13. *he hath made the first old*] The very expression, "a New Covenant," used in the disparaging connexion in which it stands, superannuates the former covenant, and stamps it as *antiquated*. The verse is a specimen of the deep sense which it was the constant object of Alexandrian interpreters to deduce from Scripture. The argument is analogous to that of vii. 11.

Now that which decayeth and waxeth old is ready to vanish away] Lit. "Now that which is becoming antiquated and waxing aged, is near obliteration." The expression "*near* evanescence" again shows that the Epistle was written before the Fall of Jerusalem, when the decree of dissolution which had been passed upon the Old Covenant was carried into effect. Even the Rabbis, though they made the Law an object of superstitious and extravagant veneration, yet sometimes admitted that it would ultimately cease to be—namely, when "the Evil Impulse" (Deut. xxxi. 21) should be overcome.

ready to vanish away] Comp. the expression "near a curse" (vi. 8), and Dr Kay points out the curious fact that "curse" and "obliteration" (*aphanismos* here alone in the N. T.) appear in juxtaposition in 2 Kings xxii. 19 (where our version renders it "desolation").

CH. IX. After thus tracing the contrast between the Two Covenants, the writer proceeds to shew the difference between their *ordinances of ministration* (ix. 1—x. 18). He contrasts the sanctuary (1—5), the offering, and the access (6, 7) of the Levitical Priests, in their shadowy and inefficacious ritual (9, 10), with the sanctuary (11), the offering, and the access of Christ (12), stating how far superior was the efficacy of Christ's work (13, 14). In the remainder of the chapter (15—28) he explains the perfection and indispensableness of Christ's one sacrifice for sin. His object in this great section of the Epistle is to prove to the Hebrews that Christ is "the end of the Law;" that by His sacrifice all other sacrifices have been rendered

Then verily the first *covenant* had also ordinances of 9 divine service, and a worldly sanctuary. For there was a 2 tabernacle made; the first, wherein *was* the candlestick, and the table, and the shewbread; which is called the

needless; and that unlike the brief, intermittent, and partial access of the High Priest to the Holy of Holies on the Day of Atonement, we have through Christ a perfect, universal, and continuous access to God.

1. *Then verily the first tabernacle had also ordinances*] Rather, "To resume then, even the first (*covenant*) had its ordinances." No substantive is expressed with "first," but the train of reasoning in the last chapter sufficiently shews that "Covenant," not "Tabernacle," is the word to be supplied.

had] Although he often refers to the Levitic ordinances as still continuing, he here contemplates them as obsolete and practically annulled.

and a worldly sanctuary] Rather, "and its sanctuary—a material one." The word *kosmikon*, rendered "worldly," means that the Jewish Sanctuary was visible and temporary—a *mundane* structure in contrast to the Heavenly, Eternal Sanctuary. The adjective "worldly" only occurs here and in Tit. ii. 12.

2. *made*] "prepared" or "established." He treats of the Sanctuary in 2—5, and of the Services in 6—10.

the first] By this is not meant the Tabernacle in contrast with the Temple, but "*the outer chamber* (or Holy Place)." It is however true that the writer is thinking exclusively of the Tabernacle of the Wilderness, which was the proper representative of the worship of the Old Covenant. He seems to have regarded the later Temples as deflections from the divine pattern, and he wanted to take all that was Judaic at its best. His description applies to the Tabernacle only. It is doubtful whether the seven-branched candlestick was preserved in the Temple of Solomon; there was certainly no ark or mercy-seat, much less a Shechinah, in the Herodian Temple of this period. When Pompey profanely forced his way into the Holy of Holies he found to his great astonishment *nothing whatever* (*vacua omnia*).

was] Rather, "is." The whole tabernacle is ideally present to the writer's imagination.

the candlestick] Ex. xxv. 31—39, xxxvii. 17—24. The word would more accurately be rendered "lamp-stand." In Solomon's temple there seem to have been ten (1 Kings vii. 49). There was indeed one only in the Herodian temple (1 Macc. i. 21, iv. 49; Jos. *Antt.* XII. 7. § 6, and allusions in the Talmud) It could not however have exactly resembled the famous figure carved on the Arch of Titus (as Josephus hints in a mysterious phrase, Jos. *B. J.* VII. 5. § 5), for that has marine monsters carved upon its pediment, which would have been a direct violation of the second commandment.

and the table] Ex. xxv. 23—30, xxxvii. 10—16. There were ten

3 sanctuary. And after the second vail, the tabernacle which
4 is called the holiest of all; which had the golden censer,

such tables of acacia-wood overlaid with gold in Solomon's temple (2 Chron. iv. 8, 19).

and the shewbread] Lit. "the setting forth of the loaves." The Hebrew name for it is "the bread of the face" (i.e. placed before the presence of God), Ex. xxv. 23—30; Lev. xxiv. 5—9.

which is called the sanctuary] In the O.T. *Kodesh*, "the Holy Place."

3. *after the second vail*] Rather, "behind the second veil." There were two veils in the Tabernacle—one called *Másák* (Ex. xxvi. 36, 37, LXX. *kalumma* or *epispastron*) which hung before the entrance; and "the second," called *Purocheth* (LXX. *katapetasma*) which hung between the Holy Place and the Holiest (Ex. xxvi. 31—35). The Rabbis invent *two* curtains between the Holy Place and the Holiest with a space of a cubit between them, to which they give the name *Tarkesin*, which is of uncertain origin. They had many fables about the size and weight of this curtain—that it was a hand-breadth thick, and took 300 priests to draw it, &c. &c.

the holiest of all] Lit. "the Holy of Holies," a name which, like the Latin *Sancta Sanctorum* is the exact translation of the Hebrew *Kodesh Hakkodashim*. In Solomon's Temple it was called "the Oracle."

4. *the golden censer*] The Greek word is *thumiaterion*, and it has been long disputed whether it means Censer or Altar of Incense. It does not occur in the Greek version of the Pentateuch (except as a various reading) where the "altar of incense" is rendered by *thusiasterion thumiamatos* (Ex. xxxi. 8; comp. Lk. i. 11); but it is used by the LXX. in 2 Chron. xxvi. 19; Ezek. viii. 11, and there means "censer;" and the Rabbis say that "a golden censer" was used by the High Priest on the Day of Atonement only (*Yoma*, IV. 4). "Censer" accordingly is the rendering of the word in this place in the Vulgate, Syriac, Arabic and Æthiopic versions; and the word is so understood by many commentators ancient and modern. On the other hand (which is very important) both in Josephus (*Antt.* III. 6 § 8) and in Philo (Opp. I. 504) the word *thumiaterion* means "*the Altar of Incense*," which, like the table, might be called "golden," because it was overlaid with gold; and this is the sense of the word in other Hellenistic writers of this period down to Clemens of Alexandria. The Altar of Incense was so important that it is most unlikely to have been left unmentioned. Further, it is observable that we are not told of *any* censer kept in the *Tabernacle*, but only in the Temple. The incense in the days of the Tabernacle was burnt in a *machettah* (πυρεῖον, "brazier," Lev. xvi. 12); nor could the censer have been kept in the Holiest Place, for then the High Priest must have gone in to fetch it before kindling the incense, which would have been contrary to all the symbolism of the ritual.

But it is asserted that the writer is in any case mistaken, for that *neither* the censer nor the "altar of incense" were in the Holiest.

But this is not certain as regards the censer. It is possible that some

and the ark of the covenant overlaid round about with gold, wherein *was* the golden pot that had manna, and Aaron's

golden censer-stand may have stood in the Holiest, on which the High Priest placed the small golden brazier (*machettah*, LXX. *pureion*), which he carried with him. There is indeed no doubt that the "Altar of Incense" was *not* in the *Holiest* Place, but as all authorities combine in telling us, in the Holy Place. But there was a possibility of mistake about the point because in Ex. xxvi. 35 only the table and the lampstand are mentioned; and Ex. xxx. 6 is a little vague. Yet the writer does not say that the altar of incense was *in* the Holiest. It was impossible that any *Jew* should have made such a mistake, unless he were, as Delitzsch says, "a monster of ignorance;" and if he had been unaware of the fact otherwise, he would have found from Philo in several places (*De Victim Offer.* § 4; *Quis Rer. Div. Haer.* § 46) that the Altar (which Philo also calls *thumiaterion*) was outside the Holiest. Josephus also mentions this, and it was universally notorious (*B. J.* v. 5, § 5). Accordingly, the writer only says that the Holiest "*had*" the Altar of Incense, in other words that the Altar in some sense *belonged to it*. And this is rigidly accurate; for in 1 Kings vi. 22 the altar is described as "belonging to" the Oracle (lit. "the Altar which *was to* the Oracle," *laddebīr*), and on the Day of Atonement the curtain was drawn, and the Altar was intimately associated with the High Priest's service in the Holiest Place. Indeed the Altar of Incense (since incense was supposed to have an atoning power, Num. xvi. 47) *was itself called* "Holy of Holies" (A.V. "most holy," Ex. xxx. 10) and is expressly said (Ex. xxx. 6, xl. 5) to be placed "*before* the mercy-seat." In Is. vi. 1—8 a seraph flies from above the mercy-seat to the Altar. The writer then, though he is not entering into details with pedantic minuteness, has not made any mistake; nor is there the smallest ground for the idle conjecture that he was thinking of the Jewish Temple at Leontopolis. The close connection of the Altar of Incense with the service of the Day of Atonement in the Holiest Place is illustrated by 2 Macc. ii. 1—8, where the Altar is mentioned in connexion with the Ark.

the ark of the covenant] This, as we have seen, applies only to the Tabernacle and to Solomon's Temple. "There was nothing whatever," as Josephus tells us, in the Holiest Place of the Temple after the Exile (*B. J.* v. 5. § 5). The stone on which the ark had once stood, called by the Rabbis "the stone of the Foundation," alone was visible.

overlaid round about with gold] The word "round about" means literally "on all sides," i.e. "within and without" (Ex. xxv. 11).

with gold] The diminutive χρυσίῳ here used for gold seems to imply nothing distinctive. Diminutives always tend to displace the simple forms in late dialects.

the golden pot that had manna...] The Palestine Targum says that it was an *earthen* jar, but Jewish tradition asserted that it was of gold. The LXX. inserts the word "golden" in Ex. xvi. 33 and so does Philo. It contained an "omer" of the manna, which was the daily portion for each person. The writer distinctly seems to imply that the Ark

5 rod that budded, and the tables of the covenant; and over it the cherubims of glory shadowing the mercy seat; of 6 which *we* cannot now speak particularly. Now when these

contained three things—a golden jar (*stamnos*) containing a specimen of the manna, Aaron's rod that budded, and the Stone Tables of the Decalogue. Here again it is asserted that he made a mistake. Certainly the Stone Tables were in the Ark, and the whole symbolism of the Ark represented the Cherubim bending in adoration over the blood-sprinkled propitiatory which covered the tables of the broken moral law. But Moses was only bidden to lay up the jar and the rod "*before the Testimony,*" not "*in the Ark;*" and in 1 Kings viii. 9; 2 Chron. v. 10 we are somewhat emphatically informed that "there was nothing in the Ark" except these two tables, which we are told (Deut. x. 2, 5) that Moses placed there. All that can be said is that the writer is not thinking of the Temple of Solomon at all, and that there is nothing impossible in the Jewish tradition here followed, which supposes that "before the Testimony" was interpreted to mean "in the Ark." Rabbis like Levi Ben Gershom and Abarbanel had certainly no desire to vindicate the accuracy of the Epistle to the Hebrews, and yet they say that the pot and the rod were actually at one time *in* the Ark, though they had been removed from it before the days of Solomon.

Aaron's rod that budded] Num. xvii. 6—10.

5. *the cherubims*] Rather, "the Cherubim," since *im* is the Hebrew plural termination.

of glory] Not "the glorious Cherubim" but "the Cherubim of the Shechinah" or cloud of glory. This was regarded as the symbol of God's presence, and was believed to rest between their outspread wings (see 1 Sam. iv. 22; 2 Kings xix. 15; Hag. ii. 7—9; Ecclus. xlix. 8). They were emblems of all that was highest and best in animated nature—the grandest products of creation combined in one living angelic symbol (Ezek. x. 4)—upholding the throne of the Eternal as on "a chariot" and bending in adoring contemplation of the moral law as the revelation of God's will.

the mercy-seat] The Greek word "*hilasterion*" or "propitiatory" is the translation used by the LXX. for the Hebrew *Cappóreth* or "covering." The word probably meant no more than "lid" or "cover;" but the LXX. understood it metaphorically of the covering of sins or expiation, because the blood of the expiatory offering was sprinkled upon it.

of which we cannot now speak particularly] Rather, "severally," "in detail." It was no part of the writer's immediate purpose to enter upon an explanation of that symbolism of the Tabernacle which has largely occupied the attention of Jewish historians and Talmudists as well as of modern writers. Had he done so he would doubtless have thrown light upon much that is now obscure. But he is pressing on to his point, which is to shew that even the most solemn and magnificent act of the whole Jewish ritual—the ceremony of the Day of

things were thus ordained, the priests went always into the first tabernacle, accomplishing the service *of God*. But into 7 the second *went* the high priest alone once every year, not without blood, which he offered for himself, and *for* the errors of the people: the Holy Ghost this signifying, that 8 the way into the holiest *of all* was not yet made manifest, while as the first tabernacle was yet standing: which *was* a 9 Atonement—bears upon its face the signs of complete transitoriness and inefficiency when compared with the work of Christ.

6. *Now when these things were thus ordained*] Rather, "since then these things have been thus arranged."

went always into the first tabernacle, accomplishing the service of God] Rather, "into the outer tabernacle the priests enter continually in performance of their ministrations." Their ordinary ministrations were to offer sacrifice, burn incense, and light the lamps, and in the performance of these they certainly entered the Holy Place twice daily, and apparently might do so as often as they saw fit.

7. *But into the second*] i.e. "the inner," "the Holiest." There was a graduated sanctity in the Tabernacle and in the Temple. In the Temple any one might go into the Outer Court or Court of the Gentiles; Jews into the Second Court; men only into the Third; priests only in their robes into the Holy Place; and only the High Priest into the inmost shrine (Jos. *c. Apion.* II. 8).

once every year] i.e. only on one day of the whole year, viz. on the tenth day of the seventh month Tisri, the Day of Atonement. In the course of that day he had to enter it at least three, and possibly four times, namely (1) with the incense, (2) with the blood of the bullock offered for his own sins, (3) with the blood of the goat for the sins of the people, and perhaps (4) to remove the censer (Lev. xvi. 12—16; Yoma, v. 2). But these entrances were practically one.

offered] The present "offers" is here used, as before.

for the errors of the people] Lit. "for the ignorances," but the word seems to be used in the LXX. to include sins as well as errors (v. 2, 3; Ex. xxxiv. 7; Lev. xvi. 2, 11, 34; Num. xv. 27—31).

8. *that the way into the holiest...was not yet made manifest*] Entrance into the Holiest symbolised direct access to God, and the "way" into it had not been made evident until He came who is "the way, the truth, and the life" (John xiv. 6). He is "the new and living way" (x. 19, 20).

while as the first tabernacle was yet standing] Rather, "while yet the *outer* Tabernacle is still standing," i.e. so long as there is (for the Temple, which represented the continuity of the Tabernacle and the Old Covenant, had not sunk in flames, as it did a few years later) an outer Tabernacle, through which not even a Priest was ever allowed to enter into the Holiest. Hence the deep significance of the rending of the veil of the Temple from the top to the bottom at the Crucifixion. (Matt. xxvii. 51).

figure for the time *then* present, in which were offered both gifts and sacrifices, that could not make him that did the service perfect, as pertaining to the conscience; *which stood only in meats and drinks, and divers washings, and carnal*

9. *which was a figure for the time then present*] i.e. And this outer Tabernacle is a parable for the present time. By "the present time" he means the prae-Christian epoch in which the unconverted Jews were still (practically) living. The full inauguration of the New Covenant of which Christ had prophesied as his Second Coming, began with the final annulment of the Old, which was only completed when the Temple fell, and when the observance of the Levitic system thus became (by the manifest interposition of God in history) a thing simply *impossible*. A Christian was already living in "the Future Aeon" (*Olam habba*); a Jew who had not embraced the Gospel still belonged to "the present time" (*olam hazzeh ὁ καιρὸς ὁ ἐνεστηκώς*). The meaning of the verse is that the very existence of an *outer* Tabernacle ("the Holy Place") emphasized the fact that close access to God (of which the entrance of the High Priest into the Holiest was a symbol) was not permitted under the Old Covenant.

in which...] The true reading is not καθ' ὅν but καθ' ἥν, so that the "which" refers to the word "parable" or "symbol," "in accordance with which symbolism of the outer Tabernacle, both gifts and sacrifices are being offered, such as (μὴ) are not able, so far as the *conscience* is concerned, to perfect the worshipper." He says "are offered" and "him that *does* the service," using the present (not as in the A.V. the past tense), because he is throwing himself into the position of the Jew who still clings to the Old Covenant. The introduction of "a clear conscience" (or moral consciousness) into the question may seem like a new thought, but it is not. The implied argument is this: only the innocent can "ascend the hill of the Lord, and stand in His Holy Place:" the High Priest was regarded as *symbolically* innocent by virtue of minute precautions against any ceremonial defilement, and because he carried with him the atonement for his own sins and those of the people: *he* therefore, *but he alone*, was permitted to approach God by entering the Holiest Place. The worshippers in general were so little regarded as "perfected in conscience" that only the Priests could enter even the *outer* "Holy" (vii. 18, 19, x. 1—4, 11).

10. *which stood only in meats and drinks*] The "which" of the A.V. refers to the "present time." The Greek is here elliptical, for the verse begins with the words "only upon." The meaning is that the "gifts and sacrifices" consist only in meats and drinks and divers washings—being ordinances of the flesh, imposed (only) till the season of reformation.

meats] Ex. xii.; Lev. xi.; Num. vi.

drinks] Lev. x. 8, 9; Num. vi. 2, 3; Lev. xi. 34.

divers washings] Lev. viii. 6, 12; Ex. xl. 31, 32; Num. xix. and the Levitical law *passim*. All these things had already been disparaged by Christ as meaning nothing *in themselves* (Mark vii. 1—15); and

ordinances, imposed *on them* until the time of reformation. But Christ being come a high priest of good *things* to come, by a greater and more perfect tabernacle, not made with hands, that is to say, not of this building, neither by the

St Paul had written "Let no man judge you in meat, or in drink... which are a shadow of things to come; but the body is of Christ" (Col. ii. 16, 17).

and carnal ordinances] This is a wrong reading. The "and" should be omitted, and for *dikaiomasi* we should read *dikaiomata* in the accusative case. It stands in apposition to the sentence in general, and to the "gifts and sacrifices" of the last verse; they could not assure the conscience, because they had only to do with meats, &c.— being only ordinances of the flesh, i.e. outward, transitory, superficial.

imposed on them] There is no need for the "on them." The verb means "imposed as a burden," "lying as a yoke." Comp. Acts xv. 10, 28; Gal. v. 1.

until the time of reformation] The season of reformation is that of which Jeremiah prophesied: it is in fact the New Covenant, see viii. 7—12. The "yoke of bondage," which consists of a galling and wearisome externalism, was then changed for "an easy yoke and a light burden" (Matt. xi. 29).

11—14. ASSURANCE OF CONSCIENCE, THE CONDITION OF ACCESS TO GOD, WAS SECURED THROUGH CHRIST ALONE.

11. *being come*] "Being come among us."

a high priest of good things to come] Another and perhaps better reading is "of the good things that have come" (γενομένων B, D, not μελλόντων). The writer here transfers himself from the Jewish to the Christian standpoint. The "good things" of which the Law was only "the shadow" (x. 1) were still future to the Jew, but to the Christian they had already come.

by a greater and more perfect tabernacle] The preposition *dia* rendered "by" may mean either "*through*"—in which case "the greater and better tabernacle" means the outer heavens through which Christ (anthropomorphically speaking) passed (see ver. 24 and iv. 14); or "*by means of*"—in which case "the better tabernacle" is left undefined, and may *here* mean either the human nature in which for the time "He tabernacled" (x. 20; John i. 14, ii. 19; Col. ii. 9; 2 Cor. v. 1), or as in viii. 2, the Ideal Church of the firstborn in heaven (comp. Eph. i. 3).

not made with hands] Because whatever tabernacle is specifically meant it is one which "the Lord pitched, not man."

not of this building] The word *ktisis* may mean either "building" or "creation." If the latter, then the meaning is that the better tabernacle, through which Christ entered, does not belong to the material world. But since *ktizo* means "to build," *ktisis* may mean "building," and then the word "this" by a rare idiom means

blood of goats and calves, but by his own blood he entered in once into the holy *place*, having obtained eternal re- 13 demption *for us*. For if the blood of bulls and of goats, and the ashes of a heifer sprinkling the unclean, sanctifieth

"vulgar," "ordinary" (Field, *Otium Norvicense*, III. 142); otherwise the clause would be a mere tautology.

12. *neither*] "Nor yet."

by the blood of goats and calves] "by means of the blood of goats and calves," (this is the order of the words in the best MSS.). It is not meant that the sacrifices of the Old Covenant were *useless*, but only that when they were regarded as meritorious *in themselves*—apart from the faith, and the grace of God, by which they could be blessed to sincere and humble worshippers—they could neither purge the conscience, nor give access to God. When the Prophets speak of sacrifices with such stern disparagement they are only denouncing the superstition which regarded the mere *opus operatum* as sufficient apart from repentance and holiness (Hos. vi. 6; Is. i. 10—17, &c.).

by his own blood] His own blood was the offering by which He was admitted *as our High Priest* and *Eternal Redeemer* into the Holy of Holies of God's immediate presence (xiii. 20; Rev. v. 6).

once] "once for all."

into the holy place] i.e. into the Holiest, as in Lev. xvi. 3, 9.

eternal redemption] i.e. "the forgiveness of sins" (Eph. i. 7), and ransom from sinful lives (1 Pet. i. 18, 19) to the service of God (Rev. v. 9). It should always be borne in mind that the Scriptural metaphors of Ransom and Propitiation describe the Atonement by its blessed effects *as regards man*. All speculation as to its bearing on the counsels of God, all attempts to frame a scholastic scheme out of metaphors only intended to indicate a transcendent mystery, *by its results for us* have led to heresy and error. *To whom* was the ransom paid? The question is idle, because "ransom" is only a metaphor of *our deliverance* from slavery. For nearly a thousand years the Church was content with the most erroneous, and almost blasphemous notion that the ransom was *paid by God to the devil*, which led to still more grievous aberrations. Anselm who exploded this error substituted for it *another*—the hard forensic notion of indispensable *satisfaction*. Such terms, like those of "substitution," "vicarious punishment," "reconciliation of God to us" (for "of *us* to God"), have no sanction in Scripture, which only reveals what is necessary for man, and what man can understand, viz. that the love of God in Christ has provided for him a way of escape from ruin, and the forgiveness of sins.

having obtained...for us] The "for us" is rightly supplied; but the *middle voice* of the verb shews that Christ in His love to us also regarded the redemption as dear to Himself.

13. *if the blood of bulls and of goats, and the ashes of a heifer sprinkling the unclean*] The writer has designedly chosen the two most striking sacrifices and ceremonials of the Levitical Law, namely the calf and the

to the purifying of the flesh: how much more shall the blood of Christ, who through the eternal Spirit offered himself without spot to God, purge your conscience from dead works to serve the living God?

goat offered for the sins of people and priest on the Day of Atonement (Lev. xvi.) and "the water of separation," or rather "of impurity," i.e. "to remove impurity" "as a sin-offering" described in Num. xix. 1—22 (comp. Heb. vii. 26).

of a heifer] The Jews have the interesting legend that *nine* such red heifers had been slain between the time of Moses and the destruction of the Temple.

the unclean] Those that have become ceremonially defiled, especially by having touched a corpse.

sanctifieth to the purifying of the flesh] i.e. if these things are adequate to restore a man to ceremonial cleanness which was a type of moral purity. So much efficacy they *had*; they did make the worshipper ceremonially pure before God: their further and deeper efficacy depended on the faith and sincerity with which they were offered, and was derived from the one offering of which they were a type.

14. *how much more*] Again we have the characteristic word—the key-note as it were—of the Epistle.

the blood of Christ] which is typified by "the fountain opened for sin and for uncleanness" (Zech. xiii. 1).

who through the eternal Spirit] If this be the right rendering the reference must be to the fact that Christ was "quickened by the Spirit" (1 Pet. iii. 18); that "God gave not the Spirit by measure unto Him" (John iii. 34); that "the Spirit of the Lord was upon Him" (Lk. iv. 18); that He "by the Spirit of God" cast out devils (Matt. xii. 28). For this view of the meaning see Pearson *on the Creed*, Art. III., and it is represented by the reading "Holy" for Eternal in some cursive MSS. and some versions. It may however be rendered "by *an* Eternal Spirit," namely by *His own* Spirit—by that burning love which proceeded from His own Spirit—and not by a mere "ordinance of the flesh" (vers. 10). In the Levitic sacrifices involuntary victims bled; but Christ's sacrifice was offered by the will of His own Eternal Spirit.

without spot] Christ had that *sinless perfection* which was dimly foreshadowed by the unblemished victims which could alone be offered under the Levitic law (1 Pet. i. 19).

from dead works] See vi. 1. If *sinful* works are meant, they are represented as affixing a *stain* to the conscience; they pollute as the touching of a dead thing polluted ceremonially under the Old Law (Num. xix. 11—16). But all works are "dead" which are done without love. It is to be observed that the writer—true to the Alexandrian training which instilled an awful reverence respecting Divine things—attempts even less than St Paul to explain the *modus operandi*. He tells us that the Blood of Christ redeems and purifies us as the old sacrifices could not do. Sacrifices removed ceremonial defilement —they thus "purified the flesh:" but the Blood of Christ perfects and

15 And for this cause he is the mediator of the new testament, that by means of death, for the redemption of the transgressions that were under the first testament, they which are called might receive the promise of eternal inheritance. 16 For where a testament *is*, there must also of

purifies the conscience (x. 22) and so admits us into the Presence of God. The "*how* can this be?" belongs to the secret things which God has not revealed; we only know and believe that so it *is*.

to serve the living God] Not to serve "dead works" or a mere material tabernacle, or fleshly ordinances, but to serve the Living God who can only be truly served by those who are "alive from the dead" (Rom. vi. 13).

15—28. THE INDISPENSABLENESS AND EFFICACY OF THE DEATH OF CHRIST.

15. *for this cause*] i.e. on account of the grandeur of His offering.

the mediator of the new testament] Rather, "a mediator of a NEW Covenant." Moses had been called by Philo "the Mediator" of the Old Covenant, i.e. he who came between God and Israel as the messenger of it. But Christ's intervention—His coming as One who revealed God to man—was accompanied with a sacrifice so infinitely more efficacious that it involved a NEW Covenant altogether.

by means of death] This version renders the passage entirely unintelligible. The true rendering and explanation seem to be as follows: "And on this account He is a Mediator of a *New* Covenant, that—since death" [namely the death of sacrificial victims] "occurred for the redemption of the transgressions which took place under the first covenant—those who have been called [whether Christians, or faithful believers under the Old Dispensation] may [by virtue of *Christ's* death, which the death of those victims typified] receive [i.e. actually enjoy the fruition of, vi. 12, 17, x. 36, xi. 13] the promise of the Eternal Inheritance." Volumes of various explanations have been written on this verse, but the explanation given above is very simple. The verse is a sort of reason why Christ's death was necessary. The ultimate, *a priori*, reason he does not attempt to explain, because it transcends all understanding; but he merely says that since under the Old Covenant *death* was necessary, and victims had to be slain in order that by their blood men might be purified, and the High Priest might enter the Holiest Place, so, under the New Covenant, a better and more efficacious death was necessary, both to give to those old sacrifices the only real validity which they possessed, and to secure for all of God's elect an eternal heritage.

16. *For where a testament is*] In these two verses (16, 17), and these only, *Diathēkē* is used in its Greek and Roman sense of "a will," and not in its Hebrew sense of "a covenant." The sudden and momentary change in the significance of the word explains itself, for he has just spoken of *an inheritance*, and of the *necessity for a death*. It was there-

necessity be the death of the testator. For a testament *is* 17
of force after *men* are dead: otherwise it is of no strength
at all whilst the testator liveth. Whereupon neither the 18

fore quite natural that he should be reminded of the fact that just as the Old Covenant (*Diathēkē*) required the constant infliction of *death* upon the sacrificed victims, and therefore (by analogy) necessitated the death of Christ under the New, so the word *Diathēkē* in its other sense of "Will" or "Testament" (which was by this epoch familiar also to the Jews) involved the necessity of death, because a will assigns the inheritance of a man who is dead. This may be called "a mere play on words;" but *such* a play on words is perfectly admissible in itself; just as we might speak of the "New Testament" (meaning the Book) as "a testament" (meaning "a will") sealed by a Redeemer's blood. An illustration of this kind was peculiarly consonant with the deep mystic significance attached by the Alexandrian thinkers to the sounds and the significance of words. Philo also avails himself of both meanings of *Diathēkē* (*De Nom. Mutat.* § 6; *De Sacr. Abel*, Opp. I. 586. 172). The passing illustration which thus occurs to the writer does not indeed explain or attempt to explain the eternal necessity why Christ must die; he leaves that in all its awful mystery, and merely gives prominence to the *fact* that the death *was* necessary, by saying that since under the Old Covenant death was required, so the New Covenant was inaugurated by a better death; and since a Will supposes that some one has died, so this "Will," by which *we* inherit, involves the necessity that Christ must die. The Old Covenant could not be called "a Will" in any ordinary sense; but the New Covenant was, by no remote analogy, the Will and Bequest of Christ.

there must also of necessity be the death of the testator] Wherever there is a will, the supposition that the maker of the will has died is implied, or legally involved (φέρεσθαι, *constare*).

17. *after men are dead*] This rendering expresses the meaning rightly—a will is only valid "in cases of death," "in the case of men who are dead." *Ex vi termini*, "a testament," is the disposition which a man makes of his affairs with a view to his death. The attempt to confine the word *diathēkē* to the sense of "covenant" which it holds throughout the rest of the Epistle has led to the most strained and impossible distortion of these words ἐπὶ νεκροῖς in a way which is but too familiar in Scripture commentaries. They have been explained to mean "over dead victims," &c.; but all such explanations fall to the ground when the special meaning of *diathēkē* in these two verses is recognised. The author thinks it worth while to notice, in passing, that death is the condition of inheritance by *testament*, just as death is necessary to ratify a *covenant* (Gen. xv. 7—10; Jer. xxxiv. 18).

otherwise it is of no strength at all...] The words are better taken as a question—"Since is there any validity in it at all while the testator is alive?" This is an appeal to the reader's own judgment.

18. *Whereupon*] Rather, "Wherefore;" because both "a covenant" and "a testament" involve the idea of death.

19 first *testament* was dedicated without blood. For when Moses had spoken every precept to all the people according to the law, he took the blood of calves and of goats, with water, and scarlet wool, and hyssop, and sprinkled 20 both the book, and all the people, saying, This *is* the blood of the testament which God hath enjoined 21 unto you. Moreover he sprinkled with blood both the 22 tabernacle, and all the vessels of the ministry. And almost

neither] "not even."
was dedicated] Lit. "has been handselled" or "inaugurated." The word is from the same root as "Encaenia," the name given to the re-dedication of the Temple by the Maccabees (John x. 22. Comp. Deut. xx. 5; 1 Kings viii. 63; LXX.). The perfect is used by the author, as in so many other instances.

19. *and of goats*] This is not specially mentioned, but it may be supposed that "goats" were among the burnt-offerings mentioned in Ex. xxiv. 5.

water, and scarlet wool, and hyssop] These again are not mentioned in Ex. xxiv. 6, but are perhaps added from tradition on the analogy of Ex. xii. 22; Num. xix. 6; and Lev. xiv. 4—6.

hyssop] the dry stalks of a plant resembling marjoram.

both the book] See Ex. xxiv. 6—8, where however it is not specially mentioned that the Book was sprinkled. The Jewish tradition was that it lay upon the altar (see Ex. xxiv. 7). The "book" seems to have been the written record of what was uttered to Moses in Ex. xx. 22 to xxiii. 33. This is one of several instances in which the writer shews himself learned in the Jewish legends (*Hagadoth*).

20. *This is*] In the Hebrew "Behold!" Some have supposed that the writer adopted the variation from a reminiscence of our Lord's words—"This is my blood of the new covenant which is shed for many for the remission of sins" (Matt. xxvi. 28). But if such a reference or comparison had been at all present to his mind, he would hardly have been likely to pass it over in complete silence.

which God hath enjoined unto you] Rather, "which God commanded with regard to you," i.e. which (covenant) Jehovah commanded me to deliver to you.

21. *both the tabernacle*] This again is not mentioned in the scene to which the writer seems to be referring (Ex. xxiv. 6—8), which indeed preceded the building of the Tabernacle. It is nowhere recorded in Scripture that the *Tabernacle* was sprinkled, although it is perhaps *implied* that on a later occasion this may have been done (Ex. xl. 9, 10); and Josephus, closely following the same *Hagadah* as the writer, says that such was the case (Jos. *Antt.* III. 8. § 6).

all the vessels] This again is not directly mentioned, though we are told that Aaron and his sons, and the altar, were consecrated by such a sprinkling (Lev. viii. 30), and that the "propitiatory" was so sprinkled on the Day of Atonement (Lev. xvi. 14). By these references to unre-

all *things* are by the law purged with blood; and without shedding of blood is no remission. *It was* therefore neces- 23 sary that the patterns of *things* in the heavens should be purified with these; but the heavenly *things* themselves with better sacrifices than these. For Christ is not entered into 24 the holy *places* made with hands, *which are* the figures of the true; but into heaven itself, now to appear in the presence of God for us: nor yet that he should offer him- 25 self often, as the high priest entereth into the holy *place*

corded traditions the writer shews that he had been trained in Rabbinic Schools.

22. *almost all things*] There were a few exceptions (Ex. xix. 10; Lev. v. 11—13, xv. 5, xvi. 26, &c.) The word σχεδόν, "almost," is only found in two other passages of the N. T. (Acts xiii. 44, xix. 26).

without shedding of blood] This, and not "pouring out of blood" at the foot of the altar (Ex. xxix. 16, &c.), is undoubtedly the true rendering. Comp. Lev. xvii. 11; Lk. xxii. 20. The Rabbis have a proverb, "no expiation except by blood." The writer merely mentions this as a revealed *fact*: he does not attempt to construct any theory to account for the necessity.

23. *patterns*] Rather, "copies," or outlines—*Abbilden* (not *Urbilden*), iv. 11, viii. 5.

the heavenly things themselves] Not "the New Covenant," or "the Church," or "ourselves as heirs of heaven," but apparently the Ideal Tabernacle in the Heavens, which was itself impure before Him to whom "*the very heavens are not clean.*" If this conception seem remote we must suppose that by the figure called *Zeugma* the verb "purified" passes into the sense of "handselled," "dedicated."

with better sacrifices than these] The plural is here only used generically to express *a class*. He is alluding to the *one* transcendent sacrifice.

24. *For Christ is not entered*] "For not into any Material Sanctuary did Christ enter—a (mere) imitation of the Ideal,—but into Heaven itself, now to be visibly presented before the face of God for us." The Ideal or genuine Tabernacle is the eternal uncreated Archetype as contrasted with its antitype (or "imitation") made with hands. The Ideal in the Alexandrian philosophy, so far from being an antithesis of the real, meant that which *alone* is absolutely and eternally real; it is the antithesis of the *material* which is but a perishing imitation of the Archetype. The word "to be visibly presented" (ἐμφανισθῆναι) is not the same as that used in ver. 26 (πεφανέρωται "He hath been manifested,") nor with that used in ver. 28 (ὀφθήσεται "He shall be seen,") though all these are rendered in English by the verb "appear."

25. *entereth into the holy place every year*] In this entrance of the High Priest once a year, on the Day of Atonement, into the Holiest Place culminated all that was gorgeous and awe-inspiring in the Jewish ritual. The writer therefore purposely chose it as his point of com-

26 every year with blood of others; for then must he often have suffered since the foundation of the world: but now once in the end of the world hath he appeared to put away

parison between the ministrations of the Two Covenants. For if he could shew that even the ceremonies of this day—called by the Jews "*the* Day"—were a nullity compared with the significance of the Gospel, he was well aware that no other rite would be likely to make a converted Hebrew waver in his faith. The Day of Atonement was called "the Sabbath of Sabbatism" or "perfect Sabbath." It was the *one* fast-day of the Jewish Calendar. The 70 bullocks offered during the Atonement-week were regarded as a propitiation for all the 70 nations of the world. On that day the very Angels were supposed to tremble. It was the only day on which perfect pardon could be assured to sins which had been repented of. On that day alone Satan had no power to accuse, which is inferred by "*Gematria*" from the fact that "*the Accuser*" in Hebrew was numerically equivalent to 364, so that on the 365th day of the year he was forced to be silent. On the seven days before the day of Atonement the High Priest was scrupulously secluded, and was kept awake all the preceding night to avoid the chance of ceremonial defilement. Till the last 40 years before the Fall of Jerusalem it was asserted that the tongue of scarlet cloth tied round the neck of the goat "for Azazel" ("the Scape Goat") used to turn white in token of the Remission of Sins. The function of the High Priest was believed to be attended with much peril, and the people awaited his reappearance with deep anxiety. The awful impression made by the services of the day is shewn by the legends which grew up respecting them, and by such passages as Ecclus. l. 5—16, xlv. 6—22. See an Excursus on this subject in my *Early Days of Christianity*, II. 549—552.

with blood of others] Namely of the goat and the bullock. See ver. 22. A Rabbinic book says "Abraham was Circumcised on the Day of Atonement; and on that Day God annually looks on the blood of the Covenant of the Circumcision as atoning for all our iniquities."

26. *for then must he often have suffered*] Since He could not have entered the Sanctuary of God's Holiest in the Heavens without some offering of atoning blood.

once] "Once for all."

in the end of the world] This phrase does not convey the meaning of the Greek which has "at the consummation of the ages" (Matt. xiii. 39, 49, xxiv. 3, xxviii. 20), in other words "when God's full time was come for the revelation of the Gospel" (comp. i. 1; 1 Cor. x. 11).

hath he appeared] Lit., "He has been manifested"—namely, "in the flesh" at the Incarnation (1 Tim. iii. 16; 1 Pet. i. 20, &c.).

to put away sin] The word is stronger—"for the *annulment* of sin." Into this one word is concentrated the infinite superiority of the work of Christ. The High Priest even on the Day of Atonement could offer no sacrifice which could put away sin (x. 4), but Christ's sacrifice was able to *annul* sin altogether.

sin by the sacrifice of himself. And as it is appointed unto 27 men once to die, but after this the judgment: so Christ 28 was once offered to bear the sins of many; and unto them that look for him shall he appear the second time without sin unto salvation.

by the sacrifice of himself] The object of which was, as St Peter tells us, "to bring us to God" (1 Pet. iii. 18).

27. *as*] "Inasmuch as."

it is appointed] Rather, "it is reserved;" lit., "it is laid up for."

the judgment] Rather, "a judgment." By this apparently is not meant "a day in the which He will judge the world in righteousness" (Acts xvii. 31), but a judgment which follows immediately after death.

28. *was once offered*] Christ may also be said as in ver. 14 "to *offer Himself;*" just as He is said "to be delivered for us" (Rom. iv. 25) and "to deliver up Himself" (Eph. v. 2).

to bear the sins] The word rendered "to bear" may mean "to carry them with Him on to the Cross," as in 1 Pet. ii. 24; or as probably in Is. liii. 12 "to take them *away.*"

of many] "Many" is only used as an antithesis to "few." Of course the writer does not mean to contradict the lesson which runs throughout the N.T. that Christ died for *all.* Once for all One died for all who were "many" (see my *Life of St Paul*, II. 216).

without sin] Not merely "without ($\chi\omega\rho\iota\varsigma$)" but "apart from ($\alpha\tau\epsilon\rho$) sin," i.e. apart from all connexion with it, because He shall have utterly triumphed over, and annulled it (ver. 26); Dan. ix. 24, 25; Is. xxv. 7, 8). The words do not go with "the second time" for at Christ's first coming He appeared *without* sin indeed, but *not* "apart *from* sin," seeing that "He was numbered with the transgressors" (Is. liii. 12) and was "made sin for us" (2 Cor. v. 21).

unto salvation] "It shall be said in that day, Lo, this is our God; ...we have waited for Him, we will be glad and rejoice in his salvation" (Is. xxv. 9). It is remarkable that the Sacred Writers—unlike the Mediæval painters and moralists—almost invariably avoid the more terrible aspects of the Second Advent. "How shall He appear?" asks St Chrysostom on this passage, "As a Punisher? He did not say this, but the bright side." The parallelism of these verses is Man dies once, and is judged; Christ died once and shall return—he might have said "to be man's *judge*" (Acts xvii. 31)—but he does say "He shall return...for salvation."

We may sum up some of the contrasts of this previous chapter as follows. The descendants of Aaron were but priests; Christ, like Melchisedek, was both Priest and King. They were for a time; He is a Priest for ever. They were but links in a long succession, inheriting from forefathers, transmitting to dependents; He stands alone, without lineage, without successor. They were established by a transitory ordinance, He by an eternal oath. They were sinful, He is sinless. They weak, He all-powerful. Their sacrifices were ineffectual, His

10 For the law having a shadow of good *things* to come, *and* not the very image of the things, can never with those sacrifices which they offered year by year continually make

was perfect. Their sacrifices were offered daily, His once for all. Theirs did but cleanse from ceremonial defilement, His purged the conscience. Their tabernacle was but a copy, and their service a shadow; His tabernacle was the Archetype, and His service the substance. They died and passed away; He sits to intercede for us for ever at God's right hand. Their Covenant is doomed to abrogation; His, founded on better promises, is to endure unto the End. Their High Priest could but enter once and that with awful precautions, with the blood of bulls and goats, into a material shrine; He, entering with the blood of His one perfect sacrifice into the Heaven of Heavens, has thrown open to all the right of continual and fearless access to God. What a sin then was it, and what a folly, to look back with apostatising glances at the shadows of a petty Levitism while Christ the Mediator of a New, of a better, of a final Dispensation—Christ whose blood had a real and no mere symbolic efficacy had died once for all, and Alone for all, as the sinless Son of God to obtain for us an eternal redemption, and to return for our salvation as the Everlasting Victor over sin and death!

CH. X. The first eighteen verses of this chapter are a summary, rich with fresh thoughts and illustrations, of the topics on which he has been dwelling; namely (1) The one sacrifice of Christ compared with the many Levitic sacrifices (1—10). (2) The perfectness of His finished work (11—18). The remainder of the chapter is occupied with one of the earnest exhortations (19—25) and solemn warnings (25—31), followed by fresh appeals and encouragements (32—39), by which the writer shews throughout that his object in writing is not speculative or theological, but essentially practical and moral.

1—14. THE ONE SACRIFICE AND THE MANY SACRIFICES.

1. *of good things to come*] Of *the* good things which Christ had now brought into the world (ix. 11).

not the very image of the things] "The Law," says St Ambrose, "had the *shadow*; the Gospel the image; the Reality itself is in Heaven." By the word image is meant the true historic form. The Gospel was as much closer a resemblance of the Reality as a statue is a closer resemblance than a pencilled outline.

can never] This may be the right reading, though the plural "*they* are never able," is found in some MSS. If this latter be the true reading the sentence begins with an unfinished construction (*anakoluthon*).

with those sacrifices...] Rather, "with the same sacrifices, year by year, which they offer continuously, make perfect them that draw nigh," i.e. the Priests can never with their sacrifices, which are the same year by year, perfect the worshippers. Some have given a fuller sense to the

the comers *thereunto* perfect. For then would they not 2 have ceased to be offered? because that the worshippers once purged should have had no more conscience of sins. But in those *sacrifices there is* a remembrance *again made* 3 of sins every year. For *it is* not possible that the blood 4 of bulls and of goats should take away sins. Wherefore 5

words "the same," as though it meant that even the sacrifices of the Day of Atonement cannot make any one perfect, being as they are, after all, *the same* sacrifices in their inmost nature as those which are offered every morning and evening.

2. *once purged*] having been cleansed, by these sacrifices, once for all.

conscience] Rather, "consciousness."

3. *there is a remembrance again made of sins*] This view of sacrifices—that they are "a calling to mind of sins yearly"—is very remarkable. It seems to be derived from Num. v. 15, where "the offering of jealousy" is called "an offering of memorial, *bringing iniquity to remembrance*." Philo also speaks of sacrifices as providing "not an *oblivion* of sins, but a *reminding* of them." *De plant. Noe*, § 25. *De Vit. Mos.* III. § 10 (Opp. I. 345, II. 246). But if the sacrifices thus called sins to remembrance, they also daily symbolised the means of their removal, so that when offered obediently with repentance and faith they became valid symbols.

4. *it is not possible*...] This plain statement of the nullity of sacrifices *in themselves*, and regarded as mere outward acts, only expresses what had been deeply felt by many a worshipper under the Old Covenant. It should be compared with the weighty utterances on this subject in the O.T., 1 Sam. xv. 22; Is. i. 11—17; Jer. vi. 20, vii. 21—23; Amos v. 21—24; Mic. vi. 6—8; Ps. xl. 6—8 (quoted in the next verses), and Pss. l. and li.; and above all Hos. vi. 6, which, being a pregnant summary of the principle involved, was a frequent quotation of our Lord. Any value which the system of sacrifices possessed was not theirs intrinsically (*propriâ virtute*) but relatively and typically (*per accidens*). "By a rudely sensuous means," says Lünemann, "we cannot attain to a high spiritual good." Philo in one of his finest passages shews how deeply he had realised that sacrifices were valueless apart from holiness, and that no mere external acts can cleanse the soul from moral guilt. He adds that God accepts the innocent even when they offer no sacrifices, and delights in unkindled altars if the virtues dance around them (*De plant. Noe*). The heathen had learnt the same high truths. Horace (*Od.* III. 23) sings,

"Immunis aram si tetigit manus
 Non sumptuosâ blandior hostiâ
  Mollivit aversos Penates
   Farre pio et saliente micâ."

when he cometh into the world, he saith, Sacrifice and offering thou wouldest not, but a body hast thou pre-
6 pared me: in burnt offerings and *sacrifices* for sin
7 thou hast had no pleasure. Then said I, Lo, I come (in the volume of the book it is written of

5. *when he cometh into the world, he saith*] The quotation is from Ps. xl. 6—8. The words of the Psalmist are ideally and typologically transferred to the Son, in accordance with the universal conception of the O.T. Messianism which was prevalent among the Jews. It made no difference to their point of view that *some* parts of the Psalm (e.g. in ver. 12) could only have a primary and contemporary significance. The "coming into the world" is here regarded as having been long predetermined in the divine counsels; it is regarded, as Delitzsch says, "not as a point but as a line."

Sacrifice and offering thou wouldest not] "Thou carest not for slain beast or bloodless oblation." This is in accordance with the many magnificent declarations which in the midst of legal externalism declared its nullity except as a *means* to better things (Is. i. 11; Jer. vi. 20; Hos. vi. 6; Amos v. 21; 1 Sam. xv. 22, &c.

but a body hast thou prepared me] This is the rendering of the LXX. In the Hebrew it is "*But ears hast thou digged* for me." The *text* of the Hebrew does not admit of easy alteration, so that either (1) the reading of the Greek text in the LXX. must be a clerical error, e.g. ΚΑΤΗΡΤΙΣΑΣΩΜΑ for ΚΑΤΗΡΤΙΣΑΣΩΤΙΑ, or (2) the LXX. rendering must be a sort of Targum or explanation. They regarded "a body didst Thou prepare" as equivalent to "Ears didst thou dig." The explanation is usually found in the Hebrew custom of boring a slave's ear if he preferred to remain in servitude (Ex. xxi. 6; Deut. xv. 17), so that the "bored ear" was a symbol of willing obedience. But the Hebrew verb means "to dig" rather than "to bore," and the true explanation seems to be "thou hast caused me to hear and obey." So in Is. xlviii. 8 we have "thine ear was not opened," and in l. 5, "God *hath opened my ear* and I was not rebellious." Thus in the two first clauses of each parallelism in the four lines we have the sacrifices which God does *not* desire; and in the second clause the obedience for which He does care. "The prepared body" is "the form of a servant," which Christ took upon Him in order to "open His ears" to the voice of God (Phil. ii. 7). See Rev. xviii. 13, where "bodies" means "slaves." St Paul says, "Ye are become dead to the law *by the body* of Christ" (Rom. vii. 4).

6. *burnt offerings*] Lit., "Holocausts." The word occurs here alone in the N.T. These "whole burnt offerings" typified absolute self-dedication; but the holocaust without the *self*-sacrifice was valueless.

7. *Lo, I come*] Rather, "I am come." This 40th Psalm is one of the special Psalms for Good Friday.

in the volume of the book] The word *kephalis*, here rendered volume, does not occur elsewhere in the N.T. It means the knob (*umbilicus*)

me,) to do thy will, O God. Above when he said, 8 Sacrifice and offering and burnt offerings and *offering* for sin thou wouldest not, neither hadst pleasure *therein:* which are offered by the law; then 9 said he, Lo, I come to do thy will, O God. He taketh away the first, that he may establish the second. By the which will we are sanctified through the offering of 10 the body of Jesus Christ once for all. And every priest 11 standeth daily ministering and offering oftentimes the same

of the roller on which the vellum was rolled. The word in the Hebrew is *Megillah*, "a roll." It cannot be rendered "in the chief part" or "in the beginning." The words "it is written of me" may mean in the Hebrew "*it has been prescribed to me*," and others take the clause to mean "I am come with the roll of the book which is written for me." If we ask *what* was "the book" to which the *author of the Psalm referred* the answer is not easy; it may have been the Law, or the Book of God's unwritten counsels, as in Ps. cxxxix. 16. The writer of the Epistle, transferring and applying David's words to Christ, thought doubtless of the whole O. T. (comp. Lk. xxiv. 26, 27, "He expounded unto them *in all the Scriptures* the things concerning Himself).

to do thy will] The writer has omitted the words "I delight." Slavish accuracy in quotation is never aimed at by the sacred writers, because they had no letter-worshipping theory of verbal inspiration. They held that the inspiration lay in the sense and in the thoughts of Scripture, not in its *ipsissima verba*. Hence they often consider it sufficient to give the general tendency of a passage, and frequently vary from the exact words.

8. *which are offered by the law*] Rather, "according to the Law." A whole argument is condensed into these words, which the context would enable readers to develop for themselves.

9. *then said he*] Lit., "*Then he has said.*"

He taketh away the first] namely, Sacrifices, &c.

that he may establish the second] namely, the Will of God.

10. *By the which will we are sanctified*] Rather, "we have been sanctified" because, as we have already seen, the word *hagiasmos* is not used of *progressive* sanctification, but of consecration in a pure state to God's service (ii. 11, xiii. 12, &c., and comp. John xvii. 19; 1 Thess. iv. 3, "This is the *will of God*, even your *sanctification*").

the offering of the body of Jesus Christ] The "body" is a reference to ver. 5. And because Christ thus offered His body we are bidden to offer our bodies as "a living sacrifice, holy, well-pleasing to God" (Rom. xii. 1).

11. *And every priest*] The better reading seems to be "High Priest."

standeth] None were permitted to sit in the Holy Place. Christ sat in the Holiest, far above all Heavens.

12 sacrifices, which can never take away sins: but this *man*, after he had offered one sacrifice for sins for ever, sat down 13 on the right hand of God; from henceforth expecting till 14 his enemies be made his footstool. For by one offering he hath perfected for ever them that are sanctified. 15 *Whereof* the Holy Ghost also is a witness to us: for after 16 that *he* had said before, This *is* the covenant that I will make with them after those days, saith the Lord, I will put my laws into their hearts, and in 17 their minds will I write them; and their sins and 18 iniquities will I remember no more. Now where remission of these *is*, *there is* no more offering for sin.

oftentimes] "Day by day for a continual burnt-offering" (Num. xxviii. 3; comp. vii. 27).
take away sins] The word is not the same verb (*aphairein*) as in ver. 4, but a much stronger one (*perielein*) which means "at once to strip away," as though sin were some close-fitting robe (see xii. 1).
12. *on the right hand of God*] viii. 1, i. 13.
13. *his footstool*] Ps. cx. 1; 1 Cor. xv. 25.
14. *he hath perfected*] vii. 11, 25.
them that are sanctified] "those who are in the way of sanctification" (ii. 11; comp. Acts ii. 47).
15. *Whereof*] Rather, "But."
the Holy Ghost] For "holy men of God spake as they were moved by the Holy Ghost" (2 Pet. i. 21).
for after that he had said] There is no direct completion of this sentence, but the words "again He saith" are found in some editions before ver. 17. They have no manuscript authority, but were added by Dr Paris (from the Philoxenian Syriac) in the margin of the Cambridge Bible of 1762.
16. *This is the covenant*] Jer. xxxi. 33, 34 (comp. viii. 10—12).
17. *will I remember no more*] This oblivion of sin is illustrated by many strong metaphors in Is. xliv. 22, xxxviii. 17; Jer. l. 20; Ps. ciii. 12; Mic. vii. 19, &c.
18. *there is no more offering for sin*] Since the object of all sacrifices is the purging of the soul from guilt, sacrifices are no longer needed when sins have been annulled (ix. 26). Those words form the triumphant close of the argument. To revert to Judaism, to offer sacrifices, meant henceforth faithlessness as regards Christ's finished work. And if sacrifices were henceforth abolished there was obviously an end of the Aaronic Priesthood, and therewith of the whole Old Covenant. The shadow had now been superseded by the substance, the sketch by the reality. And thus the writer has at last made good his opening words, that "at this end of the days God had revealed Himself to us by His Son," and that the New Covenant thus revealed was superior to the

Having therefore, brethren, boldness to enter into the holiest by the blood of Jesus, *by* a new and living way, which he hath consecrated for us, through the vail, that is to say, his flesh; and *having* a high priest over the house of God; let us draw near with a true heart in full assurance of faith, having *our* hearts sprinkled from an evil conscience, and *our* bodies washed with pure water. Let us hold fast

First, alike in its Agent (vii. 1—25), its Priesthood (vii. 25—ix. 12), its Tabernacle, and its sacrificial ordinances (ix. 13—x. 18).

19—25. AN EXHORTATION TO CHRISTIAN CONFIDENCE AND FELLOWSHIP.

19. *brethren*] iii. 1, 12, xiii. 22.

boldness to enter into the holiest by the blood of Jesus] Rather, "confidence in the blood of Jesus, for our entrance into the Holiest." This right of joyful confidence in our access to God through Christ is dwelt upon in Eph. ii. 18, iii. 12.

20. *by a new and living way*] The word rendered "new" is not *kainos* as elsewhere in this Epistle, but *prosphatos*, which means originally "*newly-slain*." It may be doubted however whether the writer intended the oxymoron "*newly-slain* yet *living*." That the road was "new" has already been shewn in ix. 8—12. It is called "living" not as "life-giving" or "enduring," but because "the Lord of life" is Himself the way (John xiv. 6; comp. Eph. iii. 12).

which he hath consecrated] The verb is the same as in ix. 18, "which He inaugurated for us."

through the vail, that is to say, his flesh] There is here a passing comparison of Christ's human body to the *Parocheth* or Veil (vi. 19, ix. 3) through which the High Priest passed into the Holiest, and which was rent at the crucifixion (Matt. xxvii. 51). It was *through* His Suffering Humanity that He passed to His glory.

21. *a high priest*] Lit. "a great Priest" (as in Lev. xxi. 10), here meaning a Kingly Priest (Zech. vi. 11—13).

over the house of God] See iii. 6; 1 Tim. iii. 15.

22. *Let us draw near*] We have seen throughout that the notion of *free access and approach to God* is prominent in the writer's mind.

in full assurance of faith] See vi. 11.

having our hearts sprinkled from an evil conscience] That is, having our souls—our inmost consciousness—sprinkled as it were with the blood of Christ (ix. 14, xii. 24, 1 Pet. i. 2) and so cleansed from the consciousness of guilt. So the Jewish priests were purified from ceremonial defilement by being sprinkled with blood (Ex. xxix. 21; Lev. viii. 30).

and our bodies washed] The perfect participles in these clauses—"*having been sprinkled*," "*having been washed*"—imply that it is to be done once and for ever. All Christians are priests to God (Rev. i. 5, 6); and therefore Christian Priests, before being permitted to approach to

the profession of *our* hope without wavering; (for he *is*
24 faithful that promised;) and let us consider one another
25 to provoke unto love and to good works: not forsaking the
assembling of ourselves together, as the manner of some *is;*
but exhorting *one another:* and so much the more, as ye see
the day approaching.

God, must, like the Jewish Priests (Ex. xxx. 20), be *sprinkled* with the blood of Christ, and bathed in the water of baptism (Eph. v. 26; Tit. iii. 5; 1 Pet. iii. 21).

with pure water] "I will sprinkle clean water upon you, and ye shall be clean" (Ezek. xxxvi. 25).

23. *the profession of our hope*] Rather, "the confession of our Hope." Here we have the same trilogy of Christian graces as in St Paul—Faith (ver. 22), Hope (ver. 23), and Love (ver. 24).

without wavering] "So that it do not bend." It must be not only "secure" (iii. 6, 14), but not even liable to be shaken.

for he is faithful that promised] vi. 13, xi. 11, xii. 26. The writer felt the necessity of insisting upon this point, because the sufferings of the Hebrew converts, and the long delay (as it seemed to them) of Christ's return, had shaken their constancy.

24. *to provoke unto love*] "For provocation to love." The word *paroxusmos* (whence our "paroxysm") is more generally used in a bad sense, like the English word "provocation" (see Acts xv. 39; Deut. xxix. 28; LXX.). And perhaps the writer here chose the word to remind them that the "provocation" at present prevailing among them was to hatred not to love.

25. *the assembling of ourselves together*] i.e. "our Christian gatherings." Apparently the flagging zeal and waning faith of the Hebrews had led some of them to neglect the Christian assemblies for worship and Holy Communion (Acts ii. 42). The word here used (*episunagōgē*) only occurs in 2 Thess. ii. 1, and is perhaps chosen to avoid the Jewish word "synagogue;" and the more so because the duty of attending "the synagogue" was insisted on by Jewish teachers. In the neglect of public worship the writer saw the dangerous germ of apostasy.

as the manner of some is] This neglect of attending the Christian gatherings may have been due in some cases to fear of the Jews. It shewed a fatal tendency to waver in the direction of apostasy.

exhorting one another] This implies the duty of mutual *encouragement.*

ye see the day approaching] The Day which Christians expected was the Last Day (1 Cor. iii. 13). They failed to see that the Day which our Lord had *primarily* in view in His great eschatological discourse (Matt. xxiv.) was the Close of the Old Dispensation in the Fall of Jerusalem. The signs of this were already in the air, and that approaching Day of the Lord was destined to be "the bloody and fiery dawn" of the Last Great Day—"the Day of days, the Ending-day of all days, the

For if we sin wilfully after that *we* have received the 26
knowledge of the truth, there remaineth no more sacrifice
for sins, but a certain fearful looking for of judgment and 27
fiery indignation, which shall devour the adversaries. He 28

Settling-day of all days, the Day of the promotion of Time into Eternity, the Day which for the Church breaks through and breaks off the night of this present world" (Delitzsch).

26—31. A SOLEMN WARNING OF THE PERIL OF WILFUL APOSTASY.

26. *For if we sin wilfully*] The word "wilfully" stands in contrast with sins of weakness, ignorance and error in v. 2. If the writer meant to say that, after the commission of wilful and heinous sins, "there remaineth no more sacrifice for sins," this would not only be the most terrible passage in Scripture, but would do away with the very object of Redemption, and the possibility of any Forgiveness of Sins. It would, as Kurz says, "be in its consequences truly subversive and destructive of the whole Christian soteriology." But the meaning rather is "*If we are willing sinners*," "if we are in a state of deliberate and voluntary defiance to the will of God." He is alluding not only to those sins which the Jews described as being committed presumptuously "with uplifted hand" (Num. xv. 30; Ps. xix. 13; see vi. 4—8, xii. 16, 17), but to the *deliberate continuity of such sins as a self-chosen law of life;* as for instance when a man has closed against himself the door of repentance and said "Evil be thou my good." Such a state is glanced at in 2 Pet. ii. 20, 21; Matt. xii. 43—45.

after that we have received the knowledge of the truth] Rather, "the *full* knowledge of the truth." Something more is meant than mere historical knowledge. He is contemplating Christians who have made some real advance, and then have relapsed into "desperation or the wretchlessness of unclean living."

there remaineth no more sacrifice for sins] Lit., "no sacrifice for sins is any longer left for them." They have rejected the work of Christ, and it cannot be done for them over again. There is one atoning sacrifice and that they have repudiated. He does not say that they have exhausted the infinite mercy of God, nor can we justly assert that he held such a conclusion; he only says that they have, so long as they continue in such a state, put themselves out of God's covenant, and that there are no other covenanted means of grace. For they have trampled under foot the offer of mercy in Christ and there is no salvation in any other (Acts iv. 12).

27. *but a certain fearful looking for of judgment...*] All that is left for willing apostates when they have turned their backs on the sole means of grace is "some fearful expectance of a judgment." They are "heaping up to themselves wrath against the day of wrath" (Rom. ii. 5).

and fiery indignation] Lit., "and a jealousy of fire." He is thinking of God "as a consuming fire" (xii. 29) and of the question "Shall thy jealousy burn like fire?" Ps. lxxix. 5 (comp. Ezek. xxxv. 5).

that despised Moses' law died without mercy under two or
29 three witnesses: of how much sorer punishment, suppose
ye, shall he be thought worthy, who hath trodden under
foot the Son of God, and hath counted the blood of the

which shall devour the adversaries] "Yea let fire devour thine enemies" (Is. xxvi. 11). It has so long been the custom to interpret such passages of "eternal torments" that we lose sight of the fact that such a meaning, if we may interpret Scripture historically, was in most cases not consciously present to the mind of the writers. The constant repetition of the same metaphor by the Prophets with no reference except to temporal calamities and the overthrow of cities and nations made it familiar in this sense to the N.T. writers. By "the adversaries" here are not meant "sinners," but impenitent Jews and wilful apostates who would perish in the Day of the Lord (2 Thess. i. 8). It is at least doubtful whether the writer meant to imply anything beyond that prophecy of doom to the heirs of the Old Covenant which was fulfilled a few years later when the fire of God's wrath consumed the whole system of a Judaism which had rejected its own Messiah. The word for "adversaries" only occurs in the N.T. in Col. ii. 14.

28. *He that despised Moses' law*] Especially by being guilty of the sin of idolatry (Deut. xvii. 2—7). Literally, it is "*any one*, on setting at nought Moses' law."

died] Lit., "dies." Here is another of the favourite Jewish exegetical arguments a *minori ad majus*.

without mercy] The Mosaic law pronounced on offenders an inexorable doom. "The letter killeth" (2 Cor. iii. 6).

under two or three witnesses] i.e. by the testimony of at least two (John viii. 17; 2 Cor. xiii. 1).

29. *of how much sorer punishment*] The word for "punishment" in the N.T. is in every other passage *kolasis*, which means, in accordance with its definition, and in much of its demonstrable usage, "*remedial* punishment." Here the word (though the difference is not observed by our A.V. which has created so many needless variations, and obliterated so many necessary distinctions) is *timoria* which means "vengeance" or "retribution." It need hardly be said that "*vindictive* punishment" can only be attributed to God by the figure of speech known as *anthropopathy*, i.e. the representation of God by metaphors drawn from human passions. It is also obvious that we misuse Scripture when we press casual words to unlimited inferences. "Vengeance" is here used because (1) the author is alluding to defiant and impenitent apostates, in language derived from the earthly analogies, and (2) because he is referring to the temporal ruin and overthrow of the Jewish polity at the fast-approaching Day of Christ's Coming. The passage which he proceeds to quote (Deut. xxxii. 35) refers directly to *national* and *temporal* punishments. The verb "to avenge" is only used twice in the N.T. (Acts xxii. 5, xxvi. 11)—both times of the persecution of Christians by Saul.

trodden under foot the Son of God] The writer could hardly use

vv. 30, 31.] HEBREWS, X. 157

covenant, wherewith he was sanctified, an unholy *thing*, and hath done despite unto the Spirit of grace? For we know 30 him that hath said, Vengeance *belongeth* unto me, I will recompense, saith the Lord. And again, The Lord shall judge his people. *It is* a fearful *thing* to fall into 31

stronger language to imply the extremity of wilful rebellion which he has in view. It scarcely applies to any except blaspheming infidels and to those Jews who have turned the very name of Jesus in Hebrew into an anagram of malediction, and in the Talmud rarely allude to Him except in words of scorn and execration.

the blood of the covenant] He uses the same phrase in xiii. 20.

an unholy thing] Lit., "a common thing," i.e. either "unclean" or "valueless." Clearly such conduct as this must be the nearest approach we can conceive to "the sin against the Holy Ghost," "the unpardonable sin," "the sin unto death," for which no remedy is provided in any earthly means of grace (Matt. xii. 31; 1 John v. 16).

done despite unto] Lit., "insulted;" e.g. "by blasphemy against the Holy Ghost" (Matt. xii. 31, 32). It is possible to grieve utterly that Holy Spirit (Eph. iv. 30) and so to become "reprobate." The apostates whose case is here imagined despise alike the Father (v. 5), the Son, and the Holy Spirit (vi. 4—6). They reject the very promises of their baptismal profession and abnegate the whole economy of grace. The verb for "to do despite" occurs here only in the N.T.

30. *Vengeance belongeth unto me*] The Scripture warrant adduced in support of this stern language is Deut. xxxii. 35, and a similar phrase ("O God, to whom vengeance belongeth") is used in Ps. xciv. 1, 2. It is remarkable that the citation does not agree either with the Hebrew or the LXX., but is quoted in the same form as in Rom. xii. 19, where however the application is quite different, for it is there used as an argument against avenging our own wrongs. The writer of this Epistle, as a friend of St Paul and one who was of his school, may have been familiar with this form of the quotation, or may have read it in the Epistle to the Romans, with which he seems to have been familiar (comp. xiii. 1—6 with Rom. xii. 1—21); and indeed there are traces that the quotation in this form was known in the Jewish schools. Perhaps it had become proverbial.

saith the Lord] The words are omitted in ℵ, D, and most ancient versions, and may have been added from Rom. xii. 19.

And again] Deut. xxxii. 36.

The Lord shall judge his people] In the original passage the "judgment" consists in saving His people from their enemies, as also in Ps. cxxxv. 14.

31. *It is a fearful thing to fall into the hands of the living God*] Fearful for the deliberate apostate and even for the penitent sinner (1 Chron. xxi. 13; 2 Sam. xxiv. 14; LXX. Ecclus. ii. 18), and yet better in any case than to fall into the hands of man.

of the living God] iii. 12.

32 the hands of the living God. But call to remembrance the former days, in which, after ye were illuminated, ye endured 33 a great fight of afflictions; partly, whilst ye were made a gazingstock both by reproaches and afflictions; and partly, whilst ye became companions of them that were 34 so used. For ye had compassion *of me* in my bonds, and took joyfully the spoiling of your goods, knowing in your-

32—39. WORDS OF APPEAL AND ENCOURAGEMENT.

32. *But call to remembrance the former days*] Rather, "keep in remembrance." Here, as in vi. 9—12, he mingles appeal and encouragement with the sternest warnings. The "former days" are those in which they were in the first glow of their conversion.

after ye were illuminated] The word *photizein* "to enlighten" only became a synonym for 'to baptise' at a later period. Naturally however in the early converts baptism was synchronous with the reception of the gifts of the Holy Spirit (see vi. 4). For the metaphor—that "God hath shined in our hearts"—see 2 Cor. iv. 6; 1 Pet. ii. 9.

ye endured a great fight of afflictions] Rather, "much wrestling of sufferings." These were doubtless due to the uncompromising hostility of the Jewish community (see 1 Thess. ii. 14—16), which generally led to persecutions from the Gentiles also. To the early Christians it was given "not only to believe on Christ, but also to suffer for His sake" (Phil. i. 29).

33. *ye were made a gazingstock*] Lit. "being set upon a stage" (*theatrizomenoi*). The same metaphor is used in 1 Cor. iv. 9 ("We became a *theatre*," comp. 1 Cor. xv. 32).

companions] Rather, "partakers."

that were so used] "Who lived in this condition of things."

34. *ye had compassion of me in my bonds*] This reading had more to do than anything else with the common assumption that this Epistle was written by St Paul. The true reading however undoubtedly is not τοῖς δεσμοῖς μου, but τοῖς δεσμίοις, "ye sympathised with the prisoners." The reading of our text was probably introduced from Col. iv. 18; Phil. i. 7, &c. In the first persecutions many confessors were thrown into prison (Acts xxvi. 10), and from the earliest days Christians were famed for their kindness to their brethren who were thus confined. See too xiii. 3. The verb συμπαθεῖν occurs only here and in iv. 15. St Paul uses συμπάσχειν "to suffer with" in Rom. viii. 17.

took joyfully the spoiling of your goods] Christians were liable to be thus plundered by lawless mobs. Epictetus, by whose time Stoicism had become unconsciously impregnated with Christian feeling, says, "I became poor at thy will, yea and gladly." On the supposition that the letter was addressed to Rome, "the spoiling of goods" has been referred to the edict of Claudius which expelled the Jews (and with them the Christian Jews) from Rome; or to the Neronian persecution. But the supposition is improbable.

selves that *ye* have in heaven a better and an enduring substance. Cast not away therefore your confidence, which 35 hath great recompence of reward. For ye have need of 36 patience, that, after ye have done the will of God, ye might receive the promise. For yet a little while, *and* he that 37 **shall come will come, and will not tarry. Now** 38 **the just shall live by faith: but if** *any man* **draw**

knowing in yourselves that ye have in heaven] The "in heaven" is almost certainly a spurious gloss, and the "in" before "yourselves" should be unquestionably omitted. If the true reading be ἑαυτοῖς, the meaning is "recognising that ye have *for yourselves*," but if we may accept ἑαυτούς, the reading of ℵ, we have the very beautiful and striking thought, "recognising that ye have **yourselves** as a better possession and an abiding." He points them to the tranquil self-possession of a holy heart (Lk. ix. 25, xxi. 19), the acquisition of our own souls, as a sufficient present consolation for the loss of earthly goods (Heb. xi. 26), independently of the illimitable future hope (Matt. vi. 20; Rom. viii. 18; 1 Pet. i. 4—8).

35. *your confidence*] iii. 6, iv. 16.

which hath] The Greek relative implies "seeing that it has" (*quippe quae*).

recompence of reward] The compound *misthapodosia* as before for the simple *misthos* (ii. 2, xi. 26; comp. xi. 6).

36. *of patience*] Few graces were more needed in the terrible trials of that day (vi. 12; Lk. xxi. 19; Col. i. 11; Jas. i. 3, 4).

after ye have done] The meaning perhaps rather is "by doing," or "by having done the will of God ye may win the fruition of the promise." The apparently contradictory expressions, about "receiving" and "not receiving" the promise or the promises, arise in part from the fact that "promise" is used both for the *verbal* promise, and for its actual fulfilment (ix. 15, xi. 39).

37. *yet a little while*] The original has a very emphatic phrase (μικρὸν ὅσον ὅσον) to imply the nearness of Christ's return, "yet but a very very little while." The phrase occurs in the LXX. in Is. xxvi. 20. The quotations in this and the next verse are adapted from Hab. ii. 3, 4. In the original it is "the vision" which will not tarry, but the writer quotes from the LXX., only inserting the definite article before ἐρχόμενος, and applying it to the Messiah. "The coming one" was a Messianic title (Matt. xi. 3; Lk. vii. 19; comp. Dan. vii. 13, &c.). In Matt. xxiv. 34 our Lord has said, "*This generation* shall not pass till all these things be fulfilled;" and by the time that this Epistle was written few still survived of the generation which had seen our Lord. Hence, Christians felt sure that Christ's coming was very near, though it is probable that they did not realise that it would consist in the close of the Old Dispensation, and not as yet in the End of the World.

38. *Now the just shall live by faith*] The true reading here (though not in the Hebrew) perhaps is, "But *my* righteous one shall live by faith"

39 back, my soul shall have no pleasure in him. But we are not of *them* who draw back unto perdition; but of *them* that believe to the saving of the soul.

(as in ℵ, A, K), and this is all the more probable because the "my" is omitted by St Paul, and therefore might be omitted here by the copyists. In D, as in some MSS. of the LXX., "my" is found after "faith." In the original Hebrew the passage seems to mean "But the righteous shall live by his fidelity." On the deeper meaning read into the verse by St Paul see my *Life of St Paul*, I. 369. The Rabbis said that Habakkuk had compressed into this one rule the 365 negative and 248 positive precepts of the Law.

but if any man draw back] The introduction of the words "any man" by the A.V. is wholly unwarrantable, and at first sight looks as if it were due to dogmatic bias and a desire to insinuate the Calvinistic doctrine of the "indefectibility of grace." But throughout this Epistle there is not a word which countenances the dogma of "final perseverance." The true rendering is "And 'if *he draw back* My soul approveth him not;'" i.e. "if my just man draw back" (comp. Ezek. xviii. 24, "when the righteous turneth away from his righteousness)." The verb implies that shrinking from a course once begun which is used of St Peter in Gal. ii. 12. It means, primarily, "to strike or shorten sail," and then to withdraw or hold back (comp. Acts xx. 20, 27). This quotation follows the LXX. in here diverging very widely from the Hebrew of Hab. ii. 4, which has "Behold his (the Chaldean's) soul in him is puffed up, it is not humble (lit *'level'*); but the righteous shall live by his faithfulness." All that we have seen of previous quotations shews us how free was the use made, by way of illustration, of Scripture language. Practically the writer here applies the language of the old Prophet, not in its primary sense, but to express his own conceptions (Calvin). On the possible defection of "the righteous" see Article xvi. of our Church.

39. *But we are not of them who draw back*] More tersely in the original, "But we are not of defection unto perdition, but of faith unto gaining of the soul." "Faith," says Delitzsch, "saves the soul by linking it to God...The unbelieving man loses his soul; for not being God's *neither is he his own*." He does not *possess* himself. The word for "gaining" is found also in Eph. i. 14. In these words the writer shews that in his awful warnings against apostasy he is only putting a *hypothetical* case. "His readers," he says, "though some of them may have gone towards the verge, have not yet passed over the fatal line." The word Faith is here introduced with the writer's usual skill to prepare for the next great section of the Epistle.

CH. XI. THE HEROES OF FAITH.

The main task of the writer has now been performed, but the remainder of the Epistle had also a very important purpose. It would have been fatal to the peace of mind of a Jewish convert to feel that there was a chasm between his Christian faith and the faith of his past

Now faith is the substance of *things* hoped for, the 11
evidence of things not seen. For by it the elders obtained 2
life. The writer wishes to shew that there is no painful *discontinuity* in the religious convictions of Hebrew converts. They could still enjoy the *viaticum* of good examples set forth in their O.T. Scriptures. Their faith was identical with, though transcendently more blessed than, that which had sustained the Patriarchs, Prophets, and Martyrs of their nation in all previous ages. The past history of the Chosen People was not discarded or discredited by the Gospel; it was, on the contrary, completed and glorified.

1. *Now faith*] Since he has said "we are of faith to gaining of the soul," the question might naturally arise, What then is faith? It is nowhere defined in Scripture, nor is it defined here, for the writer rather describes it in its effects than in its essence; but it is described by what it *does*. The chapter which illustrates "faith" is full of works; and this alone should shew how idle is any contrast or *antithesis* between the two. Here however the word "faith" means only "the belief which leads to faithfulness"—the hope which, apart from sight, holds the ideal to be the most real, and acts accordingly.

the substance of things hoped for] The word "*hypostasis*," here rendered "substance," as in i. 3, may mean (1) that underlying essence which gives reality to a thing. Faith gives a subjective reality to the aspirations of hope. But it may be used (2) in an ordinary and not a metaphysical sense for "basis," foundation; or (3) for "*confidence*," as in iii. 14 (comp. 2 Cor. ix. 4, xi. 17): and this seems to be the most probable meaning of the word here. St Jerome speaks of the passage as breathing somewhat of Philo ("Philoneum aliquid spirans"), who speaks of faith in a very similar way.

the evidence of things not seen] The word rendered "evidence" means "demonstration," or "test."

not seen] i.e. which are as yet invisible, because they are eternal and not temporal (2 Cor. iv. 18, v. 7). God Himself belongs to the things as yet unseen; but Faith—in *this* sense of the word, which is not the distinctively Pauline sense (Gal. ii. 16, iii. 26; Rom. iii. 25)—demonstrates the existence of the immaterial as though it were actual. The object of faith from the dawn of man's life had been Christ, who, even at the Fall, had been foretold as "the seed of the woman who should break the serpent's head." The difference between the Two Covenants was that in the New He was fully set forth as the effulgence of the Father's glory, whereas in the Old He had been but dimly indicated by shadows and symbols. Bishop Wordsworth quotes the sonnet of the poet Wordsworth on these lines:

> "For what contend the wise? for nothing less
> Than that the Soul, freed from the bonds of sense,
> *And to her God restored by evidence
> Of things not seen*, drawn forth from their recess,
> Root there—and not in forms—her holiness."

3 a good report. Through faith we understand that the worlds were framed by the word of God, so that *things* which are seen were not made of *things* which do appear. 4 By faith Abel offered unto God a more excellent sacrifice

> **2.** *For by it the elders obtained a good report*] Lit., "For therein the elders had witness borne to them." Their "good report" was won in the sphere of faith. The elders—a technical Jewish term (*Zekenîm*)—means the ancient fathers of the Church of Israel (i. 1).
>
> **3.** *Through faith*] In this chapter we find fifteen special instances of the work of faith, besides the summary enumeration in the 32nd and following verses.
>
> *we understand*] 'we apprehend with the reason'. See Rom. i. 20.
>
> *that the worlds were framed*] The word for "worlds" means literally ages (i. 2), i. e. the world regarded from the standpoint of human history. The "time-world" necessarily presumes the existence of the space-world also. See i. 2.
>
> *were framed*] "have been established" (xiii. 21; Ps. lxxiv. 16; LXX.).
>
> *by the word of God*] Rather, "by the utterance (*rhemati*) of God," namely by His fiat, as in Gen. i. ; Ps. xxxiii. 6, 9; 2 Pet. iii. 5. There is no question here as to the creation of the world by the Logos, for he purposely alters the word λόγῳ used by the LXX. in Ps. xxxiii. into *rhemati*.
>
> *so that things which are seen*...] The true reading and literal translation are "so that not from things which appear hath that which is seen come into being," a somewhat harsh way of expressing that "the visible world did not derive its existence from anything phenomenal." In other words, the clause denies the pre-existence of matter. It says that the world was made out of nothing, not out of the primeval chaos. So in 2 Macc. vii. 28 the mother begs her son "to look upon the heaven and earth and all that is therein, and consider that God made them *out of things that are not*" (ἐξ οὐκ ὄντων). If this view be correct, the writer would seem purposely to avoid Philo's way of saying that the world was made out of τὰ μὴ ὄντα, "things conceived as non-existent," by which he meant the "formless matter" (as in Wisd. xi. 17). He says that the world did not originate from *anything* phenomenal. This verse, so far from being superfluous, or incongruous with what follows, strikes the keynote of faith by shewing that its first object must be a Divine and Infinite Creator. Thus like Moses in Gen. i. the verse excludes from the region of faith all Atheism, Pantheism, Polytheism, and Dualism.
>
> **4.** *By faith Abel*] Intending, so to speak, "to pluck only the flowers which happen to come within his reach, while he leaves the whole meadow full to his readers," he begins to cull his instances from the world before the flood. His examples of faith fall into five groups. 1. Antediluvian (4—6). 2. From Noah to Abraham (7—19, including some general reflexions in 13—16). 3. The Patriarchs (20—22). 4. From Moses to Rahab (23—31). 5. Summary reference to later heroes and martyrs down to the time of the Maccabees (32—40).

than Cain, by which he obtained witness that he was righteous, God testifying of his gifts: and by it he being dead yet speaketh. By faith Enoch was translated that 5 he should not see death; and was not found, because God had translated him: for before his translation he had this testimony, that *he* pleased God. But without faith 6 *it is* impossible to please *him:* for he that cometh to God must believe that he is, and *that* he is a rewarder of them that diligently seek him. By faith Noah, being warned 7 of God of *things* not seen as yet, moved with fear, prepared an ark to the saving of his house; by the which he con-

more excellent] Lit., "more" or "greater."
a more excellent sacrifice than Cain] This we learn from Gen. iv. 5, but we are not told the exact points in virtue of which the sacrifice was superior. We may naturally infer that Abel's was a more carefully-chosen and valuable offering, but especially that it was offered in a more sincere and humble spirit of faith and love.
he obtained witness] By God's sign of approval (Gen. iv. 4; LXX.). Hence he is called "righteous" in Matt. xxiii. 35; 1 John iii. 12. The Jewish *Hagadah* was that God had shewn His approval by fire from heaven which consumed Abel's sacrifice.
testifying of his gifts] Rather, "bearing witness to his gifts."
and by it] i.e. by his faith.
he being dead yet speaketh] Another reading (D, E, I, K) is "though dead, he is still being spoken of." But the allusion seems to be to "the voice of his blood" (Gen. iv. 10), as seems clear from the reference in xii. 24. No doubt it is also meant that he speaks *by his example*, but there seems to have been some Jewish *Hagadah* on the subject, for Philo says "Abel—which is most strange—has both been slain and lives" (Opp. I. 200). He deduces from Gen. iv. 10 that Abel is still unforgotten, and hence that the righteous are immortal.

5. *Enoch was translated*] Lit., "was transferred (hence)" (Gen. v. 24; Ecclus. xliv. 16, xlix. 14; Jos. *Antt.* i. 3. § 4.
was not found, because God had translated him. Gen. v. 24 (LXX. Cod. *Alex.*).
he had this testimony] "he hath had witness born to him;" "Enoch walked with God," Gen. v. 24 (LXX. "*pleased* God").

6. *that he is...*] The object of Faith is both the existence and the Divine government of God. "We trust in the living God, who is the Saviour of all men, specially of those that believe" (1 Tim. iv. 10).
and that he is a rewarder] Rather, "and that he *becomes* (i.e. shews or proves Himself to be) a rewarder."

7. *warned of God*] The same word is used as in viii. 5, xii. 25.
moved with fear] Influenced by godly caution and reverence; the same kind of fear as that implied in v. 7.

demned the world, and became heir of the righteousness
8 which is by faith. By faith Abraham, when he was called
to go out into a place which he should after receive for
an inheritance, obeyed; and he went out, not knowing
9 whither he went. By faith he sojourned in the land of
promise, as *in* a strange *country*, dwelling in tabernacles
with Isaac and Jacob, the heirs with *him* of the same
10 promise: for he looked for a city which hath foundations,

condemned the world] His example was in condemning contrast with the unbelief of the world (Matt. xii. 41; Lk. xi. 31).

of the righteousness which is by faith] Rather, "which is according to faith" (comp. Ezek. xiv. 14). Noah is called "righteous" in Gen. vi. 9, and Philo observes that he is the first to receive this title, and erroneously says that the name Noah means "righteous" as well as "rest." St Paul does not use the phrase "the righteousness according to faith," though he has "the righteousness of faith" (Rom. iv. 13). "Faith" however in this writer never becomes the same as mystic oneness with Christ, but means general belief in the unseen; and "righteousness" is not "justification," but faith manifested by obedience. Throughout this chapter righteousness is the human condition which faith produces (xi. 33), not the divine gift which faith receives. Hence he says that Noah "became an heir of the righteousness which is according to faith," i.e. he entered on the inheritance of righteousness which faith had brought him. In 2 Pet. ii. 5 Noah is called "a preacher of righteousness;" and in Wisd. x. 4 "the righteous man."

8. *Abraham*] As was natural, the faith of "the father of the faithful" was one of the commonest topics of discussion in the Jewish Schools. Wordsworth (*Eccles. Sonnets*, XXVI.) speaks of

"*Faith*, which to the Patriarchs did dispense
Sure guidance ere a ceremonial fence
Was needful to men thirsting to transgress."

when he was called] The Greek (if ὁ καλούμενος be the right reading) can only mean literally either "he who is called Abraham," which would be somewhat meaningless; or "Abraham, who was called to go out."

to go out] from Ur of the Chaldees (Acts vii. 4).

a place which he should after receive] Gen. xii. 7.

9. *as in a strange country*] "I am a stranger and a sojourner with you" (Gen. xxiii. 3). The patriarchs are constantly called *paroikoi*, "dwellers beside," "sojourners" (Gen. xvii. 8, xx. 1, &c.).

dwelling in tabernacles] i.e. in tents (Gen. xii. 8, xiii. 3, &c.).

10. *a city which hath foundations*] Rather, "the city which hath the foundations," namely, "the Jerusalem above" (Gal. iv. 26; Heb. xii. 22, xiii. 14; Rev. xxi. 2, 14). The same thought is frequently found in Philo. The tents of the Patriarchs had no foundations; the foundations of the City of God are of pearl and precious stone (Rev. xxi. 14, 19.)

whose builder and maker *is* God. Through faith also Sara herself received strength to conceive seed, and was delivered of a child when *she* was past age, because she judged him faithful who had promised. Therefore sprang there even of one, and him as good as dead, *so many* as the stars of the sky in multitude, and as the sand which is by the sea shore innumerable. These all died in faith, not having received the promises, but having seen them afar off, and were persuaded of *them*, and embraced *them*, and confessed that they were strangers and pilgrims on the earth. For they that say such *things* declare plainly that they seek a country. And truly, if they had been mindful of that *country* from whence they came out, they might

builder and maker] Rather, "architect and builder." This is the only place in the N.T. where the word *demiourgos* occurs. It is found also in 2 Macc. iv. 1, and plays a large part in the vocabulary of Gnostic heretics. But God is called the "Architect" of the Universe in Philo and in Wisd. xiii. 1, "neither by considering the works did they acknowledge the workmaster."

11. *also Sara herself*] Rather "even." Perhaps the "even" refers to her original weakness of faith when she laughed (Gen. xviii. 12, xxi. 2; comp. Rom. iv. 19). Dr Field thinks that these words may be a gloss, and that the verse refers to Abraham, since ἔτεκεν, "was delivered," is not found in ℵ, A, D.

to conceive seed] For technical reasons the probable meaning here is "for the founding of a family" (comp. the use of the word *katabolē* in iv. 3, ix. 26 and "seed" in ii. 16, xi. 18).

who had promised] Comp. x. 23.

12. *as the stars...as the sand*] Gen. xxii. 17; Deut. i. 10.

13. *in faith*] Lit. "according to faith."

not having received the promises] They received the promises in one sense, *as* promises (ver. 17), but had not yet entered upon their fruition (comp. ver. 39 and ix. 15).

and were persuaded of them] These words are not found in all the best MSS.

and embraced them] Rather, "saluting them" (Gen. xlix. 18). "Your father Abraham rejoiced to see my day; and he saw it, and was glad" (John viii. 56).

confessed that they were strangers and pilgrims] Gen. xxiii. 4, xlvii. 9; 1 Chron. xxix. 15; Ps. xxxix. 12, &c.

14. *that they seek a country*] Rather, "that they are seeking further after a native land." Hence comes the argument of the next verse that it was not their old home in Chaldea for which they were yearning, but a heavenly native-land.

16 have had opportunity to have returned. But now they desire a better *country*, that is, a heavenly: wherefore God is not ashamed to be called their God: for he hath prepared 17 for them a city. By faith Abraham, when he was tried, offered up Isaac: and he that had received the promises 18 offered up *his* only begotten *son*, of whom it was said, That 19 in Isaac shall thy seed be called: accounting that God *was* able to raise *him* up, even from the dead; from 20 whence also he received him in a figure. By faith Isaac

15. *to have returned*] But they never attempted to return to Mesopotamia, because they were home-sick not for that land but for heaven.

16. *But now*] "But, as the case now is."

they desire] The word means, "they are yearning for," "they stretch forth their hands towards."

is not ashamed to be called their God] Rather, "is not ashamed of them, to be called their God" (Gen. xxviii. 13; Ex. iii. 6—15.)

he hath prepared for them a city] The "inheritance incorruptible and undefiled, and that fadeth not away, reserved in heaven for us" (1 Pet. i. 4). This digression is meant to shew that the faith and hopes of the Patriarchs reached beyond mere temporal blessings.

17. *By faith Abraham...offered up Isaac*] Reverting to Abraham, whose faith (1) in leaving his country, (2) in living as a stranger in Canaan, he has already mentioned, he now adduces the third and greatest instance of his faithful obedience in being ready to offer up Isaac. Both tenses, "hath offered up" (perf.) and "was offering up" (imperf.) are characteristic of the author's views of Scripture as a permanent record of events which may be still regarded as present to us. St James (ii. 21) uses the aorist.

he that had received the promises] Four verbs are used with reference to "receiving" the promises, ἀναδέχεσθαι (here), λαβεῖν (ix. 15), ἐπιτυχεῖν (xi. 33), κομίσασθαι (xi. 39). The word here used implies a joyous welcome of *special* promises. The context generally shews with sufficient clearness the *sense* in which the Patriarchs may be said both to have "received" and "not to have received" the promises. They received and welcomed special promises, and those were fulfilled; and in those they saw the germ of richer blessings which they enjoyed by faith but not in actual fruition.

18. *of whom*] Lit. "with reference to whom" (Isaac); or perhaps "to whom," i.e. to Abraham.

in Isaac shall thy seed be called] Gen. xvii. 8, 19, xxi. 12, &c.

19. *from whence*] The only place in this Epistle where ὅθεν has its local sense.

in a figure] Lit. "in a parable." For the use of the word see ix. 9. The exact meaning is much disputed. It has been rendered "as a type" (comp. Vulg. *in parabolam*), or "in a bold venture." or "unexpectedly."

blessed Jacob and Esau concerning *things* to come. By 21
faith Jacob, when he was a dying, blessed both the sons of
Joseph; and worshipped, *leaning* upon the top of his staff.
By faith Joseph, when he died, made mention of the 22

These views are hardly tenable. But how could Abraham have received Isaac back "*in a figure*" when he received him back "*in reality*"? The answer is that he received him back, figuratively, *from the dead*, because Isaac was typically, or figuratively, dead—potentially sacrificed—when he received him back. Josephus in narrating the event uses the same word (*Antt.* I. 13. § 4). But in this instance again it is possible that the key to the expression might be found in some Jewish legend. In one Jewish writer it is said (of course untruly) that Isaac *really was killed*, and raised again. The restoration of Isaac *was* undoubtedly a type of the resurrection of Christ, but it is hardly probable that the writer would have expressed so deep a truth in a passing and ambiguous expression.

20. *By faith Isaac blessed Jacob and Esau*] It is true that the blessing of Esau when rightly translated, "Behold thy dwelling shall be *away from* the fatness of the earth and *away from* the dew of blessing" (Gen. xxvii. 39) reads more like a curse; but the next verse (40) involves a promise of ultimate freedom, and Esau obtained the blessings of that lower and less spiritual life for which he was alone fitted by his character and tastes.

concerning things to come] The true reading seems to be "*even* concerning," though it is not easy to grasp the exact force of the "even."

21. *both the sons*] Rather, "each of the sons." He made a marked difference between them (Gen. xlviii. 17—19).

worshipped, leaning upon the top of his staff] In this verse there is an allusion to two separate events. The first is the blessing of Ephraim and Manasseh (Gen. xlviii. 1—20); the other an earlier occasion (Gen. xlvii. 29—31). In our version it is rendered "And Israel bowed himself upon the bed's head," but in the LXX. and Peshito as here, it is "upon the top of his staff." The reason for the variation is that having no vowel points the LXX. understood the word to be *matteh*, "staff," not *mittah*, "bed," as in Gen. xlviii. 2. If they were right in this view, the passage means that Jacob, rising from his bed to take the oath from Joseph, supported his aged limbs on the staff, which was a type of his pilgrimage (Gen. xxxii. 10), and at the end of the oath bowed his head over the staff in sign of thanks and reverence to God. The Vulgate (here following the *Itala*) erroneously renders it *adoravit fastigium virgae ejus*, Jacob "adored the top of *his* (Joseph's) staff," and the verse has been quoted (e. g. by Cornelius a Lapide) in defence of image-worship. Yet in Gen. xlvii. 31 the Vulgate has "adoravit *Deum*, conversus ad lectuli caput." Probably all that is meant is that, being too feeble to rise and kneel or stand, Jacob "bowed himself upon the head of his couch" in an attitude of prayer, just as the aged David did on his deathbed (1 Kings i. 47).

departing of the children of Israel; and gave commandment
23 concerning his bones. By faith Moses, when he was born, was hid three months of his parents, because they saw *he was* a proper child; and they were not afraid of the king's com-
24 mandment. By faith Moses, when he was come to years,
25 refused to be called the son of Pharaoh's daughter; choosing rather to suffer affliction with the people of God, than to
26 enjoy the pleasures of sin for a season; esteeming the reproach of Christ greater riches than the treasures in

22. *when he died*] The less common word for "dying" is here taken from the LXX. of Gen. l. 26.

gave commandment concerning his bones] A sign of his perfect conviction that God's promise would be fulfilled (Gen. l. 24, 25; Ex. xiii. 19; comp. Acts vii. 16).

23. *Moses...was hid*] The "faith" is of course that of his parents, Amram and Jochebed.

of his parents] This is implied in the LXX. of Ex. ii. 2, but the Hebrew only says that his *mother* concealed him.

a proper child] In Acts vii. 20 he is called "fair to God." In his marvellous beauty (see Philo, *Vit. Mos.*) they saw a promise of some future blessing, and braved the peril involved in breaking the king's decree.

the king's commandment] To drown all male children (Ex. i. 22, ii. 2).

24. *refused to be called the son of Pharaoh's daughter*] He refused the rank of an Egyptian prince. The reference is to the Jewish legends which were rich in details about the infancy and youth of Moses. See Jos. *Antt.* II. ix—xi.; Philo, Opp. II. 82; Stanley, *Lect. on Jewish Church*. The only reference to the matter in Scripture is in Ex. ii. 10; Acts vii. 22—25.

25. *with the people of God*] iv. 9.

the pleasures of sin for a season] The *brevity* of sinful enjoyment is alluded to in Job xx. 5, "The triumphing of the wicked is short, and the joy of the hypocrite but for a moment." The special sin would have been the very one to which the readers were tempted—apostasy.

26. *the reproach of Christ*] Rather, "of the Christ" (comp. xiii. 13; 2 Cor. i. 5; Rom. xv. 3; Phil. iii. 7—11; Col. i. 24). There may be in the words a reminiscence of Ps. lxxxix. 50, 51, "Remember Lord *the reproach* of thy servants...wherewith thine enemies have *reproached* the footsteps *of thine anointed*." By "the reproach of the Christ" is meant "the reproach which He had to bear in His own person, and has to bear in that of His members" (2 Cor. i. 5). It is true that in no other passage of the Epistle does the writer allude to the mystical oneness of Christ and His Church, but he must have been aware of that truth from intercourses with St Paul and knowledge of his writings. Other-

Egypt: for he had respect unto the recompence of the reward. By faith he forsook Egypt, not fearing the wrath of the king: for he endured, as seeing *him who is* invisible. Through faith he kept the passover, and the sprinkling of blood, lest he that destroyed the firstborn should touch them. By faith they passed through the Red sea as by dry *land:* which the Egyptians assaying to do were drowned. By faith the walls of Jericho fell down, after they were com- 27 28 29 30

wise we must suppose him to imply that Moses by faith realised, at least dimly, that he was suffering as Christ would hereafter suffer.

he had respect unto] Lit. "for he was looking *away from it to.*" What Moses had in view was something wholly different from sinful pleasure. The verb is found here only in the N. T.

27. *By faith he forsook Egypt*] This must allude to the Exodus, not to the flight of Moses into Midian. On the latter occasion, he distinctly did "fear the wrath of the king" (Ex. ii. 14, 15). It is true that for the moment Pharaoh and the Egyptians pressed the Israelites to depart, but it was only in fear and anger, and Moses foresaw the immediate pursuit.

he endured, as seeing] The words have also been rendered, but less correctly, "He was stedfast towards Him who is invisible, as if seeing Him."

him who is invisible] "The blessed and only Potentate...whom no man hath seen, nor can see" (1 Tim. vi. 15, 16). Perhaps we should render it "the *King* Invisible," understanding the word βασιλέα, and so emphasizing the contrast between the fear of God and the consequent fearless attitude towards Pharaoh.

28. *Through faith*] Rather, "by faith," as before.

he kept the passover] Lit. "he hath made," or "instituted." Another of the author's characteristic tenses (see ver. 17).

and the sprinkling of blood] Ex. xii. 21—23. The "faith" consisted primarily in believing the promises and obeying the command of God, and secondarily, we may believe, in regarding the sprinkled blood as in some way typical of a better propitiation (Rom. iii. 25). The word for sprinkling is not *rantismos*, as in xii. 24, but πρόσχυσις, which is found here only ("effusion"), but is derived from the verb used in Lev. i. 5 (LXX.).

he that destroyed] The term is derived from the LXX. The Hebrew (Ex. xii. 23) has *mashchith* "destruction." Comp. 1 Chr. xxi. 15; 2 Chr. xxxii. 21; 1 Cor. x. 10; Ecclus. xlviii. 21.

29. *they*] Moses and the Israelites.

were drowned] Lit., "were swallowed up" (Ex. xiv. 15—28; Ps. cvi. 9—12).

which the Egyptians assaying to do] The Greek words must mean " of which sea" (or "of which dry land") the Egyptians making trial.

30. *the walls of Jericho fell down*] Josh. vi. 12—20.

31 passed about seven days. By faith the harlot Rahab perished not with them that believed not, when she had received the spies with peace.
32 And what shall I more say? for the time would fail me to tell of Gedeon, and *of* Barak, and *of* Samson, and *of* Jephthae; *of* David also, and Samuel, and *of* the prophets:
33 who through faith subdued kingdoms, wrought righteousness, obtained promises, stopped the mouths of lions,
34 quenched the violence of fire, escaped the edge of the

31. *By faith*] Josh. ii. 9—11, "The Lord your God, He is God."
the harlot Rahab] So she is called in Josh. ii. 1; Jas. ii. 25, and it shews the faithfulness of the sacred narrative that her name is even introduced as well as that of Ruth, a Moabitess, in the genealogy of our Lord (Matt. i. 5). The Targum softens it down into "innkeeper" and others render it "idolatress." Her name was highly honoured by the Jews, who said that eight prophets—among them Baruch, Jeremiah, and Shallum—were descended from her, and the prophetess Huldah. Megillah f. 14. 2.
that believed not] Rather, "that were disobedient."
32. *the time would fail me*] The phrase is also found in Philo, *De Somniis*. The names of "the heroes of faith" here mentioned are drawn from the Books of Judges and Samuel, with a reference to the Books of Kings and Chronicles, and what is known of the history of the Prophets. There does not seem to be any special design in the arrangement of the *pairs* of names, though it is a curious circumstance that, in each pair, the hero who came earlier in time is placed after the other. In 32—34 we have instances of active, and in 35—38 of passive faith.
33. *subdued kingdoms*] The allusion is specially to the conquest of Canaan by Joshua, and to the victories of David (2 Sam. v. 17—25, xxi. 15, &c.).
wrought righteousness] The allusion is somewhat vague, but seems to refer to the justice of Judges and Kings (1 Sam. xii. 3, 4; 2 Sam. viii. 15; 1 Chron. xviii. 14, &c.), and perhaps especially to the Judgment of Solomon. "To execute judgment and justice" belonged especially to the Princes of Israel (Ezek. xlv. 9).
obtained promises] If we compare the expression with verses 13, 39, we see that the primary reference must be to temporal promises (see Josh. xxi. 43—45, &c.); but they also obtained at least a partial fruition of spiritual promises also.
stopped the mouths of lions] Samson (Judg. xiv. 5, 6), David (1 Sam. xvii. 34, 35), Daniel (Dan. vi. 22), Benaiah (2 Sam. xxiii. 20).
34. *quenched the violence of fire*] Dan. iii. 25; 1 Macc. ii. 59.
escaped the edge of the sword] David (1 Sam. xviii. 11, xix. 10, &c.), Elijah (1 K. xix. 2), Elisha (2 K. vi. 12—17; Jer. xxvi. 24, &c.).

sword, out of weakness were made strong, waxed valiant in fight, turned to flight the armies of the aliens. Women 35 received their dead raised to life again: and others were tortured, not accepting deliverance; that they might obtain a better resurrection: and others had trial of *cruel* 36 mockings and scourgings, yea, moreover of bonds and imprisonment: they were stoned, they were sawn asunder, 37 were tempted, were slain with the sword: they wandered

out of weakness were made strong] Hezekiah (2 K. xx. 5), Samson (Judg. xv. 15, xvi. 28—30), David (1 Sam. xvii. 42, 51, &c.).

turned to flight the armies of the aliens] This and the previous clause may refer specially to the Maccabees, though they also suit Joshua, the Judges, David, &c. The word used for "armies" (*parembolas*) is the word used for "camp" in xiii. 11, 13; Rev. xx. 9. It has both senses in the LXX. (Judg. iv. 16). The classic verb for "drove back" is found here only in the N.T. (*klino*).

35. *Women received their dead*] The woman of Sarepta (1 K. xvii. 22), the Shunamite (2 K. iv. 32—36).

raised to life again] Lit., " by resurrection."

were tortured] The word means, technically, "were broken on the wheel," and the special reference may be to 2 Macc. vi. 18—30, vii. (the tortures of Eleazer the Scribe, and of the Seven Brothers).

deliverance] "*The* deliverance offered them" (2 Macc. vi. 20, 21, vii. 24).

a better resurrection] Not a mere resurrection to earthly life, like the children of the women just mentioned, but "an everlasting reawakening of life" (2 Macc. vii. 9 and *passim*).

36. *mockings and scourgings*] "Seven brethren and their mother... being tormented with scourges and whips...and they brought the second for a mocking-stock...And after him was the third made a mocking-stock...And...they tortured and tormented the fourth in like manner" (2 Macc. vii. 1, 7, 10, 13, &c.). "And they sought out...Judas' friends... and he took vengeance on them and mocked them" (1 Macc. ix. 26).

of bonds and imprisonment] Joseph (Gen. xxxix. 20), Micaiah (1 K. xxii. 26, 27), Jeremiah (Jer. xx. 2, xxxvii. 15), Hanani (2 Chron. xvi. 10).

37. *they were stoned*] Zechariah (2 Chron. xxiv. 20, 21). Jewish tradition said that Jeremiah was stoned. See Matt. xxiii. 35—37; Lk. xi. 51.

were sawn asunder] This was the traditional mode of Isaiah's martyrdom. Hamburger *Talm. Wörterb.* s.v. Jesaia. Comp. Matt. xxiv. 51. The punishment was well-known in ancient days (2 Sam. xii. 31).

were tempted] This would not seem an anticlimax to a pious reader, for the intense violence of temptation, and the horrible dread lest the weakness of human nature should succumb to it, was one of the most awful forms of trial which persecutors could inflict (see Acts xxvi. 11),

about in sheepskins and goatskins; being destitute, afflicted, tormented; (of whom the world was not worthy:) they wandered in deserts, and *in* mountains, and *in* dens and caves of the earth. And these all, having obtained a good report through faith, received not the promise: God having provided some better *thing* for us, that they without us should not be made perfect.

especially if the tempted person yielded to the temptation, as in 1 K. xiii. 7, 19—26. There is no variation in the MSS. but some have conjectured *eprēsthēsan* "they were burned" for *epeirasthēsan*. In a recent outbreak at Alexandria some Jews had been burnt alive (Philo *in Flacc.* 20) and burnings are mentioned in 2 Macc. vi. 11. The reason for the position of the word, as a sort of climax, perhaps lies in the strong effort to tempt the last and youngest of the seven brother-martyrs to apostatise in 2 Macc. vii.

were slain with the sword] "They have slain thy prophets with the sword" (1 K. xix. 10). Jehoiakim "slew Urijah with the sword" (Jer. xxvi. 23). The Jews suffered themselves to be massacred on the Sabbath in the war against Antiochus (1 Macc. ii. 38; 2 Macc. v. 26).

in sheepskins and goatskins] Elijah (1 K. xix. 13; 2 K. i. 8). A hairy garment seems subsequently to have been a common dress among prophets, and it was sometimes adopted for purposes of deception (Zech. xiii. 4). Clement in his *Ep. ad Rom.* I. 17 says that Elishah and Ezekiel also wore hairy garments.

38. *was not worthy*] The world was unworthy of them though it treated them as worthless. The Greek would also admit the meaning that they outweighed in value the whole world (see Prov. viii. 11, LXX.).

in dens and caves] The Israelites in general (Judg. vi. 2). The prophets of the Lord (1 K. xviii. 4, 13). Elijah (1 K. xix. 9). Mattathias and his sons "fled into the mountains" (1 Macc. ii. 28), and many others "into the wilderness" (id. 29). Judas the Maccabe (2 Macc. v. 27). Refugees in caves (2 Macc. vi. 11). "Like beasts" (id. x. 6).

of the earth] Rather, "of the land." The writer's view rarely extends beyond the horizon of Jewish history.

39. *having obtained a good report through faith*] "Having been borne witness to through their faith," i.e. *though* they had this testimony borne to them, they did not see the fulfilment of the promises.

received not the promise] See verses 17, 33, vi. 15, ix. 15. They did not enjoy the fruition of the one great promise.

40. *God having provided some better thing for us*] Lit., "Since God provided" (or "foresaw") "some better thing concerning us." In one sense Abraham, and therefore other patriarchs "rejoiced to see Christ's day," and yet they did but see it in such dim shadow that "many prophets and kings desired to see what ye see, and saw not, and hear the things which ye hear, and did not hear them" (Matt.

> Wherefore seeing we also are compassed about with so 12
> great a cloud of witnesses, let us lay aside every weight, and

xiii. 17), though all their earnest seekings and searchings tended in this direction (1 Pet. i. 10, 11).

that they without us should not be made perfect] "Not unto themselves but unto us they did minister" (1 Pet. i. 12). Since in their days "the fulness of the times" had not yet come (Eph. i. 10) the saints could not be brought to their completion—the end and consummation of their privileges—apart from us. The "just" had not been, and could not be, "perfected" (xii. 23) until Christ had died (vii. 19, viii. 6). The implied thought is that if Christ had come in *their* days—if the "close of the ages" had fallen in the times of the Patriarchs or Prophets—the world would long ago have ended, and we should never have been born. Our *present* privileges are, as he has been proving all through the Epistle, incomparably better than those of the fathers. It was necessary in the economy of God that their "perfectionment" should be delayed until ours could be accomplished; in the future world we and they shall equally enjoy the benefits of Christ's redemption.

CH. XII. An exhortation to faithful endurance (1—3) and a reminder that our earthly sufferings are due to the fatherly chastisement of God (4—13). The need of earnest watchfulness (14—17). Magnificent concluding appeal founded on the superiority and grandeur of the New Covenant (18—24), which enhances the guilt and peril of apostasy (25—29).

1—3. AN EXHORTATION TO PATIENT STEADFASTNESS.

1. *Wherefore*] The Greek word is a very strong particle of inference not found elsewhere in the N. T. except in 1 Thess. iv. 8.

seeing we also are compassed] The order of the Greek is "Let us also, seeing we are compassed with so great a cloud of witnesses...run with patience."

a cloud] A classical Greek and Latin, as well as Hebrew, metaphor for a great multitude. Thus Homer speaks of "a cloud of foot-soldiers." We have the same metaphor in Is. lx. 8, "who are these who fly as clouds" (Heb.). Here, as St Clemens of Alexandria says, the cloud is imagined to be "holy and translucent."

of witnesses] The word has not yet fully acquired its sense of "martyrs." It here probably means "witnesses to the sincerity and the reward of faith." The notion that they are also witnesses of our Christian race lies rather in the word περικείμενον, "surrounding us on all sides," like the witnesses in a circus or a theatre (1 Cor. iv. 9).

let us lay aside every weight] Lit., "stripping off at once cumbrance of every kind." The word "weight" was used, technically, in the language of athletes, to mean "superfluous flesh," to be reduced by training. The training requisite to make the body supple and sinewy was severe and long-continued. Metaphorically the word comes to mean "pride," "inflation."

the sin which doth so easily beset *us*, and let us run with patience the race that is set before us, looking unto Jesus the author and finisher of *our* faith; who for the joy that was set before him endured the cross, despising the shame, and is set down at the right hand of the throne of God.

and the sin which doth so easily beset us] The six words "which doth so easily beset us" represent one Greek word, *euperistaton*, of which the meaning is uncertain, because it occurs nowhere else. It means literally "well standing round," or "well stood around." (1) If taken in the latter sense it is interpreted to mean (a) "thronged," "eagerly encircled," and so "*much admired*" or "much applauded," and will thus put us on our guard against sins which are popular; or (β) "easily avoidable," with reference to the verb *peri-istaso*, "avoid" (2 Tim. ii. 16; Tit. iii. 9). The objections to these renderings are that the writer is thinking of private sins. More probably it is to be taken in the *active* sense, as in the A.V. and the R.V. of the sin which either (a) "presses closely about us to attack us;" or (β) which "closely clings (*tenaciter inhaerens*, Erasmus) to us" like an enfolding robe (*statos chiton*). The latter is almost certainly the true meaning, and is suggested by the participle *apothemenoi*, "stripping off" (comp. Eph. iv. 22). As an athlete lays aside every heavy or dragging article of dress, so we must strip away from us and throw aside the clinging robe of familiar sin. The metaphor is the same as that of the word *apekdusasthai* (Col. iii. 9), which is the parallel to *apothesthai* in Eph. iv. 22. The gay garment of sin may at first be lightly put on and lightly laid aside, but it afterwards becomes like the fabled shirt of Nessus eating into the bones as it were fire.

with patience] Endurance (*hupomonē*) characterised the faith of all these heroes and patriarchs, and he exhorts *us* to endure because Christ also endured the cross (*hupomeinas*).

the race that is set before us] One of the favourite metaphors of St Paul (Phil. iii. 12—14; 1 Cor. ix. 24, 25; 2 Tim. iv. 7, 8).

2. *looking unto Jesus*] It is not possible to express in English the thought suggested by the Greek verb *aphorōntes*, which implies that we must "look away (from other things) unto Jesus." It implies "the concentration of the wandering gaze into a single direction."

the author] The word is the same (ἀρχηγόν) as that used in ii. 10. In Acts iii. 15, v. 31 it is rendered "a Prince," as in Is. xxx. 4 (LXX.). By His faithfulness (iii. 2) he became our captain and standard-bearer on the path of faith.

and finisher] He leads us to "the end of our faith," which is the salvation of our souls (1 Pet. i. 9).

of our faith] Rather, "of faith."

endured the cross, despising the shame] Lit., "endured *a cross*, despising shame."

is set down] Rather, "hath sat down" (i. 3, viii. 1, x. 12).

For consider him that endured such contradiction of sinners 3
against himself, lest ye be wearied and faint in your minds.
Ye have not yet resisted unto blood, striving against sin. 4
And ye have forgotten the exhortation which speaketh unto 5

3. *consider*] Lit., "compare yourselves with." Contrast the comparative immunity from anguish of your lot with the agony of His (John xv. 20).

that endured...] Who hath endured at the hand of sinners such opposition.

such contradiction of sinners against himself] The Greek word for "contradiction" has already occurred in vi. 16, vii. 7. Three uncials (א, D, E) read "against *themselves*." Christ was a mark for incessant "contradiction,"—"a sign which is spoken against" (Lk. ii. 34).

lest ye be wearied and faint in your minds] The correction of the R. V., "*that ye wax not weary, fainting in your souls*," will be reckoned by careless and prejudiced readers among the changes which they regard as meaningless. Yet, as in hundreds of other instances, it brings out much more fully and forcibly the exact meaning of the original. "*That ye wax not weary*" is substituted for "lest ye be weary" because the Greek verb, being in the aorist, suggests a *sudden* or momentary break-down in endurance; on the other hand, "fainting" is in the present, and suggests the *gradual* relaxation of nerve and energy which culminates in the sudden relapse. Lastly the word in the original is "souls," not "minds." Endurance was one of the most needful Christian virtues in times of waiting and of trial (Gal. vi. 9).

4—13. FATHERLY CHASTISEMENTS SHOULD BE CHEERFULLY ENDURED.

4. *Ye have not yet resisted unto blood*] If this be a metaphor drawn from pugilism, as the last is from "running a race," it means that as yet they have not "had blood drawn." This would not be impossible, for St Paul adopts pugilistic metaphors (1 Cor. ix. 26, 27). More probably however the meaning is that, severe as had been the persecutions which they had undergone (x. 32, 33), they had not yet—and perhaps a shade of reproach is involved in the expression—resisted *up to the point of martyrdom* (Rev. xii. 11). The Church addressed can scarcely therefore have been either the Church of Rome, which had before this time furnished "a great multitude" of martyrs (Tac. *Ann.* XV. 44; Rev. vii. 9), or the Church of Jerusalem, in which, beside the martyrdoms of St Stephen, St James the elder, and St James the Lord's brother, some had certainly been put to death in the persecution of Saul (Acts viii. 1).

striving against sin] "in your struggles against sin." Some from this expression give a more general meaning to the clause—"You have not yet put forth your utmost efforts in your moral warfare."

5. *And ye have forgotten*] "Yet ye have utterly forgotten," or possibly the words may be intended interrogatively "Yet have ye utterly forgotten?"

you as unto children, My son, despise not thou the chastening of the Lord, nor faint when thou art
6 rebuked of him: for whom the Lord loveth he chasteneth, and scourgeth every son whom he re-
7 ceiveth. If ye endure chastening, God dealeth with you as with sons; for what son is *he* whom the father chasteneth
8 not? But if ye be without chastisement, whereof all are
9 partakers, then are ye bastards, and not sons. Furthermore we have had fathers of our flesh which corrected *us*, and we gave *them* reverence: shall we not much rather be in sub-
10 jection unto the Father of spirits, and live? For they verily

the exhortation] "the encouragement," or "strengthening consolation."
speaketh] "discourseth," or "reasoneth" (*dialegetai*).
My son...] The quotation is from Prov. iii. 11, 12, and is taken mainly from the LXX. There is a very similar passage in Job v. 17, and Philo, *de Congr. quaerend. erudit. gr.* (Opp. I. 544).
despise not] "Regard not lightly."
the chastening] Rather, "the training."
nor faint...] In the Hebrew it is "and loathe not His correction."
rebuked] Rather, "tested," "corrected."

6. *for whom the Lord loveth he chasteneth*] This blessedness of being "trained by God" ("Blessed is the man whom thou chastenest O Lord, and *teachest him* out of thy law," Ps. xciv. 12) is found in many parts of Scripture. "As many as I love, I test (ἐλέγχω) and train" (*paideuo*), Rev. iii. 19; Ps. cxix. 75; Jas. i. 12.

and scourgeth every son whom he receiveth] The writer follows the reading of the LXX., by a slight change in the vowel-points, for "*even as a father* to a son He is good to him."

7. *If ye endure chastening*] The true reading is not *ei*, "if," but *eis*, "unto." "It is for training that ye endure," or better, "Endure ye, for training," i.e. "regard your trials as a part of the moral training designed for you by your Father in Heaven."

what son is he whom the father chasteneth not] The thought, and its application to our relationship towards God are also found in Deut. viii. 5; 2 Sam. vii. 14; Prov. xiii. 24.

8. *whereof all are partakers*] He speaks of God's blessed and disciplinary chastisement as a gift in which all His sons have their share.

9. *unto the Father of spirits*] God might be called "the Father of the spirits," as having created Angels and Spirits; but more probably the meaning is "the Father of our spirits," as in Num. xvi. 22, "the God of the spirits of all flesh." God made our bodies and our souls, but our spirits are in a yet closer relation to Him (Job xii. 10, xxxii. 8, xxxiii. 4; Eccl. xii. 7; Zech. xii. 1; Is. xlii. 5, &c.). If it meant "the Author of spiritual gifts," the expression would be far-fetched and would be no contrast to "the father of our flesh." Here and in vii. 10 theo-

for a few days chastened *us* after their own pleasure; but he for *our* profit, that *we* might be partakers of his holiness. Now no chastening for the present seemeth to be joyous, 11 but grievous: nevertheless afterward it yieldeth the peaceable fruit of righteousness unto them which are exercised thereby. Wherefore lift up the hands which hang 12 down, and the feeble knees; and make straight 13 paths for your feet, lest *that which is* lame be turned

logians have introduced the purely verbal, meaningless, and insoluble dispute about Creationism and Traducianism—i.e. as to whether God separately creates the soul of each one of us, or whether we derive it through our parents by hereditary descent from Adam.

10. *after their own pleasure*] Rather, "as seemed good to them." He is contrasting the brief authority of parents, and their liability to error, and even to caprice, with the pure love and eternal justice of God.

11. *the peaceable fruit of righteousness*] The original is expressed in the emphatic and oratorical style of the writer, "but afterwards it yieldeth a peaceful fruit to those who have been exercised by it—(the fruit) of righteousness." He means that though the sterner aspect of training is never pleasurable for the time it results in righteousness—in moral hardihood and serene self-mastery—to all who have been trained in these gymnasia (γεγυμνασμένοις). See Rom. v. 2—5.

12. *Wherefore*] The poetic style, and even the metrical form of diction in these two verses (of which ver. 13 contains a complete hexameter,

καὶ τροχιὰς ὀρθὰς ποιήσατε τοῖς ποσὶν ὑμῶν

and half an iambic,

ἵνα μὴ τὸ χωλὸν ἐκτραπῇ),

reflect the earnestness of the writer, as he gives more and more elaboration to his sentences in approaching the climax of his appeal. It is most unlikely that they are quotations from Hellenistic poets, for the first agrees closely with Prov. iv. 26 (LXX.). On these accidentally metrical expressions see my *Early Days of Christianity*, I. 464, II. 14.

lift up the hands...] Lit. "straighten out the relaxed hands and the palsied knees." Make one effort to invigorate the flaccid muscles which should be so tense in the struggle in which you are engaged. The writer is thinking of Is. xxxv. 3; Ecclus. xxv. 28, and perhaps of the metaphors of the race and the fight which he has just used.

13. *lest that which is lame be turned out of the way*] Lit. "that the lame (i.e. lameness) may not be quite out of joint, but may rather be cured." The verb ἐκτραπῇ may mean "be turned out of the way," as in 1 Tim. i. 6, v. 15; 2 Tim. iv. 4; but as it is a technical term for "*spraining*," or "dislocation," it may have that meaning here, especially as he has used two medical terms in the previous verse, and has the metaphor of "healing" in his thoughts. The writer may have met with these terms in ordinary life, or in his intercourse with St Luke, with

14 out of the way; but let it rather be healed. Follow peace with all *men*, and holiness, without which no *man* shall see 15 the Lord: looking diligently lest any *man* fail of the grace of God; lest any root of bitterness springing up trouble *you*, 16 and thereby many be defiled; lest there *be* any fornicator, or

whose language he shews himself familiar throughout the Epistle. Intercourse with the beloved physician is perhaps traceable in some of the medical terms of St Paul's later Epistles (see Dean Plumptre's papers on this subject in the *Expositor*, IV. 134 (first series)).
let it rather be healed] Is. lvii. 17—19.

14—17. NEED OF EARNEST WATCHFULNESS.

14. *Follow peace with all men*] The word "men" is better omitted, for doubtless the writer is thinking mainly of peace in the bosom of the little Christian community—a peace which, even in these early days, was often disturbed by rival egotisms (Rom. xiv. 19; 2 Tim. ii. 22).

and holiness] Rather, "and the sanctification" (ix. 13, x. 10, 29, xiii. 12).

without which] We have here in succession two iambics:

οὗ χωρὶς οὐδεὶς ὄψεται τὸν Κύριον
ἐπισκοποῦντες μή τις ὑστερῶν ἀπό.

15. *lest any man fail of the grace of God*] Lit. "whether there be any man who is falling short of," or possibly "falling back from the grace of God." We have already noticed that not improbably the writer has in view some one individual instance of a tendency towards apostasy, which might have a fatal influence upon other weary or wavering brethren (comp. iii. 12).

lest any root of bitterness springing up trouble you] The words "root of bitterness" are a reference to Deut. xxix. 18, "a root that beareth gall and wormwood," or, as in the margin, "a poisonful herb." Here the LXX. in the Vatican MS. has ἐν χολῇ, "in gall," for ἐνοχλῇ, "should trouble you." But the Alexandrian MS., which the writer habitually follows in his quotations, has ἐνοχλῇ. Some have supposed that there is a curious allusion to this verse, and to the reading "*in gall*" in the apparent reference to this Epistle by the Muratorian canon as "the Epistle to the Alexandrians current under the name of Paul, but forged in the interests of Marcion's heresy," which adds that "*gall* ought not to be mixed with honey." The allusion is, however, very doubtful.

many be defiled] Rather, "*the* many." Comp. 1 Cor. v. 6 ("a little leaven"); 1 Cor. xv. 33 ("evil communications"); Gal. v. 9.

16. *any fornicator*] The word must be taken in a literal sense, since Esau was not "an idolator." It is true that Esau is not charged with fornication in the Book of Genesis (which only speaks of his heathen marriages, xxvi. 34, xxviii. 8), but the writer is probably alluding to the Jewish Hagadah, with which he was evidently familiar. There Esau is represented in the blackest colours, as a man utterly sensual, intem-

profane *person*, as Esau, who for one morsel of meat sold his birthright. For ye know how that afterward, when he would 17

perate, and vile, which is also the view of Philo (see Siegfried Philo, p. 254).

or profane person] A man of coarse and unspiritual mind (Gen. xxv. 33). Philo explained the word "hairy" to mean that he was sensuous and lustful.

for one morsel of meat] "for one meal" (Gen. xxv. 29—34).

17. *For ye know how that afterward*] The verse runs literally "for ye know that even, afterwards, when he wished to inherit the blessing, he was rejected—for he found no opportunity for a change of mind—though with tears he earnestly sought for it." It is clear at once that if the writer means to say "that Esau earnestly sought to repent, but could not," then he is contradicting the whole tenor of the Scriptures, and of the Gospel teaching with which he was so familiar. This would not indeed furnish us with any excuse for distorting the meaning of his language, if that meaning be unambiguous; and in favour of such a view of his words is the fact that he repeatedly dwells on the hopelessness—humanly speaking—of all wilful apostasy. On the other hand, "apostasy," when it desires to repent, ceases to be apostasy, and the very meaning of the Gospel is that the door to repentance is never closed by God, though the sinner may close it against himself. Two modes of interpreting the text would save it from clashing with this precious truth. (1) One is to say (a) that "room for repentance" means "opportunity for changing his *father's* or his *brother's* purpose;" no subsequent remorse or regret could undo the past or alter Isaac's blessing (Gen. xxvii. 33); or (β) no room for changing his own mind in such a way as to recover the blessing which he had lost; in other words, he "found no opportunity for such repentance as would restore to him the lost theocratic blessing." But in the N. T. usage the word "repentance" (μετάνοια) is always subjective, and has a deeper meaning than in the LXX. The same objection applies to the explanation that "he found no room to change *God's* purpose" to induce God "to repent" of His rejection of him, since God "is not a man that He should repent" (Num. xxiii. 19). (2) It seems simpler therefore, and quite admissible, to regard "for he found no place for repentance" as a parenthesis, and refer "it" to the lost blessing. "Though he earnestly sought the lost blessing, even with tears, when (perhaps forty years after his shameful indifference) he wished once more to inherit it, yet *then* he found no room for repentance;" or in other words his repentance, bitter as it was, could not avert the earthly consequence of his profanity, and was unavailing to regain what he had once flung away. As far as his earthly life was concerned, he heard the awful words "too late." The text gives no ground for pronouncing on Esau's future fate, to which the writer makes no allusion whatever. His "repentance," if it failed, could only have been a spurious repentance—remorse for earthly foolishness, not godly sorrow for sin, the *dolor amissi*, not the *dolor admissi*. This is the sense of "*locus poenitentiae*," the Latin translation of τόπος μετανοίας. The

have inherited the blessing, he was rejected: for he found no place of repentance, though he sought it carefully with tears.

18 For ye are not come unto the mount that might be touched, and that burned with fire, nor unto blackness, and 19 darkness, and tempest, and the sound of a trumpet, and the voice of words; which *voice* they that heard intreated that 20 the word should not be spoken to them any more: (for they could not endure that which was commanded, And if *so much as* a beast touch the mountain, it shall be

phrase itself occurs in Wisd. xii. 10. The abuse of this passage to support the merciless severity of the Novatians was one of the reasons why the Epistle was somewhat discredited in the Western Church.

with tears] "In former days he might have had it without tears; afterwards he was rejected, however sorely he wept. Let us use the time" (Lk. xiii. 28). Bengel.

18—29. THE MERCY AND SUBLIMITY OF THE NEW COVENANT AS CONTRASTED WITH THE OLD (18—24) ENHANCE THE GUILT AND PERIL OF THE BACKSLIDER (25—29).

18. *For ye are not come*] At the close of his arguments and exhortations the writer condenses the results of his Epistle into a climax of magnificent eloquence and force, in which he shews the transcendent beauty and supremacy of the New Covenant as compared with the terrors and imperfections of the Old.

unto the mount that might be touched, and that burned with fire] Unless we allow the textual evidence to be overruled by the other considerations, which are technically called "paradiplomatic evidence," the verse should be rendered "For ye have not come near to a palpable and enkindled fire." In any case the allusion is to Ex. xix. 16—19; Deut. iv. 11, and generally to "the fiery law."

blackness, and darkness, and tempest] Deut. iv. 11, v. 22.

19. *the sound of a trumpet*] Ex. xix. 16, 19, xx. 18.

the voice of words] Deut. iv. 12.

intreated] The verb means literally "to beg off."

that the word should not be spoken to them any more] Lit. "that no word more should be added to them" (Deut. v. 22—27, xviii. 16; Ex. xx. 19).

20. *they could not endure that which was commanded, And if so much as a beast...*] Rather, "they endured not the injunction, If even a beast..." (Ex. xix. 12, 13). This injunction seemed to them to indicate an awful terror and sanctity in the environment of the mountain. It filled them with alarm. The Jewish Hagadah said that at the utterance of each commandment the Israelites recoiled twelve miles, and were only brought forward again by the ministering angels. St Paul, in different style, contrasts "the Mount Sinai which gendereth to bond-

stoned, or thrust through with a dart: and so terrible 21
was the sight, *that* Moses said, I exceedingly fear and quake;)
but ye are come unto mount Sion, and unto the city of the 22
living God, the heavenly Jerusalem, and to an innumerable
company of angels, to the general assembly, and church of 23

age" with " the Jerusalem which is free and the mother of us all" (Gal.
iv. 24—26).

or thrust through with a dart] This clause is a gloss added from Ex.
xix. 13. Any *man* who touched the mountain was to be stoned, any
beast to be transfixed (Ex. xix. 13): but the quotation is here abbreviated,
and the allusion is summary as in vii. 5 ; Acts vii. 16.

21.   *the sight*] "the splendour of the spectacle" (τὸ φαντα*ζ*όμενον,
here only in N.T.). The true punctuation of the verse is And—so fearful was the spectacle—Moses said...

I exceedingly fear and quake] No such speech of Moses at Sinai is
recorded in the Pentateuch. The writer is either drawing from the
Jewish Hagadah or (by a mode of citation not uncommon) is compress-
ing two incidents into one. For in Deut. ix. 19 Moses, after the apostasy of Israel in worshipping the Golden Calf, said; "I was afraid
(LXX. καὶ ἔκφοβός εἰμι) of the anger and hot displeasure of the Lord,"
and in Acts vii. 32 we find the words "becoming a-tremble" (ἔντρομος
γενόμενος) to express the fear of Moses on seeing the Burning Bush
(though here also there is no mention of any trembling in Ex. iii. 6).
The tradition of Moses' terror is found in Jewish writings. In Shabbath
f. 88. 2 he explains "Lord of the Universe I am afraid lest they (the
Angels) should consume me with the breath of their mouths." Comp.
Midrash Koheleth f. 69. 4.

22.   *unto mount Sion*...] The true Sion is the anti-type of all the
promises with which the name had been connected (Ps. ii. 6, xlviii. 2,
lxxviii. 68, 69, cxxv. 1; Joel ii. 32; Mic. iv. 7). Hence the names of
Sion and "the heavenly Jerusalem" are given to "the city of the living
God" (Gal. iv. 26; Rev. xxi. 2). Sinai and Mount Sion are contrasted
with each other in six particulars. Bengel and others make out an
elaborate sevenfold antithesis here.

to an innumerable company of angels...] This punctuation is suggested by the word "myriads," which is often applied to angels (Deut.
xxxiii. 2; Ps. lxviii. 17; Dan. vii. 10). But under the New Covenant
the Angels are surrounded with attributes, not of terror but of beauty
and goodness (i. 14; Rev. v. 11, 12).

23.   *to the general assembly*] The word *Panēguris* means a general
festive assembly, as in Cant. vi. 13 (LXX.). It has been questioned
whether both clauses refer to Angels—"To myriads of Angels, a Festal
Assembly, and Church of Firstborn enrolled in Heaven"—or whether
two classes of the Blessed are intended, viz. "To myriads of Angels,
(and) to a Festal Assembly and Church of Firstborn." The absence of
"and" before *Panēguris* makes this latter construction doubtful, and
the first construction is untenable because the Angels are never called in

the firstborn, which are written in heaven, and to God the
24 Judge of all, and to the spirits of just *men* made perfect, and
to Jesus the mediator of the new covenant, and to the blood
of sprinkling, that speaketh better *things* than *that of* Abel.

the N. T. either "a Church" (but see Ps. lxxxix. 5) or "Firstborn." On
the whole the best and simplest way of taking the text seems to be
"But ye have come...to Myriads—a Festal Assembly of Angels—and
to the Church of the Firstborn...and to spirits of the Just who have been
perfected."

and church of the firstborn, which are written in heaven] Rather,
"who have been enrolled in heaven." This refers to the Church of
living Christians, to whom the Angels are "ministering spirits," and
whose names, though they are still living on earth, have been enrolled
in the heavenly registers (Lk. x. 20; Rom. viii. 16, 29; Jas. i. 18) as
"a kind of firstfruits of His creatures" unto God and to the Lamb
(Rev. xiv. 4). These, like Jacob, have inherited the privileges of firstborn which the Jews, like Esau, have rejected.

to God the Judge of all] Into whose hands, rather than into the
hands of man, it is a blessing to fall, because He is "the righteous
Judge" (2 Tim. iv. 8).

and to the spirits of just men made perfect] That is, to saints now
glorified and perfected—i.e. brought to the consummation of their
course—in heaven (Rev. vii. 14—17). This has been interpreted only
of the glorified saints of the Old Covenant, but there is no reason to
confine it to them. The writer tells the Hebrews that they have come
not to a flaming hill, and a thunderous darkness, and a terror-stricken
multitude, but to Mount Sion and the Heavenly Jerusalem, where they
will be united with the Angels of joy and mercy (Lk. xv. 10), with
the happy Church of living Saints, and with the spirits of the Just
made perfect. The three clauses give us a beautiful conception of "the
Communion of the Saints above and the Church below" with myriads
of Angels united in a Festal throng, in a Heaven now ideally existent
and soon to be actually realised.

24. *the mediator of the new covenant*] Rather, "Mediator of a New
Covenant." The word for "new" is here νέας ("new in time"), not
καινῆς ("fresh in quality"), implying not only that it is "fresh" or
"recent," but also young and strong (Matt. xxvi. 27—29; Heb. ix. 15,
x. 22).

that speaketh better things than that of Abel] The allusion is explained by ix. 13, x. 22, xi. 4, xiii. 12. "The blood of Abel cried for
vengeance; that of Christ for remission" (Erasmus). In the original
Hebrew it is (Gen. iv. 10) "The voice of thy brother's *bloods* crieth from
the ground," and this was explained by the Rabbis of his blood
"sprinkled on the trees and stones." It was a curious Jewish Hagadah
that the dispute between Cain and Abel rose from Cain's denial that
God was a Judge. The "sprinkling" of the blood of Jesus, an expression borrowed from the blood-sprinklings of the Old Covenant (Ex.
xxiv. 8), is also alluded to by St Peter (1 Pet. i. 2).

See *that* ye refuse not him that speaketh: for if they escaped 25
not who refused him that spake on earth, much more *shall
not* we *escape*, if we turn away from him that *speaketh* from
heaven: whose voice then shook the earth: but now he hath 26
promised, saying, Yet once *more* I shake not the earth
only, but also heaven. And this *word*, Yet once *more*, 27
signifieth the removing of those *things* that are shaken, as of

25. *him that speaketh*] Not Moses, as Chrysostom supposed, but God. The speaker is the same under both dispensations, different as they are. God spoke alike from Sinai and from heaven. The difference of the places whence they spoke involves the whole difference of their tone and revelations. Perhaps the writer regarded Christ as the speaker alike from Sinai as from Heaven, for even the Jews represented the Voice at Sinai as being the Voice of Michael, who was sometimes identified with "the Shechinah," or the Angel of the Presence. The verb for "speaketh" is χρηματίζοντα, as in viii. 5, xi. 7.

if they escaped not] ii. 2, 3, iii. 17, x. 28, 29.

much more] On this proportional method of statement, characteristic of the writer, as also of Philo, see i. 4, iii. 3, vii. 20, viii. 6.

26. *whose voice then shook the earth*] Ex. xix. 18; Judg. v. 4; Ps. cxiv. 7.

but now he hath promised, saying, Yet once more] Rather, "again, once for all." The quotation is from Hagg. ii. 6, 7, "yet once, it is a little while" (comp. Hos. i. 4).

but also heaven] "For the powers of the heavens shall be shaken" (Lk. xxi. 26).

27. *And this word, Yet once more*] The argument on the phrase "*Again, yet once for all*," and the bringing it into connexion with the former shaking of the earth at Sinai resembles the style of argument on the word "to-day" in iii. 7—iv. 9; and on the word "new" in viii. 13.

the removing...] The rest of this verse may be punctuated "Signifies the removal of the things that are being shaken as of things which have been made, in order that things which cannot be shaken, may remain." The "things unshakeable" are God's heavenly city and eternal kingdom (Dan. ii. 44; Rev. xxi. 1, &c.). The material world—its shadows, symbols and all that belong to it—are quivering, unreal, evanescent (Ps. cii. 25, 26; 2 Pet. iii. 10; Rev. xx. 11). It is only the Ideal which is endowed with eternal reality (Dan. ii. 44, vii. 13, 14). This view, which the Alexandrian theology had learnt from the Ethnic Inspiration of Plato, is the reverse of the view taken by materialists and sensualists. *They* only believe in what they can taste, and see, and "grasp with both hands;" but to the Christian idealist, who walks by faith and not by sight, the Unseen is visible (ὡς ὁρῶν τὸν Ἀόρατον (xi. 27), τὰ γὰρ ἀόρατα αὐτοῦ...νοούμενα καθορᾶται, Rom. i. 20), and the Material is only a perishing copy of an Eternal Archetype. The earthquake which dissolves and annihilates things sensible is

things that are made, that those *things* which cannot be
28 shaken may remain. Wherefore we receiving a kingdom
which cannot be moved, let us have grace, whereby we may
29 serve God acceptably with reverence and godly fear: for our
God *is* a consuming fire.

13
2 Let brotherly love continue. Be not forgetful to enter-

powerless against the Things Invisible. The rushing waters of the cataract only shake *the shadow* of the pine.

28. *Wherefore*] This splendid strain of comparison and warning ends with a brief and solemn appeal.

let us have grace] Or "let us feel thankfulness, whereby, &c."

with reverence and godly fear] Another well-supported reading is μετ' εὐλαβείας (v. 7, xi. 7) καὶ δέους "with godly caution and fear." The word δέος for "fear" does not occur elsewhere in the N.T. The same particles καὶ γὰρ "for indeed" are used in iv. 2.

29. *for our God is a consuming fire*]. The reference is to Deut. iv. 24, and the special application of the description to one set of circumstances shews that this is not—like "God is light" and "God is love"—a description of the whole character of God, but an anthropomorphic way of expressing His hatred of apostasy and idolatry. Here the reference is made to shew why we ought to serve God with holy reverence and fear.

CH. XIII. Concluding Exhortations to Love (1); Hospitality (2); Kindness to Prisoners and the Suffering (3); Purity of Life (4); Contentment (5); Trustfulness (6); Submission to Pastoral Authority (7, 8); Steadfastness and Spirituality (9); The Altar, the Sacrifice, and the Sacrifices of the Christian (10—16); The Duty of Obedience to Spiritual Authority (17). Concluding Notices and Benedictions (18—25).

We may notice that the style of the writer in this chapter offers more analogies to that of St Paul than in the rest of the Epistle; the reason being that these exhortations are mostly of a general character, and probably formed a characteristic feature in all the Christian correspondence of this epoch. They are almost of the nature of theological *loci communes*.

1. *Let brotherly love continue*] Not only was "brotherly love" (*philadelphia*) a new and hitherto almost undreamed of virtue but it was peculiarly necessary among the members of a bitterly-persecuted sect. Hence all the Apostles lay constant stress upon it (Rom. xii. 10; 1 Thess. iv. 9; 1 Pet. i. 22; 1 John iii. 14—18, &c.). It was a special form of the more universal "Love" ('Αγάπη), and our Lord had said that by it the world should recognise that Christians were His disciples (John xiii. 35). How entirely this prophecy was fulfilled we see alike from the fervid descriptions of Tertullian, from the mocking admissions of Lucian in his curious and interesting tract "on the death of Peregrinus," and from the remark of the Emperor Julian (*Ep.* 49), that their

tain strangers: for thereby some have entertained angels unawares. Remember *them that are* in bonds, as bound 3 with *them;* and them which suffer adversity, as being yourselves also in the body. Marriage *is* honourable in all, and 4

"kindness towards strangers" had been a chief means of propagating their "atheism." But brotherly-love in the limits of a narrow community is often imperilled by the self-satisfaction of an egotistic and dogmatic orthodoxy, shewing itself in party rivalries. This may have been the case among these Hebrews as among the Corinthians; and the neglect by some of the gatherings for Christian worship (x. 25) may have tended to deepen the sense of disunion. The disunion however was only incipient, for the writer has already borne testimony to the kindness which prevailed among them (vi. 10, x. 32, 33).

2. *to entertain strangers*] The hospitality of Christians (what Julian calls ἡ περὶ ξένους φιλανθρωπία) was naturally exercised chiefly towards the brethren. The absence of places of public entertainment except in the larger towns, and the constant interchange of letters and messages between Christian communities—a happy practice which also prevailed among the Jewish Synagogues—made "hospitality" a very necessary and blessed practice. St Peter tells Christians to be hospitable to one another ungrudgingly, and unmurmuringly, though it must sometimes have been burdensome (1 Pet. iv. 9; comp. Rom. xii. 13; Tit. i. 8; 1 Tim. iii. 2). We find similar exhortations in the Talmud (Berachoth f. 63. 2; Shabbath f. 27. 1). Lucian (*De Mort. Peregr.* 16) and the Emperor Julian (*Ep.* 49) notice the unwonted kindness and hospitality of Christians.

have entertained angels unawares] Abraham (Gen. xviii. 2—22. Lot (Gen. xix. 1, 2). Manoah (Judg. xiii. 2—14). Gideon (Judg. vi. 11—20). Our Lord taught that we may even entertain Him—the King of Angels—unawares. "I was *a stranger*, and ye took Me in" (Matt. xxv. 35—40). There is an allusion to this "entertaining of angels" in Philo, *De Abrahamo* (Opp. II. 17). The classic verb rendered "unawares" (*elathon*) is not found elsewhere in the N.T. in this sense, and forms a happy paronomasia with "forget not."

3. *Remember them that are in bonds*] Comp. Col. iv. 18.

as bound with them] Lit., "as having been bound with them." In the perfectness of sympathy *their* bonds are your bonds (1 Cor. xii. 26), for you and they alike are Christ's Slaves (1 Cor. vii. 22) and Christ's Captives (2 Cor. ii. 14 in the Greek). Lucian's tract (referred to in the previous note) dwells on the effusive kindness of Christians to their brethren who were imprisoned as confessors.

as being yourselves also in the body] And therefore as being yourselves liable to similar maltreatment. "In the body" does not mean "in the body of the Church," but "human beings, born to suffer." You must therefore "weep with them that weep" (Rom. xii. 15). The expressions of the verse (κακουχουμένων, ὡς καὶ αὐτοὶ ὄντες ἐν σώματι read like a reminiscence of Philo (*De Spec. Legg.* § 30) who says ὡς ἐν τοῖς ἑτέρων σώμασιν αὐτοὶ κακούμενοι "as being yourselves also afflicted

the bed undefiled: but whoremongers and adulterers God
5 will judge. *Let your* conversation *be* without covetousness;
and be content with such *things* as ye have: for he hath

in the bodies of others;" but if so the reminiscence is only verbal, and the application more simple. Incidentally the verse shews how much the Christians of that day were called upon to endure.

4. *Marriage is honourable in all*] More probably this is an exhortation, "Let marriage be held honourable among all," or rather "in all respects," as in ver. 18. Scripture never gives even the most incidental sanction to the exaltation of celibacy as a superior virtue, or to the disparagement of marriage as an inferior state. Celibacy and marriage stand on an exactly equal level of honour according as God has called us to the one or the other state. The mediæval glorification of Monachism sprang partly from a religion of exaggerated gloom and terror, and partly from a complete misunderstanding of the sense applied by Jewish writers to the word "Virgins." Nothing can be clearer than the teaching on this subject alike of the Old (Gen. ii. 18, 24) and of the New Covenant (Matt. xix. 4—6; John ii. 1, 2; 1 Cor. vii. 2). There is no "forbidding to marry" (1 Tim. iv. 1—3) among Evangelists and Apostles. They shared the deep conviction which their nation had founded on Gen. i. 27, ii. 18—24 and which our Lord had sanctioned (Matt. xix. 4—6). The warning in this verse is against unchastity. If it be aimed against a tendency to disparage the married state it would shew that the writer is addressing some Hebrews who had adopted in this matter the prejudices of the Essenes (1 Tim. iv. 3). In any case the truth remains "*Honourable* is marriage in all;" it is only lawless passions which are "passions of dishonour" (Rom. i. 26).

and the bed undefiled] A warning to Antinomians who made light of unchastity (Acts xv. 20; 1 Thess. iv. 6).

whoremongers] Christianity introduced a wholly new conception regarding the sin of fornication (Gal. v. 19, 21; 1 Cor. vi. 9, 10; Eph. v. 5; Col. iii. 5, 6; Rev. xxii. 15) which, especially in the depraved decadence of Heathenism under the Empire, was hardly regarded as any sin at all. Hence the necessity for constantly raising a warning voice against it (1 Thess. iv. 6, &c.).

God will judge] The more because they often escape altogether the judgment of man (1 Sam. ii. 25; 2 Sam. iii. 39).

5. *your conversation*] The word here used is not the one generally rendered by "conversation" in the N.T. (*anastrophē* as in ver. 7, "general walk" Gal. i. 13; Eph. ii. 3, or ("citizenship" *politeuma*, as in Phil. i. 27, iii. 20), but "turn of mind" (*tropos*).

without covetousness] *Aphilarguros* not merely without covetousness (*pleonexia*) but "without love of money." It is remarkable that "covetousness" and "uncleanness" are constantly placed in juxtaposition in the N.T. (1 Cor. v. 10, vi. 9; Eph. v. 3, 5; Col. iii. 5).

be content] The *form* of the sentence "Let your turn of mind be without love of money, being content" is the same as "Let love be without pretence, hating" in Rom. xii. 9. The few marked similarities

vv. 6—8.] HEBREWS, XIII. 187

said, I will never leave thee, nor forsake thee. So 6
that we may boldly say, The Lord *is* my helper, and
I will not fear what man shall do unto me. Re- 7
member them which have the rule over you, who have
spoken unto you the word of God: whose faith follow, considering
the end of *their* conversation. Jesus Christ the 8

between this writer and St Paul only force the radical dissimilarity
between their styles into greater prominence; and as the writer had
almost certainly read the Epistle to the Romans a striking syntactical
peculiarity like this may well have lingered in his memory.

he hath said] More literally "Himself hath said." The "Himself"
of course refers to God, and the phrase of citation is common in the
Rabbis (הוא אמר). "He" and "I" are, as Delitzsch says, used by
the Rabbis as mystical names of God.

I will never leave thee, nor forsake thee] These words are found (in
the third person) in Deut. xxxi. 6, 8; 1 Chron. xxviii. 20, and *similar*
promises, in the first person, in Gen. xxviii. 15; Josh. i. 5; Is. xli. 17.
The very emphatic form of the citation (first with a double then with a
triple negation) "I will in no wise fail, neither will I ever in any wise
forsake thee" does not occur either in the Hebrew or the LXX., but it
is found in the very same words in Philo (*De Confus. Ling.* § 32), and
since we have had occasion to notice again and again the thorough
familiarity of the writer with Philo's works, it is probable that he
derived it from Philo, unless it existed in some proverbial or liturgical
form among the Jews. The triple negative οὐδ' οὐ μὴ is found in Matt.
xxiv. 21.

6. *we may boldly say*] Rather, "we boldly say."
The Lord is my helper] Ps. cxviii. 6.
I will not fear what man...] Rather, "I will not fear. What shall
man do unto me?"

7. *them which have the rule over you, who have spoken*] Rather,
"your leaders, who spoke to you;" for, as the next clause shews, these
spiritual leaders were dead. At this time the ecclesiastical organisation
was still unfixed. The vague term "leaders" (found also in Acts xv. 22),
like the phrase "those set over you" (*proistamenoi*, 1 Thess. v. 12)
means "bishops" and "presbyters," the two terms being, in the Apostolic
age, practically identical. In later ecclesiastical Greek this word
(ἡγούμενοι) was used for "Abbots."

whose faith follow, considering the end of their conversation] In the
emphatic order of the original, "and earnestly contemplating the issue
of their conversation, imitate their faith."

the end] Not the ordinary word for "end" (*telos*) but the very
unusual word *ekbasin*, "outcome." This word in the N.T. is found
only in 1 Cor. x. 13, where it is rendered "escape." In Wisd. ii. 17
we find, "Let us see if his words be true, and let us see what shall
happen at his end" (ἐν ἐκβάσει). It here seems to mean *death*, but
not necessarily a death by martyrdom. It merely means "imitate

9 same yesterday, and to day, and for ever. Be not carried about with divers and strange doctrines. For *it is* a good *thing* that the heart be established with grace; not with meats, which have not profited them that have been occu-

them, by being faithful unto death." The words *exodos*, "departure" (Lk. ix. 31; 2 Pet. i. 15) and *aphixis* (Acts xx. 29) are similar euphemisms for death.

8. *Jesus Christ the same*] Rather, "is the same" (comp. i. 12). The collocation "Jesus Christ" is in this Epistle only found elsewhere in ver. 21 and x. 10. He commonly says "Jesus" in the true reading (ii. 9, iii. 1, vi. 20, &c.) or "Christ" (iii. 6, 14, v. 5, &c.). He also has "the Lord" (ii. 3), "our Lord" (vii. 14), and "our Lord Jesus" (xiii. 20). "Christ Jesus," which is so common in St Paul, only occurs as a very dubious various reading in iii. 1.

yesterday, and to day, and for ever] See vii. 24. The order of the Greek is "yesterday and to-day the same, and to the ages." See i. 12; Mal. iii. 6; Jas. i. 17. The unchangeableness of Christ is a reason for not being swept about by winds of strange teaching.

9. *Be not carried about*...] Lit. "With teachings various and strange be ye not swept away." From the allusion to various kinds of food which immediately follows we infer that these "teachings" were not like the Gnostic speculations against which St Paul and St John had to raise a warning voice (Eph. iv. 14; Col. ii. 8; 1 John iv. 1), but the minutiae of the Jewish Halachah with its endless refinements upon, and inferences from, the letter of the Law. This is the sort of teaching of which the Talmud is full, and most of it has no *real* connection with true Mosaism.

it is a good] "a beautiful, or excellent thing" (*kalon*).

with grace] By the favour or mercy of God as a pledge of our real security.

not with meats] Not by minute and pedantic distinctions between various kinds of clean and unclean food (ix. 10). The word *bromata*, "kinds of food," was never applied to sacrifices. On the urgency of the question of "meats" to the Early Christians see my *Life of St Paul*, I. 264.

which have not profited them that have been occupied therein] These outward rules were of no real advantage to the Jews under the Law. As Christianity extended the Rabbis gave a more and more hostile elaboration and significance to the *Halachoth*, which decided about the degrees of uncleanness in different kinds of food, as though salvation itself depended on the scrupulosities and micrologies of Rabbinism. The reader will find some illustrations of these remarks in my *Life of St Paul*, I. 264. The importance of these or analogous questions to the early Jewish Christians may be estimated by the allusions of St Paul (Rom. xiv.; Col. ii. 16—23; 1 Tim. iv. 3, &c.). No doubt these warnings were necessary because the Jewish Christians were liable to the taunt "You are breaking the law of Moses; you are living Gentile-fashion (ἐθνικῶς) not Jewish-wise (Ἰουδαϊκῶς); you neglect the *Kashar* (rules which regu-

pied therein. We have an altar, whereof they have no right 10

late the slaughter of clean and unclean animals, which the Jews scrupulously observe to this day); you feed with those who are polluted by habitually eating swines' flesh.' These were appeals to "the eternal Pharisaism of the human heart," and the intensity of Jewish feeling respecting them would have been renewed by the conversions to Christianity. The writer therefore reminds the Hebrews that these distinctions involve no real advantage (vii. 18, 19).

10—16. THE ONE SACRIFICE OF THE CHRISTIAN, AND THE SACRIFICES WHICH HE MUST OFFER.

10. *We have an altar*] These seven verses form a little episode of argument in the midst of moral exhortations. They revert once more to the main subject of the Epistle—the contrast between the two dispensations. The connecting link in the thought of the writer is to be found in the Jewish boasts to which he has just referred in the word "meats." Besides trying to alarm the Christians by denunciations founded on their indifference to the Levitical Law and the oral traditions based upon it, the Jews would doubtless taunt them with their inability henceforth to share in eating the sacrifices (1 Cor. ix. 13) since they were all under the *Cherem*—the ban of Jewish excommunication. The writer meets the taunt by pointing out (in an allusive manner) that of the most solemn sacrifices in the whole Jewish year—and of those offered on the Day of Atonement—not even the Priests, not even the High Priest himself, could partake (Lev. vi. 12, 23, 30, xvi. 27). But of our Sacrifice, which is Christ, and from (ἐξ) our Altar, which is the Cross —on which, as on an Altar, our Lord was offered—*we* may eat. The "Altar" is here understood of the Cross, not only by Bleek and De Wette, but even by St Thomas Aquinas and Estius; but the mere figure implied by the "altar" is so subordinate to that of our participation in spiritual privileges that if it be regarded as an objection that the Cross was looked on by Jews as "the accursed tree," we may adopt the alternative view suggested by Thomas Aquinas—that the Altar means Christ Himself. To eat from it will then be "to partake of the fruit of Christ's Passion." So too Cyril says, "He is Himself the Altar." We therefore have loftier privileges than they who "serve the tabernacle." The other incidental expressions will be illustrated as we proceed; but, meanwhile, we may observe that the word "Altar" is altogether subordinate and (so to speak) "out of the Figure." There is no reference whatever to the material "table of the Lord," and only a very indirect reference (if any) to the Lord's Supper. Nothing can prove more strikingly and conclusively the writer's total freedom from any conceptions resembling those of the "sacrifice of the mass" than the fact that here he speaks of *our* sacrifices as being "the bullocks of our lips." The Christian Priest is only a Presbyter, not a Sacrificing Priest. He is only a Sacrificing Priest in exactly the same sense as every Christian is metaphorically so called, because *alike* Presbyter and people offer "*spiritual* sacrifices," which

11 to eat which serve the tabernacle. For the bodies of those beasts, whose blood is brought into the sanctuary by the 12 high priest for sin, are burnt without the camp. Wherefore Jesus also, that he might sanctify the people with his own 13 blood, suffered without the gate. Let us go forth therefore 14 unto him without the camp, bearing his reproach. For here

are alone acceptable to God through Jesus Christ (1 Pet. ii. 5). The main point is "we too have one great sacrifice," and we (unlike the Jews, as regards their chief sacrifice, Lev. iv. 12, vi. 30, xvi. 27) may perpetually partake of it, and live by it (John vi. 51—56). We live not on anything material, which profiteth nothing, but on the *words* of Christ, which are spirit and truth; and we feed on Him—a symbol of the close communion whereby we are one with Him—only in a heavenly and spiritual manner.

whereof] Lit. "from which."

they have no right to eat] Because they utterly reject Him whose flesh is meat indeed and whose blood is drink indeed (John vi. 54, 55). Forbidden to eat of the type (see ver. 11) they could not of course, in any sense, partake of the antitype which they rejected.

which serve the tabernacle] See viii. 5. It is remarkable that not even here, though the participle is in the present tense, does he use the word "Temple" or "Shrine" any more than he does throughout the whole Epistle. There may, as Bengel says, be a slight irony in the phrase "who *serve the Tabernacle*," rather than "*in the Tabernacle*."

11. *are burnt without the camp*] Of the sin-offerings the Priests could not, as in the case of other offerings, eat the entire flesh, or the breast and shoulder, or all except the fat (Num. vi. 20; Lev. vi. 26, &c.). The word for "burn" (*saraph*) means "entirely to get rid of," and is not the word used for burning upon the altar. The rule that these sin-offerings should be burned, not eaten, was stringent (Lev. vi. 30, xvi. 27).

12. *that he might sanctify the people with his own blood*] Lit. "through," or "by means of His own blood." The thought is the same as that of Tit. ii. 14, "Who gave Himself for us that He might redeem us from all iniquity, and purify unto Himself a peculiar people." This sanctification or purifying consecration of His people by the blood of His own voluntary sacrifice corresponds to the sprinkling of the atoning blood on the Propitiatory by the High Priest. For "the people," see ii. 16.

suffered without the gate] ix. 26; Matt. xxvii. 32; John xix. 17, 18.

13. *Let us go forth therefore unto him*] Let us go forth out of the city and camp of Judaism (Rev. xi. 8) to the true and eternal Tabernacle (Ex. xxxiii. 7, 8) where He now is (xii. 2). Some have imagined that the writer conveys a hint to the Christians in Jerusalem that it is time for them to leave the guilty city and retire to Pella; but, as we have seen, it is by no means probable that the letter was addressed to Jerusalem.

bearing his reproach] "If ye be reproached," says St Peter, "for the

have we no continuing city, but we seek one to come. By 15
him therefore let us offer the sacrifice of praise to God continually, that is, the fruit of *our* lips giving thanks to his
name. But to do good and to communicate forget not: for 16
with such sacrifices God is well pleased. Obey them that 17

name of Christ, happy are ye" (comp. xi. 26). As He was excommunicated and insulted and made to bear His Cross of shame, so will you be, and you must follow Him out of the doomed city (Matt. xxiv. 2). It must be remembered that the Cross, an object of execration and disgust even to Gentiles, was viewed by the Jews with *religious horror*, since they regarded every crucified person as "accursed of God" (Deut. xxi. 22, 23; Gal. iii. 13; see my *Life of St Paul*, II. 17, 148). Christians shared this reproach to the fullest extent. The most polished heathen writers, men like Tacitus, Pliny, Suetonius, spoke of their faith as an "execrable," "deadly," and "malefic" superstition; Lucian alluded to Christ as "the impaled sophist;" and to many Greeks and Romans no language of scorn seemed too intense, no calumny too infamous, to describe them and their mode of worship. The Jews spoke of them as "Nazarenes," "Epicureans," "heretics," "followers of the thing," and especially "apostates," "traitors," and "renegades." The notion that there is any allusion to the ceremonial uncleanness of those who burnt the bodies of the offerings of the Day of Atonement "outside the camp" is far-fetched.

14. *one to come*] Rather, "the city which is to be" (xi. 10, 16). Our earthly city here may be destroyed, and we may be driven from it, or leave it of our own accord; this is nothing,—for our real citizenship is in heaven (Phil. iii. 20).

15. *the sacrifice of praise*] A thanksgiving (Jer. xvii. 26; Lev. vii. 12), not in the form of an offering, but something which shall "please the Lord better than a bullock which hath horns and hoofs" (Ps. lxix. 31).

continually] Even the Rabbis held that the sacrifice of praise would outlast animal sacrifices and would never cease.

the fruit of our lips giving thanks to his name] Rather, "the fruit of lips which confess to His name." The phrase "the fruit of the lips" is borrowed by the LXX. from Is. lvii. 19. In Hos. xiv. 2 we have "so will we render the calves of our lips," literally, "our lips as bullocks," i.e. "as thank-offerings." Dr Kay notices that (besides the perhaps accidental resemblance between פרי, *peri*, "fruit" and פרים, *parim*, "calves") *karpoma* and similar words were used of burnt-offerings.

16. *to communicate*] To share your goods with others (Rom. xv. 26). The substantive from this verb is rendered "distribution" in 2 Cor. ix. 13.

with such sacrifices] The verse is meant to remind them that sacrifices of well-doing and the free sharing of their goods are even more necessary than verbal gratitude unaccompanied by sincerity of action (Is. xxix. 13; Ezek. xxxiii. 31).

17. *them that have the rule over you*] See ver. 7. The repetition of the injunction perhaps indicates a tendency to self-assertion and

have the rule over you, and submit yourselves: for they watch for your souls, as they that must give account, that they may do it with joy, and not with grief: for that *is* unprofitable for you. Pray for us: for we trust we have a good conscience, in all *things* willing to live honestly. But I beseech *you* the rather to do this, that I may be restored to you the sooner.

20 Now the God of peace, that brought again from the dead our Lord Jesus, *that* great shepherd of the sheep, through

spurious independence among them. "Bishops" in the modern sense did not as yet exist, but in the importance here attached to due subordination to ecclesiastical authority we see the gradual growth of episcopal powers. See 1 Thess. v. 12, 13; 1 Tim. v. 17.

they watch] Lit. "are sleepless."
that must give account] See Acts xx. 26, 28.
with joy] See 1 Thess. ii. 19, 20.
with grief] Lit. "groaning."
unprofitable] A *litotes*—i.e. a mild expression purposely used that the reader may correct it by a stronger one—for "disadvantageous."

18. *Pray for us*] A frequent and natural request in Christian correspondence (1 Thess. v. 25; 2 Thess. iii. 1; Rom. xv. 30; Eph. vi. 18; Col. iv. 3). The "us" probably means "me and those with me," shewing that the name of the writer was well known to those addressed.

we trust] Rather, "we are persuaded."

we have a good conscience] The writer, being one of the Paulinists, whose freedom was so bitterly misinterpreted, finds it as necessary as St Paul had done, to add this profession of conscientious sincerity (Acts xxiii. 1, xxiv. 16; 1 Cor. iv. 4; 2 Cor. i. 12). These resemblances to St Paul's method of concluding his letters are only of a general character, and we have reason to suppose that to a certain extent the beginnings and endings of Christian letters had assumed a recognised form.

willing] i.e. "desiring," "determining."
honestly] Honourably.

19. *that I may be restored to you the sooner*] So St Paul in Philem. 22. We are unable to conjecture the circumstances which for the present prevented the writer from visiting them. It is clear from the word "restored" that he must once have lived among them.

20. *the God of peace.* The phrase is frequent in St Paul (1 Thess. v. 23; 2 Thess. iii. 16; Rom. xv. 33, xvi. 20; Phil. iv. 9).

that brought again from the dead] Among many allusions to the Ascension and Glorification of Christ this is the only direct allusion in the Epistle to His Resurrection (but comp. vi. 2, xi. 35). The verb ἀνήγαγεν may be "raised again" rather than "brought up," though there may be a reminiscence of "the shepherd" (Moses) who "brought up" his people from the sea in Is. lxiii. 11.

the blood of the everlasting covenant, make you perfect in ²¹ every good work to do his will, working in you *that which is well pleasing in his sight*, through Jesus Christ; to whom *be glory for ever and ever. Amen.* And I beseech you, ²² brethren, suffer the word of exhortation: for I have written a letter unto you in few *words*. Know ye that *our* brother ²³ Timothy is set at liberty; with whom, if he come shortly, I

through the blood of the everlasting covenant] Rather, "by virtue of (lit. "in") the blood of an eternal covenant." The expression finds its full explanation in ix. 15—18. Others connect it with "the Great Shepherd." He became the Great Shepherd by means of His blood. So in Acts xx. 28 we have "to shepherd the Church of God, which He purchased for Himself by means of His own blood." A similar phrase occurs in Zech. ix. 11, "By (or "because of") *the blood of thy covenant* I have sent forth thy prisoners out of the pit."

21. *make you perfect*] Not the verb so often used to express "perfecting" but another verb—"may He fit" or "stablish" or "equip" you."

to do his will, working in you...] In the Greek there is a play on the words "to *do* His will, *doing* in you." There is a similar play on words in Phil. ii. 13.

to whom be glory for ever and ever] Lit. "to whom be the glory (which is His of right) unto the ages of the ages." The same formula occurs in Gal. i. 5; 2 Tim. iv. 18. The doxology may be addressed to Christ as in 2 Pet. iii. 18.

22. *suffer the word of exhortation*] "Bear with the word of my exhortation." Comp. Acts xiii. 15. This is a courteous apology for the tone of severity and authority which he has assumed.

for] "for indeed," as in xii. 29.

I have written a letter] This is the only place in the N. T. (except Acts xv. 20, xxi. 25) where *epistello* has this sense. Usually it means "I enjoin."

in few words] "briefly," considering the breadth and dignity of the subject, which has left him no room for lengthened apologies, and for anything but a direct and compressed appeal. Or the force of the words may be "bear with my exhortation, for I have not troubled you at any great length" (comp. δι' ὀλίγων, 1 Pet. v. 12). Could more meaning have been compressed into a letter which could be read aloud in less than an hour, but which was to have a very deep influence on many centuries?

23. *Know ye*] Or perhaps "*Ye know,*" or "know."

is set at liberty] The word probably means (as in Acts iii. 13, iv. 21) "has been set free from prison." It is intrinsically likely that Timothy at once obeyed the earnest and repeated entreaty of St Paul, shortly before his martyrdom, to come to him at Rome (2 Tim. iv. 9, 21), and that, arriving before the Neronian persecution had spent its force, he had been thrown into prison. His comparative youth, and the unoffend-

24 will see you. Salute all them that have the rule over you,
25 and all the saints. They of Italy salute you. Grace *be*
with you all. Amen.

¶ Written to the Hebrews from Italy by Timothy.

ing gentleness of his character, together with the absence of any definite charge against him, may have led to his liberation. All this however is nothing more than reasonable conjecture. The word *apolelumenos* may mean no more than official, or even ordinary, "sending forth" on some mission or otherwise, as in Acts xiii. 3, xv. 30, xix. 41, xxiii. 22.

if he come shortly, I will see you] Lit. "if he come sooner," i.e. earlier than I now expect (comp. κάλλιον, Acts xxv. 10; βέλτιον, 2 Tim. i. 18).

24. *Salute all them that have the rule over you*] This salutation to *all* their spiritual leaders implies the condition of Churches, which was normal at that period—namely, little communities, sometimes composed separately of Jews and Gentiles, who in default of one large central building, met for worship in each other's houses.

They of Italy] This merely means "the Italians in the place from which I write," just as "they of Asia" means Asiatic Jews (Acts xxi. 27. Comp. xvii. 13, vi. 9, &c.). The phrase therefore gives no clue whatever to the place from which, or the persons to whom, the Epistle was written. It merely shews that some Christians from Italy—perhaps Christians who had fled from Italy during the Neronian persecution—formed a part of the writer's community; but it suggests a not unnatural inference that it was written *to* some Italian community from some other town *out of* Italy. Had he been writing *from* Italy he would perhaps have been more likely to write "those *in* Italy" (comp. 1 Pet. v. 13).

25. *Grace be with you all. Amen*] This is one of the shorter forms of final conclusion found in Col. iv. 18; 1 Tim. vi. 21; 2 Tim. iv. 22; Tit. iii. 15.

The superscription "Written to the Hebrews from Italy by Timothy" is wholly without authority, though found in K and some versions. It contradicts the obvious inference suggested by xiii. 23, 24. We have no clue to the bearer of the Epistle, or the local community for which it was primarily intended, or the effect which it produced. But it would scarcely be possible to suppose that such a composition did not have a powerful influence in checking all tendency to retrograde into Judaism from the deeper and far more inestimable blessings of the New Covenant. The Manuscripts ℵ and C have only "To the Hebrews." A has "It was written to the Hebrews from Rome."

INDEX.

Aaron, 20, 121
Abel, 182
Abraham, 12, 22, 164, 185
Adonizedek, 116
Alexandria, Church of, 28
Alexandrian MS., 31, 62, 178
altar of incense, 135
Ambrose, St, 43, 73, 148
Amraphel, 115
Antar, poem of, 74
Antioch, 28
Antiochus, 172
Apollos, 48
Aquila, 48
Ark, the, 95, 136
Athanasius, 82
Atonement, Great Day of, 14, 23, 58, 80, 96, 125, 134, 135, 137, 144, 146, 189, 191
Augustine, St, 61

Barnabas, 43, 48, 128
Baur, quoted, 17
Bengel, quoted, 94, 180, 190
Beni-Hanan, the, 98
Berith, 30, 124
Bleek, 38, 51, 82, 86, 189
Boethusim, the, 98
brotherly love, 184

Cain, 182
Cajetan, Cardinal, 46, 65
Caleb, 88
Calvin, 65, 105, quoted, 30, 45
Canon of Muratori, 43
Chaluka, 110
Chokhmah, 55
Chrysostom, St, 26, 100, 106, 147, 183
Cicero, quoted, 117
Claudius, 158
Clement, St, of Alexandria, 44, 45, 173
Clement of Rome, 43, 48, 56, 59, 92, 128
confidence, 84
conversation, 186
Corinth, Church of, 27
counted worthy, 82
Covenant, the new, 17, 21, 24, 52, 124, 131, 132, 143; the old, 21, 24, 52, 83, 124, 131, 132, 143
Cyril, 189

David, 90
Day of Atonement, 14, 23, 58, 80, 96, 125, 134, 135, 137, 144, 146, 189, 191
dead works, 142
Delitzsch, 50, 160

Demiurge, the, 52
demons, 78
de Wette, 189
Dispensation, the old, 17, 18, 25, 159; the new, 20, 25
divers manners, 53

Ebrard, 27
elders, 162
Elijah, 172
Elisha, 172
Elohim, 70, 71
embitterment, 85
entreaties, 99
Epictetus, 158
Erasmus, 46, quoted, 30, 174, 182
Esau, 178, 179
Estius, 189
eternal judgment, 104
Eupolemos, 114
Euripides, 93
Eusebius, 30, 46, 118
Ezra, 52

faithful, 82
fear of death, 99
Field, Dr, quoted, 127, 165
forerunner, 113
foundation, 103
Fulgentius, 73

Gaius, 43
Gematria, 83, 146
Gethsemane, 99
Gideon, 185
Grotius, 88

Halachoth, the, 188
Hebrews, sense of word, 10, 11
Hebrews, Epistle to, divisions of, 20; analysis of, 22 to 25; date of, 29; character of, 30, 31; author of, 41, 42; title of, 51
heresy, the Apollinarian, 100; the Monothelite, 100
High Priest, the, 40, 96, 125, 128, 147
High Priesthood, the, 21, 96
Hilary of Poictiers, 43
Hippolytus, St, 43, 118
holocausts, 150
Holy of Holies, the, 137, 140, 153
Homer, quoted, 173
Horace, quoted, 117, 149
household, 83
hypostasis, 57, 161

ideal archetype, the, 23, 24
incense, altar of, 135
Irenaeus, St, 43, 116

Jamnia, 28
Jehoiakim, 172
Jehovah, 81, 82, 92
Jerome, St, 73, 114, quoted, 50
Jerusalem, Church of, 26
Jewish Christians, 24, 26
Joshua, 21, 88
justification, 34
Justin Martyr, 49

Kamhits, the, 98
Kantheras, the, 98
Korah, 97

Leontopolis, 126
Logos, 36, 54, 64, 81, 92, 114, 125
Lot, 185
Lucian, 185
Luke, St, 48, 177, 178
Lünemann, 82
Luther, 18, 35, 46, 48

Maimonides, 94
Manoah, 185
Marah, 85
Marcion, 43, 178
Mark, St, 48
Mâsâk, 134
Megillah, 151, 170
Melanchthon, 46
Melchizedek, 21, 22, 36, 50, 98, 101, 113, 114, 115, 116, 117, 119, 121
mercy seat, the, 136
Middoth, 25
Midrash Tanchuma, 78
Mill, Dr, quoted, 104
Milton, quoted, 63
Monophysite, 73
Mosaic Law, the, 16, 156
Moses, 129, 181, 192
Muratori, Canon of, 43

near a curse, 108
Noah, 164
Noumena, 18
Novatian, 43

oath, 123
Olam habba, 70, 106, 138
Onias, 126
Origen, 46, 51

Pantaenus, 44
Paraclete, 87
Parocheth, 134
Paul, St, 42 ff., 114, 130, 154, 175, 180, 181, 187, 193
pegarim, 88
Pentateuch, the, 79

perfectionment, 34, 72
Peripatetics, the, 96
Peter, St, 183, 185, 190
Philo, 12, 35, 37, 38, 39, 40, 41, 47, 57, 64, 91, 96, 106, 111, 125, 134, 149, 176
Plato, 37, 183
Pompey, 133
prayers, 99
Priesthood, the High, 21, 96
Primasius, 82
Priscilla, 48
prophets, 53, 54

Rabbi Hillel, 25
Ravenna, 28
Reuss, quoted, 26
Robertson Smith, quoted, 60, 78, 79

saints, 109
Salem, 114, 115
Salumias, 114
salvation, 100
Shechinah, the, 56, 95, 118, 133, 183
Shepherd, the Great, 193
Siddim, the Vale of, 109
Silas, 48
slave, 84
Socrates, 19
Sulfatara, the, 109
sons of oil, 98
soul, 93
Spenser, quoted, 66
spoils, 120
Stanley, Dean, 114
Stoics, the, 96, 99
sundry times, 52
synagogue, 154

Tabernacle, the, 19, 20, 23
Targum, the, 64, 71, 170
tempted, 95
Tennyson, quoted, 112, 113
Terence, quoted, 95
Tertullian, 34, 184
Theodoret, 26, 30, 100
Theodotion, 80
Theophylact, 100
Thomas Aquinas, St, 189
Timothy, 26, 47, 193
Titus, 48
to-day, 90, 91, 183
Traducianism, 177

Urim, 20
Uzziah, 97, 122

vail, the, 112, 134
Vatican MS., the, 31, 178
Via crucis, 72
Victorinus of Pettau, 43
Virgil, quoted, 95, 115

Wordsworth, quoted, 161, 164

THE CAMBRIDGE BIBLE FOR SCHOOLS AND COLLEGES.

GENERAL EDITOR, THE VERY REV. J. J. S. PEROWNE, DEAN OF PETERBOROUGH.

Opinions of the Press.

"*It is difficult to commend too highly this excellent series.*"—Guardian.

"The modesty of the general title of this series has, we believe, led many to misunderstand its character and underrate its value. The books are well suited for study in the upper forms of our best schools, but not the less are they adapted to the wants of all Bible students who are not specialists. We doubt, indeed, whether any of the numerous popular commentaries recently issued in this country will be found more serviceable for general use."—Academy.

"One of the most popular and useful literary enterprises of the nineteenth century."—Baptist Magazine.

"Of great value. The whole series of comments for schools is highly esteemed by students capable of forming a judgment. The books are scholarly without being pretentious: and information is so given as to be easily understood."—Sword and Trowel.

"*The value of the work as an aid to Biblical study, not merely in schools but among people of all classes who are desirous to have intelligent knowledge of the Scriptures, cannot easily be over-estimated.*"—The Scotsman.

The Book of Judges. J. J. LIAS, M.A. "His introduction is clear and concise, full of the information which young students require, and indicating the lines on which the various problems suggested by the Book of Judges may be solved."—*Baptist Magazine.*

1 Samuel, by A. F. KIRKPATRICK. "Remembering the interest with which we read the *Books of the Kingdom* when they were appointed as a subject for school work in our boyhood, we have looked with some eagerness into Mr Kirkpatrick's volume, which contains the first instalment of them. We are struck with the great improvement in character, and variety in the materials, with which schools are now supplied. A clear map inserted in each volume, notes suiting the convenience of the scholar and the difficulty of the passage, and not merely dictated by the fancy of the commentator, were luxuries which a quarter of a century ago the Biblical student could not buy."—*Church Quarterly Review.*

"To the valuable series of Scriptural expositions and elementary commentaries which is being issued at the Cambridge University Press, under the title 'The Cambridge Bible for Schools,' has been added **The First Book of Samuel** by the Rev. A. F. KIRKPATRICK. Like other volumes of the series, it contains a carefully written historical and critical introduction, while the text is profusely illustrated and explained by notes."—*The Scotsman.*

II. Samuel. A. F. KIRKPATRICK, M.A. "Small as this work is in mere dimensions, it is every way the best on its subject and for its purpose that we know of. The opening sections at once prove the thorough competence of the writer for dealing with questions of criticism in an earnest, faithful and devout spirit; and the appendices discuss a few special difficulties with a full knowledge of the data, and a judicial reserve, which contrast most favourably with the superficial dogmatism which has too often made the exegesis of the Old Testament a field for the play of unlimited paradox and the ostentation of personal infallibility. The notes are always clear and suggestive; never trifling or irrelevant; and they everywhere demonstrate the great difference in value between the work of a commentator who is also a Hebraist, and that of one who has to depend for his Hebrew upon secondhand sources."—*Academy*.

"The Rev. A. F. KIRKPATRICK has now completed his commentary on the two books of Samuel. This second volume, like the first, is furnished with a scholarly and carefully prepared critical and historical introduction, and the notes supply everything necessary to enable the merely English scholar—so far as is possible for one ignorant of the original language—to gather up the precise meaning of the text. Even Hebrew scholars may consult this small volume with profit."—*Scotsman*.

I. Kings and Ephesians. "With great heartiness we commend these most valuable little commentaries. We had rather purchase these than nine out of ten of the big blown up expositions. Quality is far better than quantity, and we have it here."—*Sword and Trowel*.

I. Kings. "This is really admirably well done, and from first to last there is nothing but commendation to give to such honest work."—*Bookseller*.

II. Kings. "The Introduction is scholarly and wholly admirable, while the notes must be of incalculable value to students."—*Glasgow Herald*.

"It is equipped with a valuable introduction and commentary, and makes an admirable text book for Bible-classes."—*Scotsman*.

"It would be difficult to find a commentary better suited for general use."—*Academy*.

The Book of Job. "Able and scholarly as the Introduction is, it is far surpassed by the detailed exegesis of the book. In this Dr DAVIDSON's strength is at its greatest. His linguistic knowledge, his artistic habit, his scientific insight, and his literary power have full scope when he comes to exegesis.... The book is worthy of the reputation of Dr Davidson; it represents the results of many years of labour, and it will greatly help to the right understanding of one of the greatest works in the literature of the world."—*The Spectator*.

"In the course of a long introduction, Dr DAVIDSON has presented us with a very able and very interesting criticism of this wonderful book. Its contents, the nature of its composition, its idea and purpose, its integrity, and its age are all exhaustively treated of.... We have not space to examine fully the text and notes before us, but we can, and do heartily, recommend the book, not only for the upper forms in schools, but to Bible students and teachers generally. As we wrote of a previous volume in the same series, this one leaves nothing to be desired. The notes are full and suggestive, without being too long, and, in itself, the introduction forms a valuable addition to modern Bible literature."—*The Educational Times*.

"Already we have frequently called attention to this exceedingly valuable work as its volumes have successively appeared. But we have never done so with greater pleasure, very seldom with so great pleasure, as we now refer to the last published volume, that on the **Book of Job**, by Dr DAVIDSON, of Edinburgh.... We cordially commend the volume to all our readers. The least instructed will understand and enjoy it; and mature scholars will learn from it."—*Methodist Recorder*.

Job—Hosea. "It is difficult to commend too highly this excellent series, the volumes of which are now becoming numerous. The two books before us, small as they are in size, comprise almost everything that the young student can reasonably expect to find in the way of helps towards such general knowledge of their subjects as may be gained without an attempt to grapple with the Hebrew; and even the learned scholar can hardly read without interest and benefit the very able introductory matter which both these commentators have prefixed to their volumes. It is not too much to say that these works have brought within the reach of the ordinary reader resources which were until lately quite unknown for understanding some of the most difficult and obscure portions of Old Testament literature."—*Guardian*.

Ecclesiastes; or, the Preacher.—"Of the Notes, it is sufficient to say that they are in every respect worthy of Dr PLUMPTRE'S high reputation as a scholar and a critic, being at once learned, sensible, and practical. . . . An appendix, in which it is clearly proved that the author of *Ecclesiastes* anticipated Shakspeare and Tennyson in some of their finest thoughts and reflections, will be read with interest by students both of Hebrew and of English literature. Commentaries are seldom attractive reading. This little volume is a notable exception."—*The Scotsman*.

"In short, this little book is of far greater value than most of the larger and more elaborate commentaries on this Scripture. Indispensable to the scholar, it will render real and large help to all who have to expound the dramatic utterances of **The Preacher** whether in the Church or in the School."—*The Expositor*.

"The '*ideal* biography' of the author is one of the most exquisite and fascinating pieces of writing we have met with, and, granting its starting-point, throws wonderful light on many problems connected with the book. The notes illustrating the text are full of delicate criticism, fine glowing insight, and apt historical allusion. An abler volume than Professor PLUMPTRE'S we could not desire."—*Baptist Magazine*.

Jeremiah, by A. W. STREANE. "The arrangement of the book is well treated on pp. xxx., 396, and the question of Baruch's relations with its composition on pp. xxvii., xxxiv., 317. The illustrations from English literature, history, monuments, works on botany, topography, etc., are good and plentiful, as indeed they are in other volumes of this series."—*Church Quarterly Review*, April, 1881.

"Mr STREANE'S **Jeremiah** consists of a series of admirable and well-nigh exhaustive notes on the text, with introduction and appendices, drawing the life, times, and character of the prophet, the style, contents, and arrangement of his prophecies, the traditions relating to Jeremiah, meant as a type of Christ (a most remarkable chapter), and other prophecies relating to Jeremiah."—*The English Churchman and Clerical Journal.*

Obadiah and Jonah. "This number of the admirable series of Scriptural expositions issued by the Syndics of the Cambridge University Press is well up to the mark. The numerous notes are excellent. No difficulty is shirked, and much light is thrown on the contents both of Obadiah and Jonah. Scholars and students of to-day are to be congratulated on having so large an amount of information on Biblical subjects, so clearly and ably put together, placed within their reach in such small bulk. To all Biblical students the series will be acceptable, and for the use of Sabbath-school teachers will prove invaluable."—*North British Daily Mail.*

"It is a very useful and sensible exposition of these two Minor Prophets, and deals very thoroughly and honestly with the immense difficulties of the later-named of the two, from the orthodox point of view."—*Expositor.*

"**Haggai and Zechariah.** This interesting little volume is of great value. It is one of the best books in that well-known series of scholarly and popular commentaries, 'the Cambridge Bible for Schools and Colleges' of which Dean Perowne is the General Editor. In the expositions of Archdeacon Perowne we are always sure to notice learning, ability, judgment and reverence.... The notes are terse and pointed, but full and reliable."—*Churchman.*

"**The Gospel according to St Matthew**, by the Rev. A. CARR. The introduction is able, scholarly, and eminently practical, as it bears on the authorship and contents of the Gospel, and the original form in which it is supposed to have been written. It is well illustrated by two excellent maps of the Holy Land and of the Sea of Galilee."—*English Churchman.*

"**St Matthew**, edited by A. CARR, M.A. **The Book of Joshua**, edited by G. F. MACLEAR, D.D. **The General Epistle of St James**, edited by E. H. PLUMPTRE, D.D. The introductions and notes are scholarly, and generally such as young readers need and can appreciate. The maps in both Joshua and Matthew are very good, and all matters of editing are faultless. Professor Plumptre's notes on 'The Epistle of St James' are models of terse, exact, and elegant renderings of the original, which is too often obscured in the authorised version."—*Nonconformist.*

"**St Mark**, with Notes by the Rev. G. F. MACLEAR, D.D. Into this small volume Dr Maclear, besides a clear and able Introduction to the Gospel, and the text of St Mark, has compressed many hundreds of valuable and helpful notes. In short, he has given us a capital manual of the kind required—containing all that is needed to illustrate the text, i.e. all that can be drawn from the history, geography, customs, and manners of the time. But as a handbook, giving in a clear and succinct form the information which a lad requires in order to stand an examination in the Gospel, it is admirable......I can very heartily commend it, not only to the senior boys and girls in our High Schools, but also to Sunday-school teachers, who may get from it the very kind of knowledge they often find it hardest to get."—*Expositor.*

"With the help of a book like this, an intelligent teacher may make 'Divinity' as interesting a lesson as any in the school course. The notes are of a kind that will be, for the most part, intelligible to boys of the lower forms of our public schools; but they may be read with greater profit by the fifth and sixth, in conjunction with the original text."—*The Academy.*

"**St Luke.** Canon FARRAR has supplied students of the Gospel with an admirable manual in this volume. It has all that copious variety of illustration, ingenuity of suggestion, and general soundness of interpretation which readers are accustomed to expect from the learned and eloquent editor. Any one who has been accustomed to associate the idea of 'dryness' with a commentary, should go to Canon Farrar's **St Luke** for a more correct impression. He will find that a commentary may be made interesting in the highest degree, and that without losing anything of its solid value. . . . But, so to speak, it is *too good* for some of the readers for whom it is intended."—*The Spectator.*

"Canon FARRAR's contribution to The Cambridge School Bible is one of the most valuable yet made. His annotations on **The Gospel according to St Luke**, while they display a scholarship at least as sound, and an erudition at least as wide and varied as those of the editors of St Matthew and St Mark, are rendered telling and attractive by a more lively imagination, a keener intellectual and spiritual insight, a more incisive and picturesque style. His *St Luke* is worthy to be ranked with Professor Plumptre's *St James*, than which no higher commendation can well be given."—*The Expositor.*

"**St Luke.** Edited by Canon FARRAR, D.D. We have received with pleasure this edition of the Gospel by St Luke, by Canon Farrar. It is another instalment of the best school commentary of the Bible we possess. Of the expository part of the work we cannot speak too highly. It is admirable in every way, and contains just the sort of information needed for Students of the English text unable to make use of the original Greek for themselves."—*The Nonconformist and Independent.*

"As a handbook to the third gospel, this small work is invaluable. The author has compressed into little space a vast mass of scholarly information. . . The notes are pithy, vigorous, and suggestive, abounding in pertinent illustrations from general literature, and aiding the youngest reader to an intelligent appreciation of the text. A finer contribution to 'The Cambridge Bible for Schools' has not yet been made."—*Baptist Magazine.*

"We were quite prepared to find in Canon FARRAR's **St Luke** a masterpiece of Biblical criticism and comment, and we are not disappointed by our examination of the volume before us. It reflects very faithfully the learning and critical insight of the Canon's greatest works, his 'Life of Christ' and his 'Life of St Paul', but differs widely from both in the terseness and condensation of its style. What Canon Farrar has evidently aimed at is to place before students as much information as possible within the limits of the smallest possible space, and in this aim he has hit the mark to perfection."—*The Examiner.*

The Gospel according to St John. "Of the notes we can say with confidence that they are useful, necessary, learned, and brief. To Divinity students, to teachers, and for private use, this compact Commentary will be found a valuable aid to the better understanding of the Sacred Text."—*School Guardian.*

"The new volume of the 'Cambridge Bible for Schools'—the **Gospel according to St John,** by the Rev. A. PLUMMER—shows as careful and thorough work as either of its predecessors. The introduction concisely yet fully describes the life of St John, the authenticity of the Gospel, its characteristics, its relation to the Synoptic Gospels, and to the Apostle's First Epistle, and the usual subjects referred to in an 'introduction'."—*The Christian Church.*

"The notes are extremely scholarly and valuable, and in most cases exhaustive, bringing to the elucidation of the text all that is best in commentaries, ancient and modern."—*The English Churchman and Clerical Journal.*

"(1) **The Acts of the Apostles.** By J. RAWSON LUMBY, D.D. (2) **The Second Epistle of the Corinthians,** edited by Professor LIAS. The introduction is pithy, and contains a mass of carefully-selected information on the authorship of the Acts, its designs, and its sources. ......The Second Epistle of the Corinthians is a manual beyond all praise, for the excellence of its pithy and pointed annotations, its analysis of the contents, and the fulness and value of its introduction."—*Examiner.*

"The concluding portion of the **Acts of the Apostles,** under the very competent editorship of Dr LUMBY, is a valuable addition to our school-books on that subject. Detailed criticism is impossible within the space at our command, but we may say that the ample notes touch with much exactness the very points on which most readers of the text desire information. Due reference is made, where necessary, to the Revised Version; the maps are excellent; and we do not know of any other volume where so much help is given to the complete understanding of one of the most important and, in many respects, difficult books of the New Testament."—*School Guardian.*

"The Rev. H. C. G. MOULE, M.A., has made a valuable addition to THE CAMBRIDGE BIBLE FOR SCHOOLS in his brief commentary on the **Epistle to the Romans.** The 'Notes' are very good, and lean, as the notes of a School Bible should, to the most commonly accepted and orthodox view of the inspired author's meaning; while the Introduction, and especially the Sketch of the Life of St Paul, is a model of condensation. It is as lively and pleasant to read as if two or three facts had not been crowded into well-nigh every sentence."—*Expositor.*

"**The Epistle to the Romans.** It is seldom we have met with a work so remarkable for the compression and condensation of all that is valuable in the smallest possible space as in the volume before us. Within its limited pages we have 'a sketch of the Life of St Paul,' we have further a critical account of the date of the Epistle to the Romans, of its language, and of its genuineness. The notes are numerous, full of matter, to the point, and leave no real difficulty or obscurity unexplained."—*The Examiner.*

"**The First Epistle to the Corinthians.** Edited by Professor LIAS. Every fresh instalment of this annotated edition of the Bible for Schools confirms the favourable opinion we formed of its value from the examination of its first number. The origin and plan of the Epistle are discussed with its character and genuineness."—*The Nonconformist.*

"**The Second Epistle to the Corinthians.** By Professor LIAS. **The General Epistles of St Peter and St Jude.** By E. H. PLUMPTRE, D. D. We welcome these additions to the valuable series of the Cambridge Bible. We have nothing to add to the commendation which we have from the first publication given to this edition of the Bible. It is enough to say that Professor Lias has completed his work on the two Epistles to the Corinthians in the same admirable manner as at first. Dr Plumptre has also completed the Catholic Epistles."—*Nonconformist.*

The Epistle to the Ephesians. By Rev. H. C. G. MOULE, M.A. "It seems to us the model of a School and College Commentary—comprehensive, but not cumbersome; scholarly, but not pedantic."—*Baptist Magazine.*

The Epistle to the Philippians. "There are few series more valued by theological students than 'The Cambridge Bible for Schools and Colleges,' and there will be no number of it more esteemed than that by Mr H. C. G. MOULE on the *Epistle to the Philippians.*"—*Record.*

"Another capital volume of 'The Cambridge Bible for Schools and Colleges.' The notes are a model of scholarly, lucid, and compact criticism."—*Baptist Magazine.*

Hebrews. "Like his (Canon Farrar's) commentary on Luke it possesses all the best characteristics of his writing. It is a work not only of an accomplished scholar, but of a skilled teacher."—*Baptist Magazine.*

"We heartily commend this volume of this excellent work."—*Sunday School Chronicle.*

"**The General Epistle of St James,** by Professor PLUMPTRE, D.D. Nevertheless it is, so far as I know, by far the best exposition of the Epistle of St James in the English language. Not Schoolboys or Students going in for an examination alone, but Ministers and Preachers of the Word, may get more real help from it than from the most costly and elaborate commentaries."—*Expositor.*

The Epistles of St John. By the Rev. A. PLUMMER, M.A., D.D. "This forms an admirable companion to the 'Commentary on the Gospel according to St John,' which was reviewed in *The Churchman* as soon as it appeared. Dr Plummer has some of the highest qualifications for such a task; and these two volumes, their size being considered, will bear comparison with the best Commentaries of the time."—*The Churchman.*

"Dr PLUMMER's edition of **the Epistles of St John** is worthy of its companions in the 'Cambridge Bible for Schools' Series. The subject, though not apparently extensive, is really one not easy to treat, and requiring to be treated at length, owing to the constant reference to obscure heresies in the Johannine writings. Dr Plummer has done his exegetical task well."—*The Saturday Review.*

THE CAMBRIDGE GREEK TESTAMENT
FOR SCHOOLS AND COLLEGES
with a Revised Text, based on the most recent critical authorities, and English Notes, prepared under the direction of the General Editor, THE VERY REVEREND J. J. S. PEROWNE, D.D.

"*Has achieved an excellence which puts it above criticism.*"—Expositor.

St Matthew. "Copious illustrations, gathered from a great variety of sources, make his notes a very valuable aid to the student. They are indeed remarkably interesting, while all explanations on meanings, applications, and the like are distinguished by their lucidity and good sense."—*Pall Mall Gazette.*

St Mark. "The Cambridge Greek Testament of which Dr MACLEAR'S edition of the Gospel according to St Mark is a volume, certainly supplies a want. Without pretending to compete with the leading commentaries, or to embody very much original research, it forms a most satisfactory introduction to the study of the New Testament in the original....Dr Maclear's introduction contains all that is known of St Mark's life; an account of the circumstances in which the Gospel was composed, with an estimate of the influence of St Peter's teaching upon St Mark; an excellent sketch of the special characteristics of this Gospel; an analysis, and a chapter on the text of the New Testament generally."—*Saturday Review.*

St Luke. "Of this second series we have a new volume by Archdeacon FARRAR on *St Luke*, completing the four Gospels....It gives us in clear and beautiful language the best results of modern scholarship. We have a most attractive *Introduction*. Then follows a sort of composite Greek text, representing fairly and in very beautiful type the consensus of modern textual critics. At the beginning of the exposition of each chapter of the Gospel are a few short critical notes giving the manuscript evidence for such various readings as seem to deserve mention. The expository notes are short, but clear and helpful. For young students and those who are not disposed to buy or to study the much more costly work of Godet, this seems to us to be the best book on the Greek Text of the Third Gospel."—*Methodist Recorder.*

St John. "We take this opportunity of recommending to ministers on probation, the very excellent volume of the same series on this part of the New Testament. We hope that most or all of our young ministers will prefer to study the volume in the *Cambridge Greek Testament for Schools.*"—*Methodist Recorder.*

The Acts of the Apostles. "Professor LUMBY has performed his laborious task well, and supplied us with a commentary the fulness and freshness of which Bible students will not be slow to appreciate. The volume is enriched with the usual copious indexes and four coloured maps."—*Glasgow Herald.*

I. Corinthians. "Mr LIAS is no novice in New Testament exposition, and the present series of essays and notes is an able and helpful addition to the existing books."—*Guardian.*

The Epistles of St John. "In the very useful and well annotated series of the Cambridge Greek Testament the volume on the Epistles of St John must hold a high position...The notes are brief, well informed and intelligent."—*Scotsman.*

CAMBRIDGE UNIVERSITY PRESS.

THE PITT PRESS SERIES.

⁎ *Many of the books in this list can be had in two volumes, Text and Notes separately.*

I. GREEK.

Aristophanes. Aves—Plutus—Ranæ. By W. C. GREEN, M.A., late Assistant Master at Rugby School. 3s. 6d. each.
Aristotle. Outlines of the Philosophy of. By EDWIN WALLACE, M.A., LL.D. Third Edition, Enlarged. 4s. 6d.
Euripides. Heracleidae. By E. A. BECK, M.A. 3s. 6d.
——— **Hercules Furens.** By A. GRAY, M.A., and J. T. HUTCHINSON, M.A. New Edit. 2s.
——— **Hippolytus.** By W. S. HADLEY, M.A. 2s.
——— **Iphigeneia in Aulis.** By C. E. S. HEADLAM, B.A. 2s. 6d.
Herodotus, Book V. By E. S. SHUCKBURGH, M.A. 3s.
——— **Book VI.** By the same Editor. 4s.
——— **Book VIII., Chaps. 1—90.** By the same Editor. 3s. 6d.
——— **Book IX., Chaps. 1—89.** By the same Editor. 3s. 6d.
Homer. Odyssey, Books IX., X. By G. M. EDWARDS, M.A. 2s. 6d. each.
——— ——— **Book XXI.** By the same Editor. 2s.
——— **Iliad. Books XXII., XXIII.** By the same Editor.
[Nearly ready.
Lucian. Somnium Charon Piscator et De Luctu. By W. E. HEITLAND, M.A., Fellow of St John's College, Cambridge. 3s. 6d.
——— **Menippus and Timon.** By E. C. MACKIE, M.A.
[Nearly ready.
Platonis Apologia Socratis. By J. ADAM, M.A. 3s. 6d.
——— **Crito.** By the same Editor. 2s. 6d.
——— **Euthyphro.** By the same Editor. 2s. 6d.
Plutarch. Lives of the Gracchi. By Rev. H. A. HOLDEN, M.A., LL.D. 6s.
——— **Life of Nicias.** By the same Editor. 5s.
——— **Life of Sulla.** By the same Editor. 6s.
——— **Life of Timoleon.** By the same Editor. 6s.
Sophocles. Oedipus Tyrannus. School Edition. By R. C. JEBB, Litt.D., LL.D. 4s. 6d.
Thucydides. Book VII. By Rev. H. A. HOLDEN, M.A., LL.D.
[Nearly ready.
Xenophon. Agesilaus. By H. HAILSTONE, M.A. 2s. 6d.
——— **Anabasis.** By A. PRETOR, M.A. Two vols. 7s. 6d.
——— **Books I. III. IV. and V.** By the same. 2s. each.
——— **Books II. VI. and VII.** By the same. 2s. 6d. each.
Xenophon. Cyropaedeia. Books I. II. By Rev. H. A. HOLDEN, M.A., LL.D. 2 vols. 6s.
——— ——— **Books III. IV. and V.** By the same Editor. 5s.
——— ——— **Books VI. VII. VIII.** By the same Editor.
[Nearly ready.

London: Cambridge Warehouse, Ave Maria Lane.

II. LATIN.

Beda's Ecclesiastical History, Books III., IV. By J. E. B. MAYOR, M.A., and J. R. LUMBY, D.D. Revised Edition. 7s. 6d.

────── **Books I. II.** By the same Editors. [*In the Press.*

Caesar. De Bello Gallico, Comment. I. By A. G. PESKETT, M.A., Fellow of Magdalene College, Cambridge. 1s. 6d. COMMENT. II. III. 2s. COMMENT. I. II. III. 3s. COMMENT. IV. and V., COMMENT. VII. 2s. each. COMMENT. VI. and COMMENT. VIII. 1s. 6d. each.

────── **De Bello Civili, Comment. I.** By the same Editor.

Cicero. De Amicitia.—De Senectute. By J. S. REID, Litt.D., Fellow of Gonville and Caius College. 3s. 6d. each.

────── **In Gaium Verrem Actio Prima.** By H. COWIE, M.A. 1s. 6d.

────── **In Q. Caecilium Divinatio et in C. Verrem Actio.** By W. E. HEITLAND, M.A., and H. COWIE, M.A. 3s.

────── **Philippica Secunda.** By A. G. PESKETT, M.A. 3s. 6d.

────── **Oratio pro Archia Poeta.** By J. S. REID, Litt.D. 2s.

────── **Pro L. Cornelio Balbo Oratio.** By the same. 1s. 6d.

────── **Oratio pro Tito Annio Milone.** By JOHN SMYTH PURTON, B.D. 2s. 6d.

────── **Oratio pro L. Murena.** By W. E. HEITLAND, M.A. 3s.

────── **Pro Cn. Plancio Oratio,** by H. A. HOLDEN, LL.D. 4s. 6d.

────── **Pro P. Cornelio Sulla.** By J. S. REID, Litt.D. 3s. 6d.

────── **Somnium Scipionis.** By W. D. PEARMAN, M.A. 2s.

Horace. Epistles, Book I. By E. S. SHUCKBURGH, M.A., late Fellow of Emmanuel College. 2s. 6d.

Livy. Book IV. By H. M. STEPHENSON, M.A. 2s. 6d.

────── **Book V.** By L. WHIBLEY, M.A. 2s. 6d.

────── **Books XXI., XXII.** By M. S. DIMSDALE, M.A., Fellow of King's College. 2s. 6d. each.

────── **Book XXVII.** By Rev. H. M. STEPHENSON, M.A. [*Nearly ready.*

Lucan. Pharsaliae Liber Primus. By W. E. HEITLAND, M.A., and C. E. HASKINS, M.A. 1s. 6d.

Lucretius, Book V. By J. D. DUFF, M.A. 2s.

Ovidii Nasonis Fastorum Liber VI. By A. SIDGWICK, M.A., Tutor of Corpus Christi College, Oxford. 1s. 6d.

Quintus Curtius. A Portion of the History (Alexander in India). By W. E. HEITLAND, M.A., and T. E. RAVEN, B.A. With Two Maps. 3s. 6d.

Vergili Maronis Aeneidos Libri I.—XII. By A. SIDGWICK, M.A. 1s. 6d. each.

────── **Bucolica.** By the same Editor. 1s. 6d.

────── **Georgicon Libri I. II.** By the same Editor. 2s.

────── ────── **Libri III. IV.** By the same Editor. 2s.

────── **The Complete Works.** By the same Editor. Two vols. Vol. I. containing the Introduction and Text. 3s. 6d. Vol. II. The Notes. 4s. 6d.

London: Cambridge Warehouse, Ave Maria Lane.

III. FRENCH.

Corneille. La Suite du Menteur. A Comedy in Five Acts.
By the late G. MASSON, B.A. 2s.

De Bonnechose. Lazare Hoche. By C. COLBECK, M.A.
Revised Edition. Four Maps. 2s.

D'Harleville. Le Vieux Célibataire. By G. MASSON, B.A. 2s.

De Lamartine. Jeanne D'Arc. By Rev. A. C. CLAPIN,
M.A., St John's College, Cambridge. 2s.

De Vigny. La Canne de Jonc. By Rev. H. A. BULL,
M.A., late Master at Wellington College. 2s.

Erckmann-Chatrian. La Guerre. By Rev. A. C. CLAPIN,
M.A. 3s.

La Baronne de Staël-Holstein. Le Directoire. (Considérations sur la Révolution Française. Troisième et quatrième parties.) Revised and enlarged. By G. MASSON, B.A., and G. W. PROTHERO, M.A. 2s.

—— —— **Dix Années d'Exil. Livre II. Chapitres 1—8.**
By the same Editors. New Edition, enlarged. 2s.

Lemercier. Fredegonde et Brunehaut. A Tragedy in Five
Acts. By GUSTAVE MASSON, B.A. 2s.

Molière. Le Bourgeois Gentilhomme, Comédie-Ballet en
Cinq Actes. (1670.) By Rev. A. C. CLAPIN, M.A. Revised Edition. 1s. 6d.

—— **L'École des Femmes.** By G. SAINTSBURY, M.A. 2s. 6d.

—— **Les Précieuses Ridicules.** By E. G. W. BRAUNHOLTZ,
M.A., Ph.D. 2s.

—— —— **Abridged Edition.** 1s.

Piron. La Métromanie. A Comedy. By G. MASSON, B.A. 2s.

Racine. Les Plaideurs. By E. G. W. BRAUNHOLTZ, M.A. 2s.

—— —— **Abridged Edition.** 1s.

Sainte-Beuve. M. Daru (Causeries du Lundi, Vol. IX.).
By G. MASSON, B.A. 2s.

Saintine. Picciola. By Rev. A. C. CLAPIN, M.A. 2s.

Scribe and Legouvé. Bataille de Dames. By Rev. H. A.
BULL, M.A. 2s.

Scribe. Le Verre d'Eau. By C. COLBECK, M.A. 2s.

Sédaine. Le Philosophe sans le savoir. By Rev. H. A.
BULL, M.A. 2s.

Thierry. Lettres sur l'histoire de France (XIII.—XXIV.).
By G. MASSON, B.A., and G. W. PROTHERO, M.A. 2s. 6d.

—— **Récits des Temps Mérovingiens I.—III.** By GUSTAVE
MASSON, B.A. Univ. Gallic., and A. R. ROPES, M.A. With Map. 3s.

Villemain. Lascaris ou Les Grecs du XVe Siècle, Nouvelle
Historique. By G. MASSON, B.A. 2s.

Voltaire. Histoire du Siècle de Louis XIV. Chaps. I.—
XIII. By G. MASSON, B.A., and G. W. PROTHERO, M.A. 2s. 6d. PART II.
CHAPS. XIV.—XXIV. 2s. 6d. PART III. CHAPS. XXV. to end. 2s. 6d.

Xavier de Maistre. La Jeune Sibérienne. Le Lépreux de
la Cité D'Aoste. By G. MASSON, B.A. 1s. 6d.

London: Cambridge Warehouse, Ave Maria Lane.

IV. GERMAN.

Ballads on German History. By W. WAGNER, Ph.D. 2s.

Benedix. Doctor Wespe. Lustspiel in fünf Aufzügen. By KARL HERMANN BREUL, M.A., Ph.D. 3s.

Freytag. Der Staat Friedrichs des Grossen. By WILHELM WAGNER, Ph.D. 2s.

German Dactylic Poetry. By WILHELM WAGNER, Ph.D. 3s.

Goethe's Knabenjahre. (1749—1759.) By W. WAGNER, Ph.D. 2s.

—— **Hermann und Dorothea.** By WILHELM WAGNER, Ph.D. Revised edition by J. W. CARTMELL, M.A. 3s. 6d.

Gutzkow. Zopf und Schwert. Lustspiel in fünf Aufzügen. By H. J. WOLSTENHOLME, B.A. (Lond.). 3s. 6d.

Hauff. Das Bild des Kaisers. By KARL HERMANN BREUL, M.A., Ph.D., University Lecturer in German. 3s.

—— **Das Wirthshaus im Spessart.** By A. SCHLOTTMANN, Ph.D. 3s. 6d.

—— **Die Karavane.** By A. SCHLOTTMANN, Ph.D. 3s. 6d.

Immermann. Der Oberhof. A Tale of Westphalian Life, by WILHELM WAGNER, Ph.D. 3s.

Kohlrausch. Das Jahr 1813. By WILHELM WAGNER, Ph.D. 2s.

Lessing and Gellert. Selected Fables. By KARL HERMANN BREUL, M.A., Ph.D. 3s.

Mendelssohn's Letters. Selections from. By J. SIME, M.A. 3s.

Raumer. Der erste Kreuzzug (1095—1099). By WILHELM WAGNER, Ph.D. 2s.

Riehl. Culturgeschichtliche Novellen. By H. J. WOLSTENHOLME, B.A. (Lond.). 3s. 6d.

Schiller. Wilhelm Tell. By KARL HERMANN BREUL, M.A., Ph.D. 2s. 6d.

—— —— **Abridged Edition.** 1s. 6d.

Uhland. Ernst, Herzog von Schwaben. By H. J. WOLSTENHOLME, B.A. 3s. 6d.

V. ENGLISH.

Ancient Philosophy from Thales to Cicero, A Sketch of. By JOSEPH B. MAYOR, M.A. 3s. 6d.

An Apologie for Poetrie by Sir PHILIP SIDNEY. By E. S. SHUCKBURGH, M.A. The Text is a revision of that of the first edition of 1595. [*Nearly ready.*]

Bacon's History of the Reign of King Henry VII. By the Rev. Professor LUMBY, D.D. 3s.

Cowley's Essays. By the Rev. Professor LUMBY, D.D. 4s.

London: Cambridge Warehouse, Ave Maria Lane.

Milton's Comus and Arcades. By A. W. VERITY, M.A., sometime Scholar of Trinity College. [*Nearly ready.*]

More's History of King Richard III. By J. RAWSON LUMBY, D.D. 3s. 6d.

More's Utopia. By Rev. Prof. LUMBY, D.D. 3s. 6d.

The Two Noble Kinsmen. By the Rev. Professor SKEAT, Litt.D. 3s. 6d.

VI. EDUCATIONAL SCIENCE.

Comenius, John Amos, Bishop of the Moravians. His Life and Educational Works, by S. S. LAURIE, A.M., F.R.S.E. 3s. 6d.

Education, Three Lectures on the Practice of. I. On Marking, by H. W. EVE, M.A. II. On Stimulus, by A. SIDGWICK, M.A. III. On the Teaching of Latin Verse Composition, by E. A. ABBOTT, D.D. 2s.

Stimulus. A Lecture delivered for the Teachers' Training Syndicate, May, 1882, by A. SIDGWICK, M.A. 1s.

Locke on Education. By the Rev. R. H. QUICK, M.A. 3s. 6d.

Milton's Tractate on Education. A facsimile reprint from the Edition of 1673. By O. BROWNING, M.A. 2s.

Modern Languages, Lectures on the Teaching of. By C. COLBECK, M.A. 2s.

Teacher, General Aims of the, and Form Management. Two Lectures delivered in the University of Cambridge in the Lent Term, 1883, by F. W. FARRAR, D.D., and R. B. POOLE, B.D. 1s. 6d.

Teaching, Theory and Practice of. By the Rev. E. THRING, M.A., late Head Master of Uppingham School. New Edition. 4s. 6d.

British India, a Short History of. By E. S. CARLOS, M.A., late Head Master of Exeter Grammar School. 1s.

Geography, Elementary Commercial. A Sketch of the Commodities and the Countries of the World. By H. R. MILL, D.Sc., F.R.S.E. 1s.

Geography, an Atlas of Commercial. (A Companion to the above.) By J. G. BARTHOLOMEW, F.R.G.S. With an Introduction by HUGH ROBERT MILL, D.Sc. 3s.

VII. MATHEMATICS.

Euclid's Elements of Geometry. Books I. and II. By H. M. TAYLOR, M.A., Fellow and late Tutor of Trinity College, Cambridge. 1s. 6d.

—— —— **Books III. and IV.** By the same Editor. [*Nearly ready.*]

Elementary Algebra (with Answers to the Examples). By W. W. ROUSE BALL, M.A. 4s. 6d.

Other Volumes are in preparation.

London: Cambridge Warehouse, Ave Maria Lane.

The Cambridge Bible for Schools and Colleges.

GENERAL EDITOR: J. J. S. PEROWNE, D.D.,
DEAN OF PETERBOROUGH.

"*It is difficult to commend too highly this excellent series.*—Guardian.

"*The modesty of the general title of this series has, we believe, led many to misunderstand its character and underrate its value. The books are well suited for study in the upper forms of our best schools, but not the less are they adapted to the wants of all Bible students who are not specialists. We doubt, indeed, whether any of the numerous popular commentaries recently issued in this country will be found more serviceable for general use.*"—Academy.

Now Ready. Cloth, Extra Fcap. 8vo. With Maps.

Book of Joshua. By Rev. G. F. MACLEAR, D.D. 2s. 6d.
Book of Judges. By Rev. J. J. LIAS, M.A. 3s. 6d.
First Book of Samuel. By Rev. Prof. KIRKPATRICK, B.D. 3s. 6d.
Second Book of Samuel. By Rev. Prof. KIRKPATRICK, B.D. 3s. 6d.
First Book of Kings. By Rev. Prof. LUMBY, D.D. 3s. 6d.
Second Book of Kings. By Rev. Prof. LUMBY, D.D. 3s. 6d.
Book of Job. By Rev. A. B. DAVIDSON, D.D. 5s.
Book of Ecclesiastes. By Very Rev. E. H. PLUMPTRE, D.D. 5s.
Book of Jeremiah. By Rev. A. W. STREANE, M.A. 4s. 6d.
Book of Hosea. By Rev. T. K. CHEYNE, M.A., D.D. 3s.
Books of Obadiah & Jonah. By Archdeacon PEROWNE. 2s. 6d.
Book of Micah. By Rev. T. K. CHEYNE, M.A., D.D. 1s. 6d.
Haggai, Zechariah & Malachi. By Arch. PEROWNE. 3s. 6d.
Book of Malachi. By Archdeacon PEROWNE. 1s.
Gospel according to St Matthew. By Rev. A. CARR, M.A. 2s. 6d.
Gospel according to St Mark. By Rev. G. F. MACLEAR, D.D. 2s. 6d.
Gospel according to St Luke. By Arch. FARRAR, D.D. 4s. 6d
Gospel according to St John. By Rev. A. PLUMMER, D.D. 4s. 6d.
Acts of the Apostles. By Rev. Prof. LUMBY, D.D. 4s. 6d.
Epistle to the Romans. By Rev. H. C. G. MOULE, M.A. 3s. 6d.
First Corinthians. By Rev. J. J. LIAS, M.A. With Map. 2s.
Second Corinthians. By Rev. J. J. LIAS, M.A. With Map. 2s.

London: Cambridge Warehouse, Ave Maria Lane.

Epistle to the Galatians. By Rev. E. H. PEROWNE, D.D. 1s. 6d.
Epistle to the Ephesians. By Rev. H. C. G. MOULE, M.A. 2s. 6d.
Epistle to the Philippians. By Rev. H. C. G. MOULE, M.A. 2s. 6d.
Epistle to the Hebrews. By Arch. FARRAR, D.D. 3s. 6d.
General Epistle of St James. By Very Rev. E. H. PLUMPTRE, D.D. 1s. 6d.
Epistles of St Peter and St Jude. By Very Rev. E. H. PLUMPTRE, D.D. 2s. 6d.
Epistles of St John. By Rev. A. PLUMMER, M.A., D.D. 3s. 6d.
Book of Revelation. By Rev. W. H. SIMCOX, M.A. 3s.

Preparing.

Book of Genesis. By Very Rev. the Dean of Peterborough.
Books of Exodus, Numbers and Deuteronomy. By Rev C. D. GINSBURG, LL.D.
Books of Ezra and Nehemiah. By Rev. Prof. RYLE, M.A.
Book of Psalms. Part I. By Rev. Prof. KIRKPATRICK, B.D.
Book of Isaiah. By Prof. W. ROBERTSON SMITH, M.A.
Book of Ezekiel. By Rev. A. B. DAVIDSON, D.D.
Epistles to the Colossians and Philemon. By Rev. H. C. G. MOULE, M.A.
Epistles to the Thessalonians. By Rev. G. G. FINDLAY, M.A.
Epistles to Timothy & Titus. By Rev. A. E. HUMPHREYS, M.A.

The Smaller Cambridge Bible for Schools.

The Smaller Cambridge Bible for Schools *will form an entirely new series of commentaries on some selected books of the Bible. It is expected that they will be prepared for the most part by the Editors of the larger series* (*The Cambridge Bible for Schools and Colleges*). *The volumes will be issued at a low price, and will be suitable to the requirements of preparatory and elementary schools.*

Now ready.

First and Second Books of Samuel. By Rev. Prof. KIRKPATRICK, B.D. 1s. each.
Gospel according to St Matthew. By Rev. A. CARR, M.A. 1s.
Gospel according to St Mark. By Rev. G. F. MACLEAR, D.D. 1s.
Gospel according to St Luke. By Archdeacon FARRAR. 1s.
Acts of the Apostles. By Rev. Prof. LUMBY, D.D.
                                                       [*Nearly ready.*

London: Cambridge Warehouse, Ave Maria Lane.

The Cambridge Greek Testament for Schools and Colleges,

with a Revised Text, based on the most recent critical authorities, and English Notes, prepared under the direction of the General Editor,

The Very Reverend J. J. S. PEROWNE, D.D.,
DEAN OF PETERBOROUGH.

Gospel according to St Matthew. By Rev. A. CARR, M.A. With 4 Maps. 4s. 6d.

Gospel according to St Mark. By Rev. G. F. MACLEAR, D.D. With 3 Maps. 4s. 6d.

Gospel according to St Luke. By Archdeacon FARRAR. With 4 Maps. 6s.

Gospel according to St John. By Rev. A. PLUMMER, D.D. With 4 Maps. 6s.

Acts of the Apostles. By Rev. Professor LUMBY, D.D. With 4 Maps. 6s.

First Epistle to the Corinthians. By Rev. J. J. LIAS, M.A. 3s.

Second Epistle to the Corinthians. By Rev. J. J. LIAS, M.A. [*In the Press.*

Epistle to the Hebrews. By Archdeacon FARRAR, D.D. 3s. 6d.

Epistle of St James. By Very Rev. E. H. PLUMPTRE, D.D. [*Preparing.*

Epistles of St John. By Rev. A. PLUMMER, M.A., D.D. 4s.

London: C. J. CLAY AND SONS,
CAMBRIDGE WAREHOUSE, AVE MARIA LANE.
Glasgow: 263, ARGYLE STREET.
Cambridge: DEIGHTON, BELL AND CO.
Leipzig: F. A. BROCKHAUS.

www.ingramcontent.com/pod-product-compliance
Lightning Source LLC
Chambersburg PA
CBHW020858230426
43666CB00008B/1230